Mencius and Aquinas

SUNY Series, Toward a Comparative Philosophy of Religions
Frank E. Reynolds and David Tracy, editors

Mencius and Aquinas

Theories of Virtue
and Conceptions of Courage

Lee H. Yearley

State University of New York Press

Published by
State University of New York Press, Albany

For information, address State University of New York Press,
State University Plaza, Albany, N.Y., 12246

Library of Congress Cataloging-in-Publication Data
Yearley, Lee H.
Mencius and Aquinas: theories of virtue and conceptions of
courage / Lee H. Yearley.
p. cm. — (SUNY series, toward a comparative philosophy of
religions)
Includes bibliographical references.
ISBN 0-7914-0431-5 (alk. paper). — ISBN 0-7914-0432-3 (pbk. :
alk. paper).
1. Virtue. 2. Virtues. 3. Courage. 4. Mencius — Ethics.
5. Thomas, Aquinas, Saint, 1225?-1274 — Ethics. 6. Ethics,
Comparative. I. Title. II. Series.
BJ1531.Y42 1990
170'.92' —dc20
89-77407
CIP

To My Wife
Sally Jeanne Gressens

Contents

Chapter One:
The Comparative Philosophy of Religions and the Study of Virtue

Chapter Two:
The Context for Mencius and Aquinas's Ideas of Virtue

Chapter Three:
Mencius and Aquinas's Theories of Virtue

Chapter Four:
Mencius and Aquinas's Conceptions of Courage

Chapter Five:
Conclusion

Foreword

Since 1981 Lee Yearley has been a major contributor to the ongoing discussions at the University of Chicago Divinity School that have generated the *Toward a Comparative Philosophy of Religions* series. He was a central participant in three conferences on "Cosmogony and Ethical Order" held between 1981 and 1984; and he contributed two essays — one on Mencius and one on Freud — to a related volume (Robin W. Lovin and Frank E. Reynolds, eds., *Cosmogony and Ethical Order: New Essays in Comparative Ethics* published in Chicago by the University of Chicago Press, 1985). Between 1986 and 1989 he participated in the six conferences on "Religion(s) in Culture and History" that generated the first volume in this present series — a collection of essays that I edited with David Tracy entitled *Myth and Philosophy* (Albany: State University of New York Press, 1990). It is, therefore, quite appropriate that the major book that he has been writing during this period now appears as Volume II in our new series.

In his study of Mencius and Aquinas, Yearley makes two important and original contributions to the development of a new kind of comparative philosophy of religions that is global in its perspective and in tune with contemporary philosophical developments and issues. The first is to bring into the comparative orbit the very lively concern of contemporary ethical philosophers with the ethics of virtue. Despite the fact that very important progress has occurred in comparative studies on the one hand, and in explorations of the ethics of virtue on the other (see, for example, Yearley's own "Recent Work on Virtue" in the January, 1990 issue of *Religious Studies Review*), previous scholars have been either unwilling or unable to break the barriers that have separated the two kinds of interest.

The second — and more general — contribution which Yearley makes is to provide a single-authored, book-length study in the comparative philosophy of religions that effectively combines careful descriptive analysis, the use of clearly articulated and highly sophisticated comparative methods, and explicit reflections on normative presuppositions and implications. There have been previous books in the comparative philosophy of religions that have dealt more or less adequately with one or even two of these very crucial and interrelated elements; but I know of no other book that effectively integrates all three elements into a single, unified field.

Early in his academic career Yearley focused his research on the Western tradition, wrote a doctoral dissertation on the natural and theological virtues in the Catholic tradition from Aquinas to Rahner, and published his first book on *The Ideas of Newman: Christianity and Human Religiosity* (University Park, Pa.: Pennsylvania State University Press, 1978). Beginning in the mid-1970s, he turned his attention to the study of the Chinese language and classical texts, and has subsequently published seven major essays on various Chinese philosophers. During the 1980s he has become increasingly concerned to explore, both theoretically and practically, the problems and possibilities of comparative methods; and to forge a connection between comparative studies and the task of normative reflection. In this present volume, Yearley draws on this rich and diversified background. What is more, he weaves the various strands into a clearly focused, highly creative synthesis.

Like all of the works in the *Toward a Comparative Philosophy of Religions* series, Yearley's comparative study of a particular aspect of philosophical ethics in China and the West will be controversial. Sinologists and Western medievalists will inevitably call into question particular points of textual interpretation. Narrowly focused area specialists as well as comparativists of other stripes will certainly challenge the methods that are employed. Normatively oriented philosophers and ethicists will doubtless have theoretical objections to raise, and substantive counter-proposals to make.

However, David Tracy and I are convinced that Yearley's book will stand the test; and that it will provide a model for other comparatively oriented philosophers of religion to follow. We are also convinced that, despite the inevitable outcries that will be heard from those whose well-domesticated disciplinary oxen have been gored, the book will stimulate creative new developments in the study of Mencius, in the study of Aquinas, and in the pursuit of an ethics of virtue that makes sense in the modern world.

Frank E. Reynolds
University of Chicago
January 20, 1990

Acknowledgments

The length of time this work has been in germination means that I am bound to overlook some whose help should be acknowledged. But I do want to thank those for whose aid I am very grateful. The National Endowment for the Humanities awarded me a Senior Fellowship and thereby gave me the support that enabled me to get this project well under way. The Henry Luce Foundation supported my year as Luce Professor of Comparative Religious Ethics at Amherst and the Five Colleges, a time during which a variety of important work, conversations, and teaching occurred. The staff in Religious Studies at Stanford University assisted with many matters relating to my work on this manuscript, and both the Dean's Office in the School of Humanities and Sciences and the Center for East Asian Studies at Stanford University provided funds that helped me to prepare the manuscript.

Many people have also contributed much through informal conversations, responses to papers they invited me to give, and the reading of all or part of versions of this manuscript. I will not attempt to name them all, but I do want to single out two ongoing groups of people I was privileged to be a part of, as well as various individuals. One group is those who participated in six conferences on comparative religious ethics held from 1980 to 1983 that received funding from both the National Endowment for the Humanities and the Luce Foundation. The other group is those who participated in the recently completed six semi-annual conferences on Religion(s) in Culture and History that were funded by the Booth-Ferris Foundation. These conferences, almost all of which took place at the University of Chicago Divinity School, provided a context for ongoing cross-cultural and cross-disciplinary conversations. I learned an immeasurable amount in both situations and also made intellectual friendships of great importance to my work.

Specific individuals, including the anonymous referees for the press, gave me both support and astute criticisms about the manuscript and related subjects. My special thanks to Robert Bellah, Carl Bielefeldt, Michael Bratman, John Carman, Chris Gamwell, Ronald Green, Jim Gustafson, Joseph Kitagawa, Van Harvey, P.J. Ivanhoe, Leon Kass, Charles Long, David Little, Tu-wei Ming, David Nivison, Giles Milhaven, Frank Reynolds, John Reeder, Jr., Kwong-loi Shun, Huston Smith, Jonathan Z. Smith, Wilfred C. Smith, David Tracy, and David Wills. Teaching and being taught by many undergraduate students as I worked on this project was also of great help and importance. Particular thanks are due to two graduate students at Stanford who helped me with final preparations on the manuscript, Bryan Van Norden and Mark Gonnerman, who worked on the index and much else. My mother, Mary Howard Yearley, although in her mid-eighties, remains a kindly but emphatic defender of good English and worked through the whole manuscript for me. These people are not, of course, responsible for any errors in interpretation, thought, or presentation that still remain.

Jennifer and John Yearley, my two children, had the ambivalent opportunity to share a significant part of their adolescence with a parent writing a book, and their patience, good humor, and restraint are much appreciated. Finally, my wife Sally Gressens is due thanks that range beyond what I can give. She supported my enterprise in myriad ways including sharing ideas and criticisms with me, and continuing to help me keep in perspective what truly was at stake in what I was doing.

Chapter 1

The Comparative Philosophy of Religions and the Study of Virtue

I. Introduction: The Importance of the Comparative Philosophy of Religious Flourishings

Speaking about anything resembling a consensus among intellectuals is risky. Nevertheless, when we consider issues in the comparative philosophy of religions, most now agree about the truth of a deceptively simple idea: the religious expressions of human beings are neither all the same nor are they all different. (Despite this, many occasionally are drawn, like moths toward flames, to discussions of the extreme positions that simple similarity or radical difference constitutes human religiosity.) Given this agreement, our most important work is to investigate the landscape between the two extreme options. We must decide how best to do comparative work within that area. This largely is a descriptive enterprise if one that relies on utilizing our imaginative powers. However, we also must see what, if any, normative conclusions we can produce or discover, a constructive enterprise that relies only in part on utilizing descriptive materials.

I am in this book, then, to map, and perhaps even make habitable, part of the middle ground between the same and the different. I also aim to reflect on the constructive implications my mapping generates. Examining two thinkers, I will chart similarities within differences and differences within similarities and also discuss the normative conclusions the process produces. The two thinkers are Mencius or Meng Tzu (fourth century B.C.E.), an early Confucian, and St. Thomas Aquinas

(1224/5-1274 C.E.), a medieval Christian. I focus on their theories of virtue, of human excellences or flourishings, and their treatments of specific virtues, especially the virtue of courage.

Mencius and Aquinas are extraordinarily significant and influential thinkers. Each combines theoretical acumen and spiritual sensitivity in a rare way. Each also served as a font of their respective traditions, even if they are not responsible for what later people did to them and for them. Finally, each has been used by modern apologists to defend a vision of human flourishing thought to be endangered by modern ideas.

Comparing the two might seem, however, to yield little more than contrasts. My own previous work both on each figure and on more general comparisons between Chinese and Western thinkers, in fact, had almost convinced me this was true. When I concentrated on their accounts of virtue, however, I saw resemblances I had not thought existed. Moreover, that concentration led me to recognize features in each thinker I had overlooked and to consider again some ideas whose force I had barely recognized before — or sometimes missed completely.

My inquiry also led me to normative conclusions. Even though most of my work generates descriptive results, I do use materials from the two thinkers to construct a position that stands, I think, as an accurate picture of how things are. (The position, however, also clarifies my description of the two thinkers.) In constructing this position, I do not attempt to examine all the problems I would were I trying only to produce a fully convincing argument, but I do aim to produce a true account. My analyses of courage; of how reason, emotions, and dispositions interact; and of how the ideas of semblances and expansions of virtue operate probably best illustrates the nature of this kind of constructive inquiry.[1]

Another normative feature of my inquiry emerged when I came to recognize that the comparing of the two thinkers contained its own flourishing and stunted forms. When I asked myself, or others asked me, what was really at stake in my work, I began to realize just how important it is to develop the virtues and skills that can enable us to compare different visions of the world. The development of any genuine human capacities is commendable, but the development of these capacities is of special importance. We each live in a nation and a world where contacts among diverse peoples and ideas grow at a remarkable pace. If we are to thrive, or perhaps even survive, we must develop those virtues that will enable us to understand, judge, and deal with ideals of human flourishing that confront us but appear to differ markedly from our own.

Some of these confrontations are notional and others are real. A notional confrontation occurs when I ask myself if I can imagine, without ceasing to be me, incarnating the virtues of a T'ang dynasty Ch'an

Buddhist monk. A real confrontation occurs when I ask myself what I can say to my daughter's desire to move into a Zen monastery in San Francisco. The distinction is helpful but too neat. In this culture, confrontations that once were notional are now becoming real. Divergent, densely constituted cultures are impinging on, or are part of, American culture in a way that has few if any historical antecedents. They present all of us with possible new ways to live and therefore with real temptations and conflicts. It is worth remembering that almost every culture appears in retrospect to have missed — almost systematically missed — the real questions that confront it. How best to deal with this diversity is, I think, for our culture to face one of those questions. We must face it for our own personal well-being, for the well-being of those we love, and for the well-being of the society that is emerging.[2]

Meeting the challenges and opportunities of this unprecedented situation will demand new virtues as well as new combinations of old virtues. All the needed virtues, however, involve wanting to do, and being able to do well, something that resembles what I do in my comparison of Mencius and Aquinas. As with all intellectual activities, comparing ideals of human excellence, doing the comparative philosophy of religious flourishings, involves intellectual virtues. We must have the dispositions that lead us to undertake such comparisons and pursue them diligently. We also must have the dispositions that enable us to construct comparisons in illuminating ways and judge what, if any, normative conclusions they produce.

Books alone rarely produce what we need to face well such complex problems. Books, however, can manifest and even clarify the needed intellectual virtues; they also can reinforce old interests and generate new ones. This book, I hope, will do that for some readers, and not just in regard to the particular figures and traditions with which I deal. My inquiry is limited to two thinkers, Mencius and Aquinas, and thus to parts of two traditions, Confucianism of the Warring States period and medieval Christianity. But the method involved in such a comparison, *mutatis mutandis*, is applicable to many other kinds of projects. (This method, like all methods, is best understood and evaluated by examining how it works on particular materials; but in the final chapter I present my general ideas on how best to compare what seem to be radically different discourses on human excellence.)

To recapitulate, I aim in my examination of Mencius and Aquinas's ideas on virtue to chart similarities within differences and differences within similarities. The inquiry also leads me to construct normative positions on matters such as the theory of the self that best explain the character of virtues. Furthermore, my whole enterprise rests on the belief that we must acquire the intellectual virtues needed for comparing ideals of religious flourishings if we are to meet successfully the challenges that our diverse society presents. Let us turn now and examine several general topics that provide us with needed background. We begin by noting general similarities and differences between Mencius and Aquinas.

II. General Differences and Similarities between Mencius and Aquinas

The philosophical and religious differences between Mencius and Aquinas are often striking. In Aquinas's theistic cosmology, for example, a deity creates and preserves the world but remains fundamentally distinct from it. In Mencius's organismic cosmology all elements are intimately interconnected; they are what they are only by means of their relationships with other elements. This distinction in cosmologies helps to generate other basic differences. In Aquinas the aseity of God, personal immortality, and judgment after death are all fundamental notions. In Mencius, however, the notion of God's aseity is not even a conceptual possibility, and personal immortality, much less judgment after death, is not a crucial problem. Moreover, fundamental conceptions also often seem to diverge sharply because of differences in cosmology. It is impossible to find evident equivalents in Mencius to Aquinas's idea of grace (gratia) or to find evident equivalents in Aquinas to Mencius's notion of a psychophysical energy that can be numinous (ch'i).[3]

Furthermore, establishing relationships between basic religious elements in each thinker can be difficult. We seem to find no equivalents in Mencius to notions such as revelation, church, or sacrament, or in Aquinas to notions such as ritual (li), fate (ming), or attention (ssu). Indeed, Mencius and Aquinas apparently fail to share a similar notion of what is involved in thinking well about religious and philosophical matters. Analytic procedures and tools are central to Aquinas, but they usually remain peripheral to Mencius. He even seems to harbor suspicions about their value, believing they can damage rather than aid the religious enterprise.

These differences between the thinkers are deep enough to affect many of the apparent resemblances that we do find. That is, they make resemblances appear superficial or insignificant, to be at so abstract a level or in so narrowly circumscribed an area that they are of little importance. Mencius and Aquinas agree, for example, that a higher power, in some fashion, is responsible for human nature's character and fulfillment; that lower aspects of human nature can imperil fulfillment; and that humans can reach a state that surpasses normal human abilities, although "transhuman" forces must empower such an actualization. But their thicker accounts of any of these matters differ in significant ways. Their under-standing of, say, the higher power's character or human nature's lower aspects appear to be fundamentally different.

The number of important differences between the two and the thin-ness of many evident comparisons must always be kept in mind. We also need to remember, however, that the two thinkers themselves believed they could harmonize positions or discourses that appeared to most people to be extremely different. Aquinas, for instance, thought he could bring together St. Paul, St. Augustine, and Aristotle; and Mencius (at times at least) Yang Chu, Mo Tzu, and Confucius. Each thinker faced differences that seem almost as insurmountable as we face in bringing together Aquinas and Mencius, yet they thought they could succeed in relating them.

Their belief, or aspiration, differs from that of most sophisticated moderns, and it rests on some grounds that should be questioned. Their historical sense often is suspect; moreover, they adhere to the doubtful ideal that there is only a single form (if with concrete variations) of human flourishing. Nevertheless, their belief and effort should still give us pause, and we ought to take it seriously enough to evaluate it. Furthermore, we also ought to remember that some significant thinkers today (e.g., Alasdair MacIntyre) disagree with the tendency of most con-temporary thinkers to focus on unbridgeable kinds of diversity. They argue such a tendency arises from a failure to examine closely the claim that great thinkers and vital traditions have resources and procedures that allow them to harmonize apparently divergent positions. Thinkers in such traditions, it is argued, can incorporate divergent positions in ways that preserve their critical insights and yet fill the lacunae in their positions and solve their previously unsolved problems.[4]

Most important to us, we also find real resemblances in Mencius and Aquinas's theories of virtue and accounts of specific virtues. Resemblances appear, for example, between their ideas on semblances of virtue and expan-sions of virtues, and in the conceptions of the self that underlie their ideas on virtue; that is, in their accounts of the character and interactions of prac-tical reason, the emotions, and dispositions. Furthermore, their treatment of the virtue of courage, in both its normal and religious forms, presents a set of fascinating similarities within differences. They agree that courage is an especially significant virtue — despite accounts of central virtues that differ sharply — because humans constantly face fears they must overcome if they are to reach desired goals. Moreover, both believe that what many think exemplifies courage is only either a semblance of courage or a minor aspect of it. Furthermore, both present a view of courage's most perfect form, its religious form, that shows striking similarities.

Once we recognize these kinds of resemblances, we are led, in turn, to reconsider whether some apparently clear differences are what they seemed to be initially. For instance, is the virtue of faith as foreign to Mencius, or the idea of a recoverable good nature as foreign to Aquinas, as each initially seemed to be? Reconsiderations like these enable us both to penetrate more deeply into each thinker and to establish more subtle relationships between them.

The best way to pursue these similarities within differences is to concentrate on the details of their respective accounts. Indeed, to my mind, the most illuminating comparisons normally occur when I focus on a narrowly defined subject matter. The lengthy, comparative analysis of a single virtue, like courage, is more productive than a general discussion of their various virtues. The comparative analysis of their understanding of the relationship of dispositions and virtues sheds more light than a general treatment of their ideas about character. Generalizations about the relationships between Mencius and Aquinas have their place, but they will adequately reflect the texture of each thinker and avoid thin resemblances only if they arise from detailed examinations.

However, we do need to consider the more theoretical background that informs our detailed examinations of Mencius and Aquinas. The remainder of this chapter, therefore, examines the role ethics, and especially virtue, plays in the comparative philosophy of religions. We begin by describing three different areas in the ethical world and end by examining the general idea of virtue, especially the notions that virtues have semblances and can be expanded. These analyses give us concepts that we will utilize in our treatment of Mencius and Aquinas. They also allow us to show how the idea of virtue functions in the comparative philosophy of religions.

III. The Comparative Philosophy of Religions and the Three Realms of Ethics

All inquiries in the comparative philosophy of religions must deal with how reason operates in those areas that are religiously significant. In comparing Aquinas and Mencius, although we could focus on reason's operations in metaphysical areas I doubt, for the reasons discussed, that we would produce rich similarities in differences. (Were the subject Aquinas and a Neo-Confucian like Wang Yang-ming, the results would be somewhat different.) Our inquiry, instead, will focus on what I call their practical theories, theories that fit between their primary and secondary theories. Concentrating on them allows us to find similarities within differences that we cannot find with either of the two other kind of theories.[5]

I discuss these three kinds of theories at length in the final chapter, but note here their general character. *Primary* theories, concerning subjects like water's effect on the growth of plants, provide explanations that allow people to predict, plan, and cope with the normal problems the world presents. Such theories appear evidentally true to most in a culture and often have a universal character. *Secondary* theories, which differ from culture to culture, usually are built from primary theories to explain peculiar or distressing occurrences, such as why water suddenly kills not nurtures plants. They utilize ideas about a class of beings (such as malevolent spirits) that differ from visible phenomena and therefore appear even to those in the culture to mix the familiar and the strange. *Practical* theories often work on the ideas primary theory produces and can link with notions in secondary theory. But practical theory presents a more theoretical account than primary theory and stays closer to normal phenomena than secondary theory. Moreover, the aim is to guide people toward full actualization and therefore concepts like virtue, obligation, and disposition are utilized. Much of practical theory, then, concerns what we call ethics.

I will focus on the part of ethics that deals with conceptions of virtue, with those human excellences found in full human flourishing. Some people may understand a focus on ethics but think it odd I choose to concentrate on conceptions of virtue rather than on an ethical idea like duty or a moral theory like contractarianism. Subjects like these, it could be argued, lead to more universal conclusions, involve a clearer notion of the reasonable than appears in notions of virtue, and command more attention in contemporary Western discussions. Moreover, many today, for whom the word virtue has an archaic ring, also either associate virtue with problematic ideals, like extreme scrupulosity, or restrict it to narrow areas, like sexual activity.

Indeed, modern thinkers often question whether the idea of virtue has the intellectual, or even ethical, content to allow for productive analysis. As Kohlberg, a leading theorist on the subject of moral education, says:

> If . . . we define our moral aims in terms of virtues and vices, we are defining them in terms of the praise and blame of others, and are caught in the pulls of being all things to all men and end up being wishy-washy. Virtues and vices do have a central significance to individuals [but only] at the conventional level of morality: our praise and blame of others is based on ascribing virtues and vices to them.

Kohlberg's critical judgment rests in part (as we shall see) on his failure to distinguish between how virtues function in first-person deliberations and in third-person ascriptions. His attitude, however, reflects that found in other more careful statements. Even more important, a number of philosophers agree with Bentham's judgment that virtues are poor conceptual soldiers:

> There is no marshalling them; they are susceptible of no arrangement; they are a disorderly body, whose members are frequently in hostility with one another. . . . Most of them are characterized by that vagueness which is a convenient instrument for the poetical but dangerous or useless to the practical moralist.[6]

These kinds of objections are significant, but they surely are not uncontroversial.

The contemporary study of virtue is burgeoning; what only ten years ago was a cottage industry threatens to become an industrial giant. Most important to us, the idea of virtue is an especially helpful tool in the comparative philosophy of religious fulfillment. Thinkers in many religious traditions often have been centrally concerned with questions about virtues. We can make highly textured comparisons among them by concentrating on their lists of virtues, conceptions of virtue, notions of how people acquire virtue, and ideas about how virtues do or should interact with each other. Moreover, the normative conclusions embedded in traditional thinker's ideas about virtue usually represent especially clearly and concretely their ideas about the best possible religious life.[7]

Let us, then, examine how the idea of virtue relates to two other features of the ethical world. This subject allows us to gain familiarity with concepts, and terms of art that will help us to analyze Mencius and Aquinas's ideas about virtue. It also allows us to treat important issues in comparative religious ethics and focus through a particular prism the questions that arise from the comparative philosophy of religions, questions such as how ethical thought relates to other forms of religious expression.

The ethical world can be organized into three realms or areas. Each is distinguished both by its content and by the forms of rational justification that operate. The first area contains *injunctions*, universal commands and prohibitions. The second contains a list of *virtues* arranged in some hierarchical order. The third contains *ways or forms of life* that are protected by the injunctions and picked out by the virtues.[8]

The area of injunctions, the focus of most previous work in comparative ethics, consists in those moral prohibitions or commands that people in a culture think present inviolable rights, duties, or claims. Some injunctions are general; for example, the notion that people ought not disregard the welfare of other human beings. Many, however, are quite specific; for example, the notion that people should not have sexual relationships with their own children. Whether the content is specific or general, a sophisticated apparatus, a casuistical system, is needed to decide how and when to apply injunctions. Questions must be answered, for instance, about who counts as a child or what human welfare means.

These injunctions protect the bare necessities needed if human life is to function adequately, if human goods are to be promoted not violated, and if humans are to be treated as integral beings not instruments to other goals. They, therefore, normally are thought to hold for all societies and thus to bind all human beings. Moreover, in traditional societies, most people think injunctions reflect a sacred order; that is, express a religious demand. The universal form and religious basis of these injunctions, as well as the rational procedures by which people often find or argue for them, give injunctions a very special status. People believe their existence is neither subordinate to nor conditional upon other ideas; they remain in force in all circumstances.

Many modern Western ethicists both concentrate on this area and emphasize the role of rational reflection in producing the injunctions. The claim often is made that rational people can discover these injunctions if they strip away contingent human features and find those general, law-like constancies that define what, at the most fundamental level, humans are and need. These modern formulations and procedures, however, do not always adequately reflect the practices found in other cultures. The injunctions in such cultures often rest on unclear arguments, encompass actions that many Western ethicists would think improper, and are vague; for example, "one has to have special reasons to kill someone."

Furthermore, even though we often can find similar injunctions in many cultures, the actions they engender can differ considerably. A vendetta, for instance, may count as an adequate special reason to kill a child. In any culture, as Bernard Williams says, "ethical life is going to contain restraints on such things as killing, injury, and lying but these restraints can take very different forms."[9] Indeed, in almost all cases, the differences in form can be explained by how the other two realms of ethics, ways of life and notions of virtue, influence the application of apparently similar injunctions. The interactions among the three areas produce, then, those practices that people's lives embody and that they believe to be true.

The third area — ways or forms of life, the ethos of a culture — is both the vaguest and the most complex of the areas. (In so far as cultures contain various ways of life, the topic is even more complicated than my treatment will show as, for clarity's sake, I present a single way of life.) Deliberately chosen, explicit ideals of conduct are part of ways of life. Often more prominent, however, are unarticulated and unchosen ideals that inform attitudes as well as actions. Such ideals usually manifest themselves most clearly in those learned conventions that govern behavior in both significant, often profoundly disturbing moments — such as rituals for the dead — and in recurring, commonplace moments — such as what, if any, utensils to use when eating. Ways of life refer, then, to all those large and small actions that make up the distinctive texture of a society. We can identify easily large manifestations, such as how the dead are treated, and see why they are important. But smaller manifestations, often more difficult to identify, are also important. They include matters such as whether adults never talk to the young or talk only occasionally and then with an air of polite reserve; or whether people virtually never touch others or touch them only when they are either very old or very young.

Many features of a culture's way of life are elusive, but others can be recognized almost immediately. To travel from Italy to France is to recognize that the Italian virtue of animated, loud conversation has become the French vice of immoderate, troubling flamboyance. Indeed, difference in ways of life are what make people keenly aware, when traveling, that they are foreigners. For example, the appropriate way to greet a stranger varies from culture to culture. An American's tendency to smile in such meetings manifests a way of life that rests on the ideal that people ought to meet with openness because the unacquainted can and should be friendly with one another. In other ways of life, however, such a smile is thought to exemplify naiveté or unbecoming forwardness, and the traveling American soon realizes that. Ways of life, then, contain those ideas, generate those attitudes, and produce those social form that enable people within a group to interact easily and to feel relatively comfortable within an often threatening world.[10]

Most work in comparative religious ethics has focused on either injunctions or ways of life. (Indeed, much work in comparative religions echoes this distinction; one group deals with the logic of theoretical statements, another with the complexities of cultural practices.) Ways of life have been the province of anthropologists and historians of religions who, assuming cultural holism, emphasize the importance of fine grained analyses. They also argue culture determines the actual form ethical life takes; it provides the concrete guidelines that constrain both specific activities and abstract pictures of human flourishing.

Philosophical or religious ethicists, in contrast, usually work with universal injunctions. The bolder of them argue that enough similarity exists among human beings to enable us to find universals in the structure, arguments for, and even content of injunctions. Other ethicists are more hesitant. They attempt only to formulate general definitions and supposedly universal procedures of ethical reasoning, although they may also speculate about normative conclusions. Finally, some ethicists are even more hesitant. They argue that ethical universals can be found only if basic presuppositions are shared, such as that humans are rational agents and nature operates by morally neutral laws.

Anthropologists and historians work, then, at particular studies of ways of life and philosophical and religious ethicists search for those universal conclusions that may appear in injunctions. Relationships between these two integral approaches have often been neither happy nor productive. We can help to bridge this gap, I think, by focusing on virtues, because virtues connect intimately with both injunctions and ways of life. They connect with injunctions through their conceptual form and claims to universality and with ways of life through their embeddedness in particular cultural contexts.[11]

A list of virtues ordered in a hierarchical fashion constitutes our second area in ethics. The list defines what qualities are virtues; the hierarchical rank helps determine when one or another virtue should be manifested. The virtues listed will be numerous, will vary in scope, and may at times conflict; for example, impartial judiciousness may conflict with family loyalty. Such hierarchical ranking sets priorities among virtues, it gives people guidelines that help them to decide when one virtue takes precedence over another in a particular situation. It allows them to know, for example, that family loyalty is more prized than impartial judiciousness except when the possible death of an innocent person is involved.

The hierarchical ranking of virtues may be quite explicit. Adults may confidently teach it to the young and use it effortlessly in their evaluations of themselves and other people. Even if that clear an articulation is lacking, however, most people, most of the time, will still understand the relative weight to give to each virtue. Indeed, humans cannot operate well without utilizing a ranked list of virtues. (A stranger who attempts to chart the complicated schemes used may find the task daunting, but members of the society often use the schemes with ease and élan.) To proceed through their innumerable activities, people must know both which virtues exist and when they are to be manifested. They must know, for example, that being patient rather than assertive, moderate rather than flamboyant, ironic rather than sober is the correct behavior when you are told your friend has been slandered.

We ought not overestimate the clarity of the guidelines such hierarchical order produces, however, especially in reflective people and in more complex cultures. (Indeed, the notions of semblances and expansions of virtues are often important just because the guidelines are unclear.) The process of establishing priorities among virtues depends on many variables and often is complicated. A person's ranking of family loyalty and impartial judgment, for example, may depend on the age and role both of the agent and those, outside and inside the family, with whom the agent deals. In fact, the ability to use well such a scheme is itself a crucial virtue, the virtue of "practical reason." In its operations, which I will analyze closely later, we often see one of the most critical manifestations in ethics of that rationality with which the comparative philosophy of religions is concerned.

The different roles of rationality in guiding and understanding virtuous action also are seen when we examine the relationship of the realm of virtue to the realms of injunctions and ways of life. Virtues resemble injunctions in three ways. Some virtues are universal; they are necessary if any society is to be preserved and the people within it are to flourish. Courage, for example, is both essential in any person who is to be praised and required in any culture that is to have a significant social life. Moreover, as with injunctions, we can achieve considerable conceptual precision about the structure of virtues. Particular acts of courage may differ, but we can articulate precisely what is involved in using the concept of courage. Finally, most virtues relate to injunctions because people rely on them to provide principles that guide their actions. Courageous people will be guided, for instance, by the principle that innocent people ought not be hurt needlessly.

Virtues also connect intimately with ways of life, even more intimately than they do with injunctions. Both the specific list of virtues and the actual rank of any virtue depend largely on the way of life in which they are embedded. In one ethos more priority will be given to acting from impartial fairness than to acting from loyalty to blood relations, but in another ethos the reverse will occur. Similarly, evaluations of people's excellence will rest on whether honesty or the preservation of social relations is more prized, on whether scrupulous care for others' feelings or spontaneous but possibly disturbing interactions with them is more valued. The distinctive style that a virtuous act manifests, and the relative weight that a virtue receives in relationship to other virtues all arise from a way of life.

Ways of life largely determine, then, which virtues are expressed and how all virtues are ranked. Lists of virtues and their hierarchical order, in turn, help distinguish ways of life. Significant differences exist between a culture that leads people to see patriotic self-sacrifice as the paradigm of courage and one that leads them to see acts of religious asceticism as the paradigm. Moreover, other major differences appear if courage is thought to be the greatest of the virtues, to be an important virtue only if it serves benevolence, or to be a minor virtue that truly good people rarely need.

Indeed, the way of life in which a virtue is embedded, its social location, in some cases basically can determine its content. If we ask whether Odysseus's response to Cyclops was courageous or brash or whether we can call courageous Robert E. Lee's decision to lead the Confederate Army, the answer often will rest on the respondent's actual or assumed social location. Moreover, the fit of virtues and a way of life can be so close that a person in one way of life cannot embrace the list and ranking of virtues that exist in another way of life. The virtues needed for a life characterized by an overriding and revolutionary political commitment cannot coexist with the virtues needed for a life characterized by decent usefulness and normal family loyalty.[12]

We must attend closely to injunctions, ways of life, and virtues, I think, if we are to render adequately all the rich complexity of humanity's ethical life. Analyzing injunctions and studying the exact forms of ways of life are obviously very important pursuits. Nevertheless, we can best establish textured but manageable comparisons if we focus on virtues rather than either on a few general injunctions or on the almost overwhelming complexity and diversity of ways of life. Moreover, when we focus on virtue we also necessarily refer to both of the other realms. In treating virtues, we must always move between the general, usually abstract injunctions of the first area and the specific, highly variable forms of life of the third area.

The conception of virtue, and the kind of practical theory it expresses, is complex enough that I need to end this chapter with some theoretical comments about it. In the following section, I sketch out a general account of virtue, drawing on modern Western discussions, and note how it informs my analysis of Mencius and Aquinas. In the final section, I examine two features of the concept of virtue (that they can be expanded and that they have semblances) and discuss how they are utilized by many thinkers, including Mencius and Aquinas, to challenge and change ethical ideals.

IV. The General Conception of Virtue

Virtues are a group of related and relatively well-defined qualities that most individuals in a group think reflect admirable characteristics. The exact boundaries of the category always will be a matter of dispute. Perfect pitch or great natural strength surely will not count as virtues, for example, but sexual attractiveness might if it arises from character and not simply from natural beauty. That is, characteristic pattern of desires and motivations, some evidence of "will," also must be present if a quality is to count as a virtue. A virtue, then, is a disposition to act, desire, and feel that involves the exercise of judgment and leads to a recognizable human excellence or instance of human flourishing. Moreover, virtuous activity involves choosing virtue for itself and in light of some justifiable life plan.

We can also differentiate virtues into two general categories: virtues of inclination or motivation like benevolence and preservative or neutralizing virtues, virtues of will power, like courage. Preservative virtues protect inclinational virtues by resisting desires that impede their actualization. Inclinational virtues, in turn, often produce the goals for which preservative virtues strive. The interactions between the two are complicated enough that a mechanical application of the distinction will obscure rather than illuminate. Nevertheless, the distinction helps us to differentiate broad classes of virtues, to unravel some especially subtle actions, and to understand the weight of what occurs when, as I shall discuss, religiously perfected courage becomes an inclinational not a preservative virtue.[13]

With either kind of virtue, the crucial predicate we use in evaluating actions (except with those in the realm of injunctions) is whether they are "in or out of character." The good equals what a person does who possesses the appropriate character traits and the bad what a person does who lacks them. Good and bad are defined in terms of what is and is not compatible with a certain kind of life. The good or flourishing person provides us, then, with the ultimate criterion by which to judge what states to seek and what acts to do. This "good person criterion" surely is circular. We use good people to identify what is good, and we know those people are good because they manifest the goods we came to know from the examples of good people. But the circle, as I shall discuss, is benign or even virtuous rather than a vicious.[14]

Most important here, when truly virtuous people deliberate, they do not think about the goodness of a virtue and the way of life it manifests. Rather they think about the situations they face and the descriptions under which their action fits. I act benevolently because the situation I face fits a description that elicits my benevolence: a suffering person whom I can aid confronts me. I do not act benevolently in order to be benevolent or to be seen as benevolent by myself or others. Indeed, if I do act that way I fall short of true benevolence. To be virtuous, then, is to pick out as relevant a range of facts and considerations and to act on them. Virtuous people do not think about their own actions in the same way as observers would comment on them; first-person deliberations and third-person ascriptions differ radically.

Two abstract considerations, however, inform a virtuous person's deliberations. One is a tendency to see certain acts as duties; the other is a propensity to consider the consequences of actions. (To use current labels, the virtuous person manifests deontological and consequentialist concerns.) In a more perfect world than we inhabit, judgments arising from virtue, duty, and a concern for consequences all easily would harmonize with each other. In this world they sometimes will not. In situations where they do conflict, virtuous people will regret whatever action they take. But the regret is not as intense as it would be if an unvirtuous action had produced a considerably less harmful result. Nor is it the kind of regret that arises when I do something I know to be virtuous — refusing to browbeat a student to obtain information — even though it causes results I abhor — the possible destruction of a promising academic career. My regret is intense, but it concerns a world that produces such impossible choices not the virtuous action.[15]

The relationship of virtuous action to notions of duty or consequences constitutes the first of the three areas in which cluster most Western discussions of virtue. In this area, most academic philosophers, many public philosophers, and some theologians connect ideas of virtue to other modern theories of morality, especially deontological or contractarian theories. (Earlier thinkers, like Sidgwick, did discuss extensively the relationship of virtue to utilitarianism.) The major issue is whether notions of virtue either provide a needed supplement to modern theories or even can replace them. A more direct inquiry into the character of virtue occurs in the other two areas.

Analysts in the second area examine those characteristics of mind and actions relevant to ideas about virtue. When they examine topics such as the character of practical judgments, emotions, and dispositions, their approach usually is abstract and stresses conceptual rigor. Other topics, such as the significance of narrative, community, and tradition, usually demand other abilities and approaches. Analysts will give detailed, nuanced descriptions of exemplary lives, for instance, or employ the explorative, tentative form of the essay. Virtue theorists must worry about all these topics, and respond to all these genres, if they are adequately to explore how character is produced, how it affects action, and how it is to be understood and evaluated.[16]

Finally, the last and least developed area of discussion concerns how ideas of virtue relate to theories of the good, to the subject of axiology. Virtue theorists, especially those drawn to traditional formulations, often believe that one kind of life manifests more fully the human good than does another kind. They think, for example, that a life committed to theoretical reflection is better than one that is not. Examining different notions of human flourishing and the justifications for them that can be presented, then, is obviously important.[17]

Those topics that arise from inquiries into the characteristics of mind and action will be most prominent in the discussion of Mencius and Aquinas. However, I also will briefly discuss their conception of the relationship of virtues to injunctions and treat at greater length their axiological judgments. In all three areas, the questions that Aquinas and especially Mencius address at times will differ from those that modern Westerners address. Their distant cultures and times explain some of these differences. Others, however, arise because they work from traditional religious visions. Unlike all modern Westerners, save for a few theologians, Mencius and Aquinas highlight hierarchies among virtues or within a virtue that rest on religious criteria. Both also will argue that the highest forms of virtue can be understood only if people recognize the significance of a correct religious view of the world and allow for the presence of transhuman powers and the communities they affect. With courage, for instance, they present a hierarchy of actions that culminates in effortless acts of self-sacrifice, arises from higher powers and appropriate communities, and manifests toward life a distinctively religious attitude.[18]

Nevertheless, notions drawn from modern discussions of virtue can help us understand their accounts. One last such notion is the idea that virtues are "corrective." Virtues correct some difficulty thought to be natural to human beings, some temptation that needs to be resisted, or some motivation that needs to be made good. No need, for example, would exist for benevolence if humans lacked selfish impulses; nor for industry if they lacked a propensity to idleness; nor for perseverance if they lacked a tendency to surrender before it is proper; nor for courage if they lacked an inclination to be dissuaded by fear from doing what should be done. Ideas about virtues, then, rest on a picture of human weakness and need. (This connection helps to explain why relating virtues to vices often can reveal much about the character of virtue.) Specific virtues can be correlated with the problems they correct to produce a picture of what human nature is "before" virtues change it. Moreover, such correlations can show us what conflicts will exist if virtue's correction is imperfect. This means we can use Mencius and Aquinas's ideas about virtue to identify what they believe are a human being's basic needs, problems, and possibilities.[19]

In making these correlations, however, we need to realize that inclinational and preservative virtues correct problems in different ways. Inclinational virtues correct a general human tendency, such as to self-indulgence or selfishness. In a fully virtuous person, they do not correct present tendencies. I need not feel the pull of selfishness to be benevolent. Preservative virtues, in contrast, usually correct a present psychological state. Courageous people legitimately fear the loss of life or reputation that their action may bring, and they must overcome that present fear. Some perfected preservative virtues, such as moderation about alcohol, may only correct a general human tendency. Even then, however, the situation in which the virtue is exercised must be one where a normal person would actually feel the contrary impulse. Moreover, with most people and most kinds of moderation, such as that used in sexual expression, the virtue never can reach that perfect a state. (Indeed, as we will discuss, when a preservative virtue like courage corrects only a general human tendency the agent must be transformed by some extraordinary power.)

Some issues about the character of correction, then, are complicated. Nevertheless, using that idea as well as others drawn from modern analyses of virtue can help us to understand and evaluate Mencius and Aquinas's accounts. Let us turn now to our last introductory topic: how thinkers challenge and reform the ideals of virtue regnant in their times by means of the ideas of expansions and semblances of virtue. Mencius and Aquinas, especially in their work on courage, illustrate how this process works, but I shall present here a theoretical account of the process and its implications.

V. Expansions and Semblances of Virtue

Reflective people often can feel uneasy with the understandings of virtue that operate most widely in their culture. One way such people can challenge and possibly reform the common understanding is to *expand* a virtue, to extend the range and thus the meaning of a particular virtue. Another way is to use the conception of *semblances* of virtue to identify differences among apparently similar kinds of virtuous activity, and therefore also to develop more subtle ways to evaluate behavior and character. The goal of both strategies is to make people's conceptions of virtue more religiously meaningful and philosophically sophisticated.

The need for such changes often is especially pronounced with the virtue of courage, and examining it illustrates well the point. Mencius and Aquinas, for example, both think the behavior that many believe exemplifies courageous action is either only a small part of courage or a semblance of it. They agree, then, with those moderns who think courage, as it is commonly understood, fits well only into either a harsher age or a questionable ideal of human life. But they disagree with those moderns who conclude that therefore courage is not a virtue. Expanding the meaning of courage and distinguishing between real courage and its semblances is Mencius and Aquinas's response.

Contemporary critics claim courage was a crucial virtue only when heroic societies were the norm. In those times (and in some unfortunate places today), a society or person was under constant threat of physical attack. People could preserve themselves, their families, and all else they valued only through the simplest, rawest kind of courage. They had to do battle with an enemy bent on mass destruction. This situation helps to produce a heroic perspective on the world. Right and wrong are drawn in strong hues; dramatic conflict continually is seen and often even sought. Self-sacrifice for ideals and destruction of enemies operate with robust fullness, and both honor received and physical heroism shown are among a society's most valued treasures. (Such a perspective also normally reflects and reinforces a social structure that manifests clear hierarchical distinctions between males and females and aristocrats and common people.)

Today, however, critics argue far fewer face the constant threat of physical attack. Therefore, courage and the heroic ideal it serves should also pass away. People ought to cultivate virtues such as imagination, irony, and political adeptness instead. These virtues allow people to avoid situations in which courage would otherwise be needed. Moreover, they provide people with a fuller picture of human fulfillment than do courage and the virtues that cohere with it. Rather then seeing difficulties to confront courageously, people should either cultivate virtues that allow them to find an imaginative compromise or view a situation with ironic detachment.[20]

This argument surely has cogency, and even poignancy, in late-twentieth-century America. The character and public reception of fictional figures like Rambo and real figures like Oliver North easily can lead one to doubt the value of courage. Even more reflective and eloquent examples of a kind of courage can lead one to shudder. Consider, for example, General Skobeleff, whom William James quotes as follows:

> I believe that my bravery is simply the passion and at the same time the contempt of danger. The risk of life fills me with an exaggerated rapture. The fewer there are to share it, the more I like it. The participation of my body in the event is required to furnish me an adequate excitement. Everything intellectual appears to me to be reflex; but a meeting of man to man, a duel, a danger into which I can throw myself headforemost, attracts me, moves me, intoxicates me. I am crazy for it, I love it, I adore it. I run after danger as one runs after women; I wish it never to stop. Were it always the same, it would bring me a new pleasure. When I throw myself into an adventure in which I hope to find it, my heart palpitates with the uncertainty; I could wish at once to have it appear and yet to delay. A sort of painful and delicious shiver shakes me; my entire nature runs to meet the peril with and impetus that my will would in vain try to resist.[21]

The general may be an extreme example, but as James notes, Garibaldi voiced similar ideas; and other laudable figures have expressed nearly the same sentiments. Indeed, the presence of these kinds of virtue makes us see the weight of Nietzsche's aphorism: "Prayer to men. — 'Forgive us our virtues' — thus one should pray to men."[22] Furthermore, we all know that societies, or at least governments, often proclaim the value of courage when the goals at which they aim are most suspect. As an Eastern European proverb says, when they begin to talk about courage, it is time to emigrate.

Many traditional thinkers, including Mencius and Aquinas, have recognized these problems. They also argue, however, that courage always has an important place. The strain, sacrifice, and drama of risk-taking and the resolution it manifests are both needed and valuable. Using the notions of expansions of courage and of semblances of courage, they develop an account that preserves courage and meets the difficulties presented by common understandings of it. They distinguish among the various manifestations of courage, develop other aspects of courage, and identify which forms are integral. For example, they distinguish true courage from those semblances of it that manifest only anger or a balancing of different fears. They also expand the notion of courage in a way that makes it an integral part of any correct religious attitude and a virtue that includes all undertakings that involve arduous striving. I will examine these transformations of courage later, but I need here to analyze the two general procedures that underlie them. Expanding virtues and identifying their semblances are two processes that reveal much about the character of virtues.

The procedure that thinkers use in the *expansion* of a virtue is relatively simple, even if the actual working out of any expansion often is complicated. They identify the general characteristics a virtue embodies and then gather under it all activities that manifest those characteristics. Expanding most people's overly narrow picture of the virtue of benevolence, for example, would involve arguing that the sympathetic reaction it embodies ought to reach beyond those linked by blood ties, shared roles, or a common community. Significant difficulties well may occur when thinkers try to convince people that such an expansion is justified. They must answer questions, for instance, about issues such as the difference, if any, between benevolence toward family and benevolence toward associates. But the general procedure that underlies the process of expansion is straightforward.

The notion that virtues have *semblances* is more complicated, but it also illuminates much, and therefore I will consider it at some length. Real virtues have both counterfeits and semblances. (These three conceptions and the phenomena they identify can be placed on a spectrum with counterfeit virtues and real virtues at either end and semblances of virtue in the middle.) Genuinely virtuous activity, then, contrasts with apparently similar activities intended to deceive others and with activities that resemble real virtue but lack important elements in it. For instance, a person whose amiability is counterfeit aims to use another for his or her own profit. A person whose amiability rests only on a belief that amiability helps society function smoothly possesses a semblance of the virtue. A person who possesses real amiability has a genuine affection for people that arises from a sensitivity both to their winning qualities and to the pleasures of social intercourse.

The concept of counterfeit virtues is easily understood and reveals little of theoretical interest about virtues. (Being able to identify them, of course, often is very important if we are to negotiate our way through life.) I will focus, therefore, on the relationship between virtues and their semblances. Understanding that relationship allows us to specify the exact character of virtues and to see how thinkers use these notions both to guide people toward real virtues and to criticize prevailing but erroneous ideas of virtue.

To be able to guide and criticize in this fashion often is especially important to religious thinkers. Their communities contain many people who either have lost touch with their tradition's more exalted picture of virtues or cannot consistently distinguish between that picture and its semblances. Mencius, for example, worries about what he calls the "village honest man" (hsiang-yüan). To many this type of person represents the epitome of virtue. Mencius, however, labels him the thief of virtue. Such people, he thinks, mistake the true self for the self in its social roles, misunderstand what should motivate virtuous activity, and therefore impede their own and others' development. Aquinas has similar concerns. A false picture of the virtues involved in martyrdom (defined broadly as a surrender of the self to serve God) leads people astray. They violate Christian ideals about the need to love the self, to respect created goods, and to examine closely apparently personal directives from God.

Thinkers who reflect on virtue recognize, then, that religious traditions will always contain a tension between what many, or even most, people think is true action or belief and what the opinion of advanced adherents reveal. As Czeslaw Milosz graphically puts the point: "[religious] doctrine is very difficult because it contains, as it were, several geological strata. One would not immediately guess that the . . . [ordinary adherent's] naive questions and answers have about as much connection with what underlies them as plant life has with the seething core of the planet."[23] In extreme cases, truly virtuous activity can differ considerably from what conventionally virtuous people do. Conventional people, for example, believe that virtuous action rests on an allegiance to generally accepted rules and therefore provides predictable, reliable results. They fail to see that real virtue rests on character, sensitivity to situations, and religious insight. That difference can lead the conventional to declare unethical the activity of a truly virtuous person who attacks normal social or religious practice in the name of a higher vision.

In more ordinary cases, the differences in the action taken are less pronounced but the differences in motivation can be great. Conventional people often mistake semblances of virtue for real virtues by not understanding that a virtuous person chooses virtuous action for itself, not for its consequences. A semblance of virtue exists if an agent chooses a virtuous action for consequences, such as material gain or enhanced reputation, that a nonvirtuous person would desire. A semblance of courage exists, for example, if I challenge the sexist actions of my boss, despite the possible loss of a job, in order to win the regard of fellow workers. In a case like this my aim resembles that of the nonvirtuous person; I just believe virtue not vice will best allow me to attain it.

Moreover, conventional people fail to realize that truly virtuous agents choose virtue for their own reasons and not because of some second-hand support such as custom or authority. That is, they choose it as part of a rational, justifiable life plan. Virtuous people's choice need not imply, as we discussed, that thought about the virtue's value enters into their deliberations. But the actions do arise from discrete acts of attention, the intelligent activation of dispositions, and a previous cultivation of the desired state. Virtue arises from choice, then, not simply from association. It comes from intelligently activated dispositions, not simply routine reactions; and it involves the choosing of virtue for itself and in view of a whole life plan.

The person embracing virtue and the person embracing semblances of virtue, then, dispute not about means to an end they both pursue but about the components of the human good. That dispute can concern only relatively unimportant components, such as whether fine food is necessary for a good life. But it also can concern the most basic components, such as whether encountering possible death to protect other people is ever justified. In many cases, especially ones involving courage, the conflict is dramatic.

The outline and implication of such conflicts is developed well in Terence Irwin's analysis of Plato's account of how different is the mad love of the truly virtuous from the slavish love of the "prudent." Normal, prudent people consider the truly virtuous to be imprudent, even mad, because their idea of humanity's ultimate end differs so markedly from that of the virtuous. This

> dispute about ultimate ends partly explains why other people think the really virtuous man is mad; they neither share nor sympathize with his ultimate end, but prefer the non-lover's virtue. . . . [Moreover, they think] the virtuous man's madness makes him indifferent to the consequences of his actions . . .[and so] think he is imprudent.[24]

Self-love operates in both kinds of people; both are concerned for their future states. But conventionally prudent people (the slavish for Plato) display their concern in a cautious attitude, a humdrum thrift, that leads them to think the truly virtuous must be indifferent to their future states. They fail to understand that the truly virtuous think a person should chose the virtuous state for itself, choose it because it is a part of a good life.

Both types of people realize that their choices may involve the loss of real goods. But the virtuous also think that the goods almost all people pursue — goods such as wealth, honor, or power — are real goods only for someone who lives virtuously. Such goods can be real only if people see them as what helps to constitute a way of life that fulfills human capacities in a harmonious way, not just as what satisfies normal human appetites.

Even more important, unlike slavish people, virtuous people recognize not only *acquisitive* but also *expressive* motives for action. They will choose a virtuous action not only because it contributes to goods they pursue but also because it expresses their conception of the good. The differences in attitude appear clearly when questions arise about whether to undertake some kinds of courageous action. The difference, for instance, means that

> the virtuous man who acts for the sake of what is admirable will prefer to do a single admirable action, even with disastrous consequences to himself, than to live on without having done it. Self sacrifice is [then] an extreme case of the virtuous man's normal attitude to virtuous action; he regards it as worthwhile because it expresses his conception of what is good and admirable, and the best life demands that kind of activity, with no further questions about its contribution to his happiness. . . . [The truly virtuous man] will plan a life which does not sacrifice more important future interest to present satisfaction, but he will not prefer his future on any terms over present actions which express his idea of himself. His decision will sometimes need courage, to override future directed desires and do what he thinks best; and this kind of courage will distinguish [him].[25]

Both acquisitive and expressive motives lead truly virtuous people to act in ways which the conventional will label imprudent. They choose the virtuous state, even if the consequences are disastrous, because this state of being is itself a part of the good life they want to acquire and express.

Such a dramatic choice is not, however, made recklessly. It arises from careful deliberation and from the cultivation of those dispositions that undergird good judgment. (It also arises from a recognition of the goods present in the world; in fact, only virtuous people fully appreciate those goods.) This kind of choice is a harmonious extension of these people's usual attitude to virtuous activity. Its possibly catastrophic consequences serve only to make strikingly clear the fundamental distinctions between truly virtuous people and people who manifest only semblances of virtue.

Both Mencius and Aquinas utilize the distinction between virtue and its semblances. When they couple it with expansions of the range of virtues, they can both challenge and reform regnant notions of virtue. Moreover, we can use these two ideas, as I shall examine more fully later, to pursue two normative aspects of this kind of comparative philosophy of religions: the construction of an accurate account of some areas of life and the acquisition of those intellectual virtues needed to do comparative work on ideals of religious flourishing.

Let us now examine more systematically Mencius and Aquinas's ideas on virtue. In the next chapter, I will briefly introduce each thinker and then examine three topics that establish a context for our more detailed study. The topics are their lists of virtues, their ideas about the relationships among injunctions and ways of life, and their understanding of human failures to be virtuous. The following chapters will contain lengthy investigations of their theories of virtue and their ideas about the virtue of courage.

Chapter 2

The Context for Mencius and Aquinas's Ideas of Virtue

I. Issues in the Interpretation of Mencius and Aquinas

Thomas Aquinas (1224/25-1274 C.E.) is one of the West's most influential and representative thinkers. In productivity and range he has few equals, and his combination of philosophic acumen and spiritual sensitivity is equally rare. Similar claims can be made about Mencius's (fourth century B.C.E., c. 390 to 310/305 B.C.E.) thought, spirituality, and influence in China, although his range and productivity are limited in comparison with those of Aquinas. The stature and influence of each thinker, as well as their cultural and temporal distance from us, is great enough to require comment on how we can best approach them.

Mencius's (Meng Tzu) ideas appear in a book called the *Mencius*, a collection of both sayings by Mencius and reports of discussions that involve him or his followers. The subject matter varies considerably. Much of it concerns political topics that arise from Mencius's attempts to counsel kings. But the book also contains, for instance, poetic aphorisms, mystical statements, and theoretical analysis of the tendencies of human nature. More than the usual interpretative difficulties dog attempts to understand the text, and only some of these problems are shared by the texts of Aquinas. Ancient Chinese culture is markedly different from our own, and significant gaps exist in our grasp of the relevant context. Mencius, for example, debates with people about whom we know little; and he sometimes, perhaps often, utilizes a technical vocabulary the exact meaning of which is unclear. Moreover, Mencius's style ranges from straightforward expositions to presentations that are closer to poetry than prose. The Chinese in the text, although often strikingly powerful or beautiful, also is sometimes cryptic; interpretations and translations of some passages can differ markedly.

Furthermore, the text is "layered": it reflects different levels and kinds of understanding. Some differences reflect how Mencius tailors his statements to the person to whom he talks. In a few cases we know the person involved and can grasp the effect of such tailoring. With many important passages, however, we know almost nothing about the context. Other differences probably arise from changes in Mencius's ideas on a subject. We can only speculate on whether a statement is early or late, although we do have criteria that allow us to distinguish more from less sophisticated ideas. Using such criteria is always controversial (if also, in this case, unavoidable), but we need to exercise special care because there are hints that Mencius's idea of argument or picture of religious perfection differs substantially from contemporary Western pictures.

The text of the *Mencius*, then, is extraordinarily rich but can be ambiguous or even mysterious. I will use a version of the interpretative principle of charity in dealing with it; that is, I aim to give an account that makes theoretical sense if at all possible. I also, however, aim to interpret the text within the context in which it was written. Combining the two can be difficult, and not just because of lacunae in our understanding of the context. Interpreting someone in context can lead to highlighting what, to us, are peculiar ideas or formulations. Interpreting someone in terms of the most sensible, to us, reconstructions of their ideas can lead to highlighting plausible ideas or formulations. (It also can lead us, for reasons I will discuss later, to using terms drawn from Western thought.) The balancing act required is difficult and some falls are inevitable. When I fall I will land on the side that emphasizes the sense and coherence of the ideas themselves. Work in the comparative philosophy of religions demands that we attempt to balance, of course, but the tendency to fall toward that side also is, I think, one defining feature of such work.

I will be little concerned with relating Mencius to his Confucian predecessors, notably Confucius, or successors, notably the great Neo-Confucian commentators on him. Understanding these relationships is important, complicated, and often has been the focus of Western and Chinese scholarship. For our purposes, however, Mencius is best understood as working with a set of problems, terms, and views — a discourse — that is shared by most fourth century B.C.E. Chinese thinkers. I fit, then, with those scholars who stress the intellectual and religious context in which classical Chinese thinkers work more than the intellectual and religious traditions to which they belong.[1]

How to relate to one's own predecessors, as well as to the predecessors of one's opponents, is one problem, of course, for fourth century B.C.E. thinkers. Mencius, for example, sees himself as defending the Confucian message especially against that being propagated by followers of Yang Chu and Mo Tzu. Nevertheless, Mencius, I think, is best understood on most issues by seeing the foes and friends he is currently engaged with, rather than by interpreting him through past figures in his tradition.

Mencius's relationship to the people and texts that follow him is a fascinating and important story, but different than the one with which I am concerned. At times, however, the relationship of Mencius to close successors illuminates features of Mencius especially clearly, and these we will briefly consider. (Hsün Tzu's debate with Mencius and those positions in the *Chuang Tzu* that seem aimed at Mencius are examples.) The comments on Mencius and use of him by more distant successors, especially his Neo-Confucian commentators, can be illuminating, as they were men of extraordinary brilliance, learning, and insight. Nevertheless, their interpretations usually are set within the context of a search for an enlightenment that lets an underlying Mind shine forth. Their secondary theories, then, differ enough from those of Mencius that their understanding of his positions can be problematic, whatever may be the merits of their own positions. I will briefly discuss this issue when, in the next chapter, I consider "discovery and development" models of human nature as they relate to Mencius, but let us now turn to Aquinas.[2]

We face with Aquinas some of the same interpretative issues we face with Mencius. But we also possess a plethora of texts, close analyses, and historical information about his culture and his opponents, which makes our task much easier. For example, Aquinas's texts, like Mencius's, are layered; they reflect different levels and kinds of understanding. The job of sorting out the layers is far simpler, however, even though it often also rests on distinguishing between more and less sophisticated ideas. We can accurately date almost all of Aquinas's work. Moreover, tracing out his more and less complicated presentations often is relatively easy; for instance, he will present an evidently general investigation of a topic and then, at another place, probe it in more detailed fashion.

With Aquinas, as with Mencius, I will use both the interpretative principle of charity and interpret his work in the context in which it was written. The same problems, and "solutions," noted earlier then also will be present.

Moreover, as in my interpretation of Mencius, I will only rarely examine Aquinas's relationships to those brilliant successors who commented on him and used his ideas. (In the next chapter, however, I do treat the difference between what I call a Stoic reading of Aquinas and his own position.) The position of these successors, whatever its intrinsic merits, shows the kind of fundamental difference in general perspective which characterizes Mencius's successors. In contrast to my treatment of Mencius, I will examine aspects of Aquinas's relationship to his predecessors, although I will not usually assess the accuracy of his understanding of them. Aquinas's attempt to combine these predecessors, who span two millennia, is critical to his whole enterprise. I will examine both how this attempt affects his analysis and how a version of it may be of use to us when we think about how best to do the comparative philosophy of religious flourishings.[3]

One last issue in interpreting Aquinas, substantially different from any found in Mencius, needs to be discussed. Aquinas's thought can appear to be overly abstract, needlessly formal, and dogmatically inflexible. (That sense is heightened by the fact it is encased in a technical and, to us, odd and forbidding vocabulary.) His mind can seem to be a highly refined calculating machine that spins out preordained answers from preestablished formulas.

This impression, I think, is largely mistaken. Aquinas was (in one scholar's phrase) "a man in a hurry," and he chose an impersonal, spare style that left the reader to fill in the background and examples. But a vital, flexible quality usually characterizes his analysis. Even the strange and apparently inflexible form of articles in *Summa Theologiae* (with their objections and answers to objections) can be seen as a way to reproduce a discussion in which Aquinas hones positions by responding to specific questions. Furthermore, we often see him modify previous treatments as new ideas or problems become significant for him.

Aquinas does employ a technical apparatus that, at times, can obscure rather than aid his inquiry. But his actual procedure is a common and productive one, especially when ethics is the topic. He starts from diverse and often conflicting common or traditional opinions. He then attempts to harmonize them, to resolve their apparent discrepancies, by making distinctions among the meanings of apparently similar words or sentences.

Despite this similarity to contemporary Western procedures, a variety of features distinguish him, and Mencius, from most modern inquiries, and recognizing that must inform our interpretation. Aquinas's thought is circumscribed by both authoritative texts and accepted methods of analysis in a way that resembles Mencius's but differs from almost all modern Western thinkers. Moreover, despite his deep sense of the fragility of human understanding, his assurance about conclusions, as with Mencius's assurance, differs from the assurance of virtually any sophisticated modern. He never doubts that a reality exists, separate from human knowing, even though he may question any human's ability to grasp it adequately. Most important, like Mencius, he does not believe real alternative conceptual schemes are possible; that is, that fundamentally different yet defensible ways to describe the world can exist.[4]

The differences between contemporary thinkers and both Mencius and Aquinas, and the difficulties in interpreting both of them, should induce caution in us. But much of the productivity in examining them, and some of the excitement, lies in working through such differences and difficulties. Let us, then, begin our investigation. I will start with separate analyses of Aquinas and Mencius's lists of virtues and the analytic procedures they manifest. I then compare features of their two lists of virtues and examine one last characteristic of the context in which their conceptions of virtue operate: the relationship of the realms of injunctions and ways of life in their ethical thinking.

II. Aquinas's List of Virtues

Sketching the lists of virtues that appear in Mencius and Aquinas, in large part, is a bloodless exercise in which thin descriptions must predominate. Nevertheless, this process enables us to present a variety of crucial material, introduces important aspects of each figure, and even allows us to raise some interesting comparative questions. We will begin with Aquinas's list, including two ideas that underlie his construction of it, then turn to Mencius's list, and end by comparing the two lists.

Aquinas's treatment of specific virtues is astonishingly complex and lengthy, covering over a million words and 170 separate questions in the *Summa Theologiae* alone. The major features of his list, however, are relatively simple. *Acquired natural virtues*, like courage, guide people's normal life. The fully flourishing religious life, however, is informed by the *infused virtues*, like faith, that are produced by God and aim toward Him. The *Gifts of the Holy Spirit*, in turn, make a person more responsive to divine promptings and therefore deepen the activities involved in both kinds of virtue.

The most important acquired natural virtues are called cardinal virtues; they are practical wisdom, justice, courage, and moderation. Of the infused virtues, the most important are called *theological virtues*; they are faith, hope, and charity. Aquinas also gathers other virtues under each of these seven virtues, calling them *parts of virtues*; caution, for example, is a separate virtue that is an integral part of practical wisdom. All these natural and infused virtues interact and affect each other in various ways. Indeed, their interactions manifest one of Aquinas's central principles, the idea that grace does not destroy but presupposes and perfects nature.

In his list of virtues, then, Aquinas divides human excellences among acquired virtues and infused virtues, and he identifies seven of them as especially important. By using the notion that *virtues have parts*, however, he can incorporate a great variety of other virtues under each of the cardinal and theological virtues and relate them systematically to each other and to the principal virtue. The parts of a virtue can be of three kinds. A component or integral part (*pars integralis*) is an element needed for the primary virtue's full functioning, a quality that combines with others to shape the virtue's action. Memory, caution, and teachableness are component parts of practical wisdom, for example. The kind or type (*pars subjectiva*) of a primary virtue is a separate virtue that fits within the general category of a primary virtue but that differs in important ways from other virtues that also fit. Practical wisdom contains domestic, military, and political kinds, for instance. Finally, an allied or subordinate virtue (*pars potentialis*) shares the primary virtue's general attributes, and even may surpass it in some respect, but fails to express fully the primary virtue's paradigmatic characteristics. *Gnome*, the wit to judge when exceptions to a rule are needed, is an allied virtue of practical wisdom. We will return to the implications of the idea that virtues have parts, but here we only need note that Aquinas uses the idea to list, relate, and examine a great variety of separable human excellences.

The four cardinal or hinge (*cardo*) natural virtues, as noted, are practical wisdom (*prudentia*), justice (*justitia*), courage (*fortitudo*), and moderation (*temperantia*). Practical wisdom, an intellectual virtue, concerns reason's guidance of conduct; justice concerns people's actions toward others; and courage and moderation concern that control of the emotions needed for the realization of all excellences. Practical wisdom covers, then, all those complicated operations that govern appropriate descriptions of the world and actions in it; decisions, for example, about when to be angry and when to be forgiving. Justice concerns people's relationships with other beings; rendering what is due is justice's goal and the action itself, not the intent behind it, is the crucial component. Courage and moderation, the two preservative virtues, concern people's relationship to their emotions, especially the forming of them that enables people to overcome obstacles to correct thought, feeling, and action.

The *infused virtues* differ from the acquired virtues in two crucial respects. God produces them, and He is the object they seek and, in a sense, reach. Human beings, then, are "divinized" through them; they receive dispositions that produce new kinds of activity and manifest a new level of being. Faith (*fides*), hope (*spes*), and charity (*caritas*), the theological virtues, are the most critical infused virtues because their relationship to God and animation of activity is especially pronounced and important. Faith differs markedly from most other intellectual operations. Love animates its assent and a real, albeit incomplete, relationship with God is produced, especially when charity informs it. Similarly, hope's distinguishing mark is a confidence that arises from the affective rather than the cognitive faculties; it moves toward God as a good that faith presents but that is difficult to attain. Mediating between presumption and despair, hope manifests a certitude about God's power not about any human's abilities.

Finally, charity concerns a relationship with God that, if analogically, can be described best in terms of Aristotle's ideal friendship. That is, charity is characterized by a sharing of "desires" with God , a wish for continuing companionship with Him, an awareness of the relationship, and all those other attributes, such as joy and peace, that are features of true friendship. Charity animates people, then, to pursue a specific kind of life. That life makes them fitting subjects for the friendship of a being whose friendship is a basic good, and one that actualizes all aspects of human well-being. Through charity people are not just subject to God, they actually participate in His life (*participatio*), if always only as a creature.

Other infused virtues guide the actions of a person, notably toward created things, that are relatively untouched by the theological virtues. Almost all natural virtues have a corresponding infused form and several crucial virtues, such as patience or penance, exist only in infused form. Aquinas, however, says little explicitly about the character of specific infused virtues other than the theological virtues. Their presence, nevertheless, underlies the fully flourishing religious life. That is, the full panoply of infused virtues exhibits those new dispositions, and thus new kinds of activity, that mark the participation in God's life that grace makes possible. For that reason, Aquinas can say

> only the infused virtues are perfect (*perfectae*), and deserve to be called virtues absolutely (*simpliciter*), since they direct a man well to the absolutely ultimate end. The other virtues, those namely that are acquired, are virtues in a limited sense (*secundum quid*), not without qualification (*simpliciter*). They direct a man well in respect to what is final in some particular field, not in the whole of life.[5]

God acts directly on people to produce not only the infused virtues but also the *Gifts of the Holy Spirit*. The Gifts do not belong within the category of virtue when it is strictly defined, and they surely involve some of the odder arcani of medieval theology. Nevertheless, the Gifts are important because they extend and deepen the activities and states produced by both the natural, acquired virtues and the supernatural, infused virtues. They do so by making a person more readily obedient or responsive, more tractable or docile, to the Holy Spirit's promptings (*instinctus*). The Gifts, then, allow a person to follow readily the promptings of the Holy Spirit, just as the acquired moral virtues perfect appetite's obedience to reason. Helping to stir a person to action, they are not a separable type of action but that by which some actions are produced or elicited.[6]

The organization of Aquinas's list of virtues and the analyses he makes of specific virtues rest on two notions. One is the idea of analogy and the procedures it spawns; that is, the study of resemblances that contain similarities in differences and differences in similarities. The other is the notion that virtues have parts. Each needs further examination, as each is complicated, underlies Aquinas's enterprise, and, when substantially reformulated, can be of use in our comparison of Mencius and Aquinas. The idea of analogy is the more general and defensible of the two, and we will start with it.

III. The Two Notions Underlying Aquinas's Construction and Analysis of His List of Virtues

Aquinas's list of virtues rests on the interlocking ideas of hierarchy and of similarity and difference. His examination of virtues reflects, then, his metaphysical framework. In that framework (except with aspects of God, such as his aseity) everything relates to everything else in a hierarchical fashion. Therefore every individual thing both resembles and differs from every other individual thing. The ideas of likeness (*similitudo*) and unlikeness, then, are crucial for him. Indeed, the analytic procedures these conceptions spawn characterize much of Aquinas's work: that is, he constantly examines analogies, the similar in the different and the different in the similar. (As we will see, the analysis of analogical predication underlies not only his work but also when reformulated, the comparative philosophy of religious flourishings.)[7]

Aquinas thinks that examining resemblances and differences will always produce a hierarchy. But the form of the hierarchy depends on which criteria are employed, on which questions are being asked. This means that when we discuss a virtue and relate it to other virtues we must always specify the hierarchy, and thus the criteria, that we employ. The relationship between acquired intellectual and ethical virtues exemplifies this procedure. The intellectual virtues surpass the ethical virtues if the criterion is the value of the object reached: they perfect reason, a higher object than the appetites the moral virtues perfect. But the reverse is true if the criterion is the effect of virtue on people's normal activity; in that case the perfection of the appetites is most crucial. Ethical virtues, then, surpass intellectual virtues when the criterion is what we need for normal human life. But the intellectual virtues surpass the ethical insofar as they reach a higher object and prefigure more perfectly humanity's ultimate goal, the beatific vision. The shifting of criteria exhibited in this example illustrates how Aquinas analyzes specific virtues and the problems related to them. (In this case, for instance, the procedure undergirds his analysis of the problem of how the active and contemplative lives relate.) That is, his procedure is to articulate, sort out, and then respond to the different kinds of questions that appear when he uses the notions of hierarchy and of similarity and differences.[8]

The procedure also appears when Aquinas identifies semblances of virtue and expands some virtues. It leads him, however, to declare every virtue both is a semblance of another virtue and is the standard against which some other virtue is measured as a semblance. For instance, acquired virtues are semblances of virtue if we use infused virtues as the standard of measurement. But any specific, acquired virtue will resemble more or less closely the integral form of that virtue. Acquired courage always is a semblance of infused courage and yet a particular instance of acquired courage will be only a semblance of real acquired courage. Indeed, he can identify the "same" phenomenon (e.g., giving up one's life for one's country) both as a semblance and as a standard. That identification depends on which criteria of value or sort of explanation he uses and thus on which hierarchies he employs. A single phenomenon, then, will be described, explained, and evaluated differently depending on what questions are asked.

Aquinas's general procedure for analyzing virtues and constituting lists of virtues, I think, is powerful and productive. Another feature of his treatment, his use of the idea that virtues have parts, seems to be considerably less productive. We need to examine the idea more closely, however, to see not only the problems but also the possibilities in it. Moreover, that examination points us toward ideas that will be important when we discuss the comparison with Mencius as well as the general issue of comparison.

Aquinas's inclination to organize phenomena into one systematically articulated, even rigid, hierarchical whole is never both so clear and so suspect as in his use of the idea that virtues have parts. By means of that idea he heroically attempts to harmonize Greek, Roman, Stoic, biblical, and early Christian ideas on what defines specific virtues, on which virtues are most important, and on what schemes best organize the different virtues.[9] The example of courage illustrates well the problems he faces. With courage he tries to combine three quite different notions. One is the idea that courage refers to the qualities needed to triumph in hand-to-hand combat. Another is the idea that courage is a general enabling virtue in situations involving fear and confidence. A third is the idea that courage underlies the detachment crucial to survival in bad times.

In trying to solve this problem Aquinas treats four major virtues as parts of courage. Two are central to the Christian life, perseverance and patience. Two are central to classical Greek schemes of human excellence, magnanimity ("great souledness") and magnificence ("great makings," such as financing large public projects). Each is called a component part of courage if the action concerns death, but an allied virtue if the action concerns difficulties less pressing than death.

Some failures or distortions are inevitable in any analysis that is driven by the aspiration to harmonize such apparently different virtues. Moreover, Aquinas's penchant for symmetry, tendency to be ahistorical, and drive for a comprehensive intellectual synthesis does exacerbate the inherent difficulties. Three problems in Aquinas's analysis are especially clear, I think. First, he disguises the importance of some virtues and therefore impedes rather than furthers our understanding of them. Magnanimity and patience are virtues of extraordinary significance, but neither their centrality nor their distinctive character is clear if we treat them as parts of courage. Second, needless complexities are introduced with some virtues to make them fit as parts of courage. A virtue like magnificence, for example, almost always will be a subordinate virtue of courage rather than a component part of it; expensive projects rarely involve facing death.

Most important, utilizing the idea that a virtue like courage has parts runs the risk of introducing into our understanding a rational coherence that falsifies the actual state of affairs. The rational construct fails to reflect well the real differences made by ways of life, by a virtue's social location. Patience's links to magnificence, for example, are far from obvious; the two virtues reflect extremely different cultural contexts and ideals. Part of a classical Greek picture of human perfection was to fund large public projects just as part of a Christian picture was to undergo with patience certain deprivations. These differences must be captured if we are to give an adequate account of the virtues.

In fact, to put the point more generally, a revealing untidiness often appears when we compare objectively the different lists of virtues that humans have created. Their separate lists of virtues are a monument to contingency, the diversity of possible ways of life, and the importance of social location. The ideals virtues represent and the ideas they utilize arose at different times and places, served different purposes, and reflected different perspectives. Any attempt to organize such virtues into one harmonious whole, then, must present an extremely misleading picture.

Moreover, the attempt to construct such a harmony arises in significant part from adopting a very problematic position: the position that only a single form of human flourishing occurs or, at the least, that there is a unity among somewhat different forms of human flourishing. Embracing that position leads people to avoid facing fully the important question, noted earlier, of whether certain human virtues present contradictory possibilities and therefore can never be realized in any single life. Magnificence and patience, impartial judiciousness and family loyalty, revolutionary commitment and ordinary decency seem (at times, at least) to be incompatible yet integral goods. These considerations have led many moderns to believe conflicts among ideals of human flourishing must or even should exist. Moreover, these moderns think that position fits better not just with the facts they see but also with the religious ideals they treasure. For instance, they doubt that people can always identify precisely the highest good and then continuously live in contact with it.[10]

Aquinas is not unaware of these problems, and his idea that virtues have parts can be helpful to us. At times, useful notions appear despite the problematic scaffolding; in these cases we must read through the structure to grasp what of value is being said. At other times, however, the structure's form generates productive questions. Aquinas claims, for instance, that no specific types exist with courage, no analogy exists to practical wisdom's domestic and military forms. This claim leads us to ask, as we will examine later, whether semblances of courage often function as do the types seen in other virtues.

Most important, analyzing the different parts of a virtue can help us to see the range of activities and states a virtue covers. We, then, can expand our notion of what a virtue is by seeing connections that we otherwise might miss, and do so in a systematic way. (This is true even if, as noted earlier, Aquinas's attempts to relate those connections technically often generate needless complexities.) For example, when we expand courage by relating it to magnificence we illuminate the character of both virtues. Magnificence — the undertaking of great projects — is a component part of courage in that it involves arduous striving. Courage surpasses it, however, and makes it an allied virtue because the courageous person faces dangers that threaten a person's life. The magnificent person, in contrast, faces dangers that only threaten to deplete financial or spiritual resources.

The connection of the two shows how undertaking any extraordinary project is an instance of courage, an allied virtue of it. It allows us to grasp more clearly the way in which creating a substantial work of art or undertaking to use well one's fortune involves overcoming substantial fears and disabling frustrations. Moreover, the connection helps us to see how generosity of spirit must underlie courage, must be a component of it. A certain greatness of spirit and fullness of aspiration, rooted deep in the character, must fuel true courage, just as the opposite will sap it. Only a certain kind of character, then, can consistently produce truly courageous action.

The kind of analysis generated by the idea that virtues have parts also provides us with a model that, when revised, can be used for the comparative study of different lists of virtues. It will help us probe Mencius's understanding of courage, for example. Alerting us to the importance of his accounts of virtues related to courage. More generally, the idea helps us to relate Mencius and Aquinas's lists of virtues. In undertaking this task we face a problem that resembles the one Aquinas faces when he attempts to relate, say, Aristotle and St. Paul's lists. Aquinas uses the notion that virtues have parts to deal with this problem, and we can use a reformed version of it, as we will examine in the last chapter. Let us turn now to Mencius's list of virtues.

IV. Mencius's List of Virtues

Mencius's list of virtues differs considerably from Aquinas's. He treats far fewer virtues, rarely provides detailed theoretical analyses, and makes little attempt to relate systematically the different virtues. Although he examines numerous virtues, including courage (*yung*), four virtues are central. Humans are defined by four potentials (*tuan*), literally "sprouts" or "germs," that when actualized are the four central virtues. These four potentials are Heaven's (*T'ien*) gift to, directive for, and empowerment of all human beings; they therefore are one of the most important ways in which Heaven makes itself present in the world. As Mencius says: "The heart of compassion is the sprout of benevolence; the heart of shame of righteousness; the heart of courtesy and modesty of propriety; the heart of right and wrong of intelligent awareness. Man has these four sprouts just as he has four limbs."[11]

One of the four potentials and its realization is a sensitivity to the sufferings of others that is actualized in helping them, in benevolence (*jen*). Another is an awareness of falling short of some standard, a repugnance manifested in shame about one's own actions and aversion toward other's actions, that is actualized in righteousness (*yi*). A third is a yielding to others or a deference toward them that is actualized in propriety (*li*). The last is a tendency to distinguish between human acts, approving of some and disapproving of others, that is actualized in intelligent awareness (*chih*).

None of these virtues corresponds exactly to virtues in Aquinas. Moreover, I assume that most readers are unfamiliar with them, and I know that finding any Western equivalents to some of them can be difficult. Therefore, I will give a more detailed account of these four virtues than I did with Aquinas's virtues and highlight how they relate to each other.

Propriety is probably the virtue in Mencius that has the least clear equivalent in any single Western virtue. (Finding an adequate single equivalent for *li* is an almost impossible task, and I will use propriety as the best of a variety of unhappy options.) Propriety covers two kinds of activity that most Westerners think differ substantially. One kind is solemn religious activities, such as funerals. The other kind falls under what we call etiquette or, more accurately, reasonable and humane learned conventions; for instance, the appropriate ways to respond to people at a formal gathering. Ritual, then, covers everything from the solemn performance of an elaborate rite to the "excuse me" after a sneeze. Mencius links the two because he believes both are sacred ceremonies that express and foster a spontaneous coordination rooted in reverence. Moreover, both exemplify learned, conventional behavior that manifests distinctly human activities rather than just instinctive reactions.

Propriety is what makes possible an actualization of the reactions of yielding or respect (*jang, tz,u* or *ching, kung*). Mencius believes these emotional reactions require conventional rules for their expression; they can find expression only through the ritual forms a society possesses. The rules or forms, in fact, are what allows people to achieve the good found in expressing and cultivating these reactions. For example, I cannot easily, or even adequately, show my respect for a cook, a host, or an elderly person unless social forms exist that allow me to express such attitudes. Furthermore, both I and others must know what those forms are and what they express. I need to know, for instance, that a slight bow and somewhat servile smile express respect not irony or rancor. The attitude of respect toward others, Mencius thinks, must express itself in a disposition to follow the conventional rules of propriety. A person observes these rules as an expression of reverence for people, their roles, and even the social organism that they embody and help preserve.

Propriety concerns, then, those human conventions that allow for the expression of certain emotions and make possible distinctively human excellences and interactions. This leads Mencius to claim that particular social forms are necessary if full human flourishing is to occur, and such a claim is bound to raise questions. Mohists or proto-Taoists, for example, will question whether the hierarchical social forms Mencius presents adequately express what they should. Mencius thinks he can answer such questions; his ability to do so, as we will discuss, is crucial to the success of his enterprise.[12]

Some features of his answer do appear in how he thinks propriety interacts with the other three virtues. Intelligent awareness (*chih*) for instance enables people to make textured judgments about what is the best course of action. Intelligent awareness names an especially complicated and important phenomenon that we will examine at length later. Briefly put, however, it arises from the tendency to differentiate among things (*shih* and *fei*). Through it people can evaluate situations one by one, and thereby manifest the valued quality called *ch'üan*, a character that originally referred to the sliding scale used in balance. Intelligent awareness, then, does not produce a set of rules to govern behavior, although a virtuous person always will observe a few general injunctions. Rather it generates that understanding of the salient characteristics of a situation that leads a person to activate dispositions at appropriate moments.[13]

Mencius's third virtue, righteousness, resembles aspects of intellectual awareness, although it generates a more powerful motivation to act; moreover, it overrules propriety, although the two relate in complex ways. I will translate *yi* by using righteousness and related grammatical forms, but the "right" is not contrasted with the good, in Mencius, as often occurs in modern Western discussions. (It is not simply a part of the realm of injunctions, as we will see.) Righteousness refers both to the virtue, a particular personal quality, and to acts exhibiting that quality. Mencius's primary focus usually is on acts, however; he speaks, for example, of what righteousness cannot do and what benevolence cannot bear.

Righteousness arises from shame (*hsiu*) and aversion (*wu*). Shame, for him, covers a multitude of reactions, some of which rest on conventional standards. It ranges from what people feel about their physical appearance, to what a wife feels toward a husband who begs for food left over after a sacrifice, to what a chariot driver feels when he uses unfair tactics to reverse his master's inept shooting performance. Aversion also ranges over many phenomena; it can arise from what people feel toward sights, sounds, contemplated acts, and even states of character.

Both righteousness and intelligent awareness concern judgments on human actions. Intelligent awareness, however, can simply distinguish among acts whereas righteousness always involves an impulse to act. The distinction resembles the difference between reading about a murder in the newspaper and knowing it is wrong (that is intelligent awareness) and seeing a murder attempted before one's eyes and being compelled to act (that is righteousness). With intelligent awareness disapproval is clear, but an impulse to act need not exist and emotional reactions like shame or aversion do not follow.[14]

Righteousness always takes precedence over propriety; propriety is defeasible and righteousness is not. Their relationship can be complicated, however. The specific guides for action manifest in propriety and the attitudes it uses fill out the general guidelines and attitudes on which righteousness operates. According to Mencius, my specific knowledge of what I owe to another may depend on what social role the person plays. Similarly, my respect for a social role may ameliorate the actions my righteousness produces; my aversion to someone's distasteful act can be modified by my reverence for the person's role.

Benevolence (*jen*), the last virtue, is a disposition to react compassionately and to act to alleviate suffering. (As Legge argued almost a century ago, Mencius's ideas on *jen* resemble Butler's understanding of benevolence, and benevolence clearly is the best rendering of the term.[15]) Benevolence rests in a pity for (*ts'e*) others in distress or a sympathy (*yin*) toward them. It gives birth to the desire to help other beings or at least not harm them. With benevolence, then, the inner state is important in a way it is not with righteousness. Both the appropriate feelings and the proper action are needed with benevolence. A right act (or in common Western terms, a just act) may be carried out by someone who lacks a full commitment to righteousness. A fully benevolent act, however, occurs only if the agent's inner state is correct.

In this sense, benevolent acts resemble acts of propriety; the full expression of either involves the presence of an appropriate inner state. Nevertheless, when the two directly conflict benevolence takes precedence. Moreover, benevolent acts are not guided by the detailed rules that guide acts of propriety and therefore the guidance of intelligent awareness is especially important. Indeed, Mencius argues for a "graded love" (similar to aspects of Aquinas's order of charity) that involves a diminution of degree as one moves out from the family. (At one place, he even delineates three levels: a special regard for family [ch'in], benevolence [jen] to all human beings, and a general regard [ai] for all beings or at least living creatures.) Intelligent awareness, then, must guide benevolence's movement by distinguishing between features that one's parents share with others and features they possess uniquely.[16]

Mencius's four central virtues of intelligent awareness, propriety, righteousness, and benevolence interact with each other in a variety of complex ways. Nevertheless, his ideas about the four fundamental qualities that constitute human flourishing are reasonably clear. The two basic human excellences are compassionate reactions and actions, and a respect for and deference to others expressed through specific, conventional social forms. They (and other virtues) are guided by intelligent awareness's perceptions and judgments and informed by the powerful motivation to action present in righteousness.

Mencius does identify other virtues and relate them to these four central virtues. We will examine some of them later, but three are especially worthy of note here. Courage (yung) concerns overcoming fear to be and do what one ought to be and do. A second, filial piety (hsiao), concerns reverence for parents. It both provides the needed source for virtuous character and limits the general attitudes and actions toward others that one should have. The third, fidelity (hsin), is truthfulness that inspires confidence. Although it has only a minor role in Mencius, it was given a rather different meaning by later Confucians and added to the list of four central virtues they took from Mencius.[17]

Let us turn now to a comparison of several significant features of Mencius and Aquinas's lists of virtues. The comparison will highlight those

situations where further examination shows that apparent similarities contain substantial differences and apparent differences some similarities.

V. A Comparison of Mencius and Aquinas's Lists of Virtues

Comparing the lists of virtues found in any thinkers presents many
problems, but special care is needed when the thinkers come from
radically different cultures and times. We must not only consider carefully
texts and contexts, but we also must understand the relationships in the
thinkers among their different kinds of theories, distinguishing, for example, among their primary, practical, and secondary theories. These matters, and more detailed comparisons of specific virtues, will be examined
in following chapters, but at this point I will only compare important general features of Mencius and Aquinas's lists of virtues. Such a comparison,
although limited in scope, can help us understand more clearly each
thinker's ideas on specific virtues. It also can enable us to treat several
general issues that arise when we compare these two thinkers.

Mencius's four virtues will be our starting point, and propriety will be
our focus because examining propriety illustrates well distinctive characteristics of the two lists. In comparing the two lists we see, I think, only similarities within differences and differences with similarities. Indeed, the discovery
of simple correspondences signals only that we have failed to probe deeply
enough. That is, correspondences appear only when we operate at a level
that fails to attend closely enough either to each thinker's specific account of
a virtue or to his placement of it in his general structure.

Mencius's benevolence (*jen*) exemplifies this situation. It could be
said to correspond to Aquinas's benevolence (*benevolentia*). Aquinas, however, distinguishes between beneficence (*beneficentia*) and benevolence
(*benevolentia*). The former covers benevolent actions and the latter only
general well-wishing; beneficence depends on but differs from that inner
state of the will specified as benevolence. More important, the virtue of
benevolence is a central one for Mencius and a peripheral one for
Aquinas. Indeed, charity (*caritas*) often plays the role for Aquinas that
benevolence does for Mencius, and charity differs in substantial ways
from benevolence. The exact meaning of benevolence in Mencius and
Aquinas differs, then, because of how they analyze the virtue and place it
in their respective lists of virtues.[18]

The relationship between Mencius's intelligent awareness (*chih*) and
Aquinas's practical wisdom (*prudentia*) is another place where we find a
resemblance but not a correspondence. (Their relationship is especially

complicated and important, and we will discuss it at considerable length in the next chapter.) Both virtues enable people to perceive the salient characteristics of a given situation. Both also guide action by empowering people to act on those descriptions of situations that correct perceptions produce. Both, then, function as a critical rational component in ethical action and therefore deeply affect the correct functioning of virtue.

They also differ, however. Each relates to other elements in Mencius or Aquinas's picture of the mind that are not present in the other thinker. Intelligent awareness, for example, links closely to *ssu*, the ability to focus on the movement of a sprout. *Ssu*, however, has no clear equivalent in Aquinas. Similarly, practical wisdom links to other theoretical intellectual virtues, such as the ability to grasp immediately the truth of some idea (*intellectus*). But Mencius notes no capacities that even resemble Aquinas's theoretical intellectual virtues.

Righteousness (*yi*) also bears certain striking resemblances to the most distilled form of Aquinas's justice. The action itself, not the intention behind it, is crucial, and a form of inviolable debt or obligation is that to which a person responds. Both, then, fit within the realm of injunctions. But the relationship between the realm of injunctions and of ways of life in each thinker differs substantially, in ways we will examine in the following section. Unlike Aquinas's justice, Mencius's righteousness covers acts the content of which clearly reflects conventional standards. He presumes, for instance, that the maintenance of rules of propriety, such as the procedure used by members of one class to summon members of another class, involves injunctions.

Although none of Mencius's central virtues correlate exactly with the virtues found in Aquinas, propriety (*li*) does seem to differ the most radically. Indeed, Mencius's emphasis on propriety illustrates two features of his general perspective that initially appear to have no analogues in Aquinas. Propriety provides us, therefore, with especially rich materials to use to examine the problems and possibilities that appear when we compare these two thinkers' lists of virtues.

The first, more specific feature, arises from Mencius's focus on an attitude often missing in Western accounts of virtue: the importance of yielding, the reaction that is actualized in propriety. Yielding corrects, Mencius thinks, a major deformation from which humans suffer. It corrects people's love of mastery and movement to self-aggrandizement, and therefore also their tendency to resent others and to seek more than they need or are due. Mencius never examines which attitudes produce a range of impediments to correct action and character. (He never develops, to use Aquinas's language, the notion that capital sins and their offspring can be specified.) But the lack of yielding seems to function in him as a major source of other vices or deformations. Both intelligent awareness and courage, for example, are corrupted by the absence of yielding. Yielding underlies intelligent awareness because only through yielding can people become truly sensitive to external situations. Only the practice of it allows them to overcome their inclination to project their own desires and ideas on to the world. Moreover, Mencius uses the idea of yielding to transform those ideas of courage that stress aggressive assertion. He both expands the idea of courage and identifies its semblances by attending to the role of yielding.

A difference from Aquinas's ideas is clear, but we must be careful not to overstate it. For example, the deformation Mencius thinks yielding corrects resembles aspects of Aquinas's central sin of pride. More important, justice, as Aquinas develops it, includes two areas that relate closely to Mencius's ideas on yielding. The "social virtues," such as wit or grace, are one area. The other area contains those virtues that concern relationships in which people incur unfulfillable debts, such as in their relationships to parents or the whole society. In each area various virtues modify the demands of justice. They operate not on the ideal of repaying debts owed but on the ideal either of expressing reverence or of nurturing harmonious coordination.

Despite these similarities, Mencius's emphasis on propriety appears to lead to a second, more striking distinction. It identifies his Confucianism as a "locative" rather than an "open" kind of religion. In open religions, such as Aquinas's Christianity, fulfillment occurs when people transcend any particular culture and reach a higher realm either here or after death. In locative religions, however, fulfillment occurs when people locate themselves within a complex social order that is thought to be sacred. Neither a differentiated religious community nor a distinct class of religious practitioners is part of a locative religion. Rather, the religio-cultural system mediates those meanings, attitudes, actions, and specific social forms that people need if they are to attain fulfillment.[19]

Many of the virtues found in a locative religion will differ substantially from those found in an open religion. For example, infused virtues or their surrogates would seem to have no place in a locative religion. Such virtues are characterized by a mode of action and being that arises from a transcendent source and goal, and no such source or goal is part of a locative religion. Indeed, Mencius's list of virtues appears to have neither equivalents to Aquinas's theological virtues nor even possible analogues to them. Moreover, it seems Mencius's presentation could never contain accounts that resemble those in Aquinas that depict God acting to "divinize" human beings; for instance, Aquinas's depiction of the courage that manifests the infused virtue of patience or the martyrdom that displays a Gift of the Holy Spirit.

These judgments surely contain much truth. They arise from combining attention to the details of each thinker's specific accounts with a sense for the more general, theoretical frameworks that inform their work. Nevertheless, they also must be considered carefully. Indeed, the very activity of comparing thinkers can allow us to see features in a thinker that we otherwise might overlook. This activity helps us to identify prized qualities in one thinker that correlate to a virtue clearly evident in another thinker. Detailed analyses in later chapters, I think, will illustrate this, but let me briefly note here how we might find correlates to infused virtues in even Mencius's locative scheme.

Aquinas's infused virtues (especially the theological virtues of faith, hope, and charity) enable people to touch realities that exceed anything they normally could or should believe in, hope for, or love. Mencius surely never labels or highlights virtues like these. Resemblances to them, however, are present in his writings. For example, Mencius is aware that humans do not seem to be naturally good and that Heaven does not seem to be active in the world. Nevertheless, he underlines the significance of belief in and hope about the heavenly (*T'ien*) source of those sprouts that define human nature's goodness. He also expresses the belief that Heaven, at times, works directly in human affairs: it intends, for instance, to send a sage to aid the world. Both these beliefs, and the hopes they engender, are held by Mencius despite all the evidence to the contrary.

Furthermore, we can agree that almost no analogue appears in Mencius to Aquinas's notion of God, much less to Aquinas's treatment of how divine and human causes might interact. (However, we must be wary about presenting too simplistic a picture of what Aquinas thinks people can know about either deity or deity's causation of human action.) Ideas in Mencius like Heaven, fate (*ming*), and psychophysical energy (*ch'i*) refer to sources of action that, in part, differ markedly from the human but interact with it. Nevertheless, Mencius has neither the conceptual apparatus, nor the interest, nor apparently the need to develop a transcendent world that resembles the one Aquinas presents. His secondary theory, then, differs strikingly from Aquinas's.

Mencius's practical theory, however, need not differ in the same fashion. Indeed, he does speak of a realm of empowering forces, of enabling abilities, that are known through truly natural inclinations and manifestations of the sacred in history. This realm resembles, if sometimes faintly, the realm Aquinas discusses in terms of that friendship with God that is charity. That is, it not only makes possible but also favors a specific understanding of obligations, ends, principles, and actions. The four virtues and other unnamed human excellences allow people to participate in it. Moreover, it produces states and activities that resemble those that Aquinas examines when discussing, for example, the infused virtue of patience.[20]

Mencius's locative perspective, a perspective exemplified in his emphasis on propriety, influences greatly the virtues that appear in his list. We must exercise both care and imagination, however, when we examine whether some kinds of virtue are not present in him, or even cannot be present in him. Few correspondences exist, but a variety of resemblances, similarities within differences and differences with similarities, well may be present, as in the case of surrogates to Aquinas's infused virtues.

A similar need to be imaginative but also to probe detailed, concrete cases appears when we consider how the locative and open perspectives will affect ideas in the realm of injunctions. A locative perspective, in general, blurs the distinction between the realms of injunctions and of ways of life more than an open perspective. But we need to examine closely that generality, and therefore we will end this chapter by discussing Mencius and Aquinas's ideas on the character and relationship of injunctions and ways of life.

VI. The Relationship of the Realms of Injunctions and Ways of Life in Mencius and Aquinas

Mencius's emphasis on propriety (*li*), his grasp of the crucial role played by conventional social forms, shows how well he understands the significance of ways of life. Indeed, like Confucians, his grasp of the role ethos plays in the production and sustenance of human excellence exceeds that found in most Western traditions. A realm of injunctions also is present in Mencius. Specifying it and understanding how it relates to ethos presents difficulties, however, as we saw when we examined propriety's connection to benevolence and righteousness. Let us, then, probe that issue, especially as probing it (as is the case with Aquinas) enables us to illuminate important features of his ethical thought and to specify tensions or difficulties within it.

Mencius clearly believes we ought never do some things and always do others. For example, he attacks a person who wants to lower taxes over an extended period, arguing that when one realizes an action is ethically wrong one should stop it immediately not slowly. (He cites, in this instance, the absurdity of slowly reducing one's thefts of a neighbor's chickens.) Moreover, the sages, he also declares, would not "perpetrate one wrongful deed or . . . kill one innocent man in order to gain the Empire." A similar point is put more abstractly, and in reference to less exalted people, when he declares that the business of an official (*shih*) is simply "To be ethical (*jen yi*). That is all. It is contrary to benevolence to kill one innocent man; it is contrary to right to take what one is not entitled to."[21] Injunctions exist for Mencius, then; some of them manifest benevolence, many of them manifest righteousness.

Mencius also includes in the category of duties, however, acts that seem to fit best within the realm of ethos. When he discusses, for example, the question of how to serve lords in a way that meets obligations both to society and higher ideals, he relates the following incident. A duke summons a gamekeeper with a pennon, to be used only for a high official, rather than with a leather cap, the appropriate means. The gamekeeper refuses to come, even though he knows the duke may put him to death for the refusal: "When the gamekeeper was summoned with what was appropriate only to a Counsellor, he would rather die than answer the summons." Mencius declares that both he and Confucius find the gamekeeper praiseworthy and even adds the following grand statement: "A man whose mind is set on high ideals never forgets that he may end in a ditch; a man of valour never forgets that he may forfeit his head."[22] The need to maintain a rule of propriety thus provides for Mencius a reason to surrender one's life.

I assume we find Mencius's position counterintuitive or simply wrong. We may be able to imagine an argument that justifies his judgment on grounds such as that the maintenance of appropriate rules and relationships underlies social stability, and that social stability in turn underlies all forms of human fulfillment. An argument like this may even inform Mencius's account. If so, however, it is liable to a devastating set of objections that query the steps leading from a plausible first principle to a very implausible conclusion.

This case illustrates, I think, how Mencius neither consistently nor clearly differentiates actions that belong, by our standards, in the realms of ethos and of injunctions. Other cases also indicate this. He often is questioned about cases where propriety and either benevolence or righteousness seem to conflict, for example. At times his responses are quite justifiable; for example, one saves a drowning sister-in-law, even though propriety forbids touching her. But in other instances, as in the case of the gamekeeper, his responses are problematic. Some of them even seem to reflect the notion that people's identity arises only from the role that they occupy. This notion, however, fits badly with his idea that human beings' four defining capacities provide them with an identity that is separable from roles.

Other of Mencius's responses highlight his failure to grasp all the implications of the notion that propriety's regulations are necessarily conventional. He does recognize that regulations can be overruled, of course, and he states emphatically that the spirit of propriety and the rules of propriety can conflict. But he does not really consider the possibility that the rules of propriety might change to fulfill better their purpose. Nor does he recognize that different rules might work more effectively in some cultural situations. Indeed, Mencius usually presumes, as did Confucius, that a perfect society had existed in the past and that any society ought to emulate its rules and organizations.[23]

The problems just noted reflect two related tensions in Mencius's thought. One is the tension between seeing virtues as linked to roles and virtues as linked to human nature. Are virtues those qualities that help a person to fulfill a social role or are virtues those qualities that help a person to fulfill natural human capacities? The other is the tension between seeing people as having something like natural rights and seeing people as valuable because of what they accomplish. Are people autonomous bearers of rights or are people valuable only in so far as they fulfill the potentialities present either in their social roles or in their natures?

These tensions often appear most clearly in Mencius's defenses of what, to us, are vulnerable positions. He claims, for example, that the general ethical inclinations implanted in people by Heaven can find correct expression only in the specific rules of propriety formulated in the past by the sages. The major problems he faces in maintaining this position is that the notion of inclinations given by Heaven and the notion of rules given by sages point in very different directions. Heaven gives only general characteristics to human nature, and it seems they could manifest themselves in different ways. The exact form the manifestations take would depend on the contingencies of a given social situation. The sages, however, gave complex and specific rules, and following them, it appears, is the only way in which the sages (and thus apparently Heaven) thought human beings could thrive. These two kinds of formulations sit uneasily together. This tension illustrates Mencius's problematic understanding of the relationship between the realms of injunctions and of ways of life.[24]

When we focus more narrowly and look just at Mencius's approach to the directives arising from injunctions and ethos, another difficulty emerges. A common Western approach to ethics distinguishes among acts or ideals that are ethically indifferent, permissible, obligatory, and supererogatory. Mencius makes few firm distinctions among the first three categories because of his emphasis on propriety (*li*), and strong arguments can be marshalled in defense of his position. Most important to consider here, however, and much more problematic is the absence of any distinction between the obligatory and the supererogatory. Mencius does not differentiate acts, or even ideals of life, on the grounds of whether they are universally binding. He does not distinguish between acts, or general states of being, that I must do or pursue (the obligatory) and those that I would never think I must pursue or perhaps even contemplate pursing (the supererogatory). Mencius seems to think that all people, for instance, are called on to sacrifice their lives in a wide variety of situations.

This position is especially striking because three elements that might alleviate the severity of the picture are missing in Mencius. No ritualized procedure for expiation of faults is built into his religious system. Moreover, he never places human actions within some larger framework — such as life after death or cycles of reincarnation — that diminishes the significance of what occurs in normal life. Finally, he never considers fully how ameliorating conditions might affect judgments on action, or modify the guilt or regret some acts normally produce. He does distinguish between what can be accomplished by those who labor with their bodies and by those who labor with their minds, and he does emphasize that insufficient material means will generate evil actions in most people. Nevertheless, no nuanced discussion about the conditions of responsibility occurs. Moreover, the distinctions he does make sit uneasily with his emphasis on the possibility of all people becoming sages.

Certain of Mencius's ideas about how intelligent awareness operates may function in ways similar to the conception of supererogation. The notion of "timely" entrance to and withdrawal from situations, for example, should lead people to avoid some situations where heroic action is demanded. Given that, people are not always obligated to pursue courses of action that would lead to dramatic choices. Moreover, Mencius does emphasize that people need to fit their actions to their stage of development. That is, they ought not undertake actions that could severely harm their self-cultivation. This notion also provides people with reasons to avoid certain demands.

Nevertheless, Mencius never gives a detailed analysis of just how a person is to decide what demands must be met and what demands avoided. Indeed, a version of the Western distinction among kinds of obligation could help him make that analysis without also forcing him to provide the kinds of rules that, for him, would impede the functioning of intelligent awareness. Such a conceptual apparatus would allow Mencius to say, for example, that people must always meet the demands of injunctions, even if self-cultivation is harmed, but need not meet other supererogatory demands if such harm is likely to occur.[25]

Mencius presents, then, a very lofty ethical ideal, and he provides few means for people to excuse, forgive, or otherwise ameliorate their failures. This approach accords with, and may even rest on, the fact that Mencius rejects any attempt to create a provisional ethics or ideal. When he is asked to provide a more accessible ethical ideal, he emphatically refuses:

Kung-sun Ch'ou said, "The Way is indeed lofty and beautiful, but to attempt it is like trying to climb up to Heaven which seems beyond one's reach. Why not substitute for it something which men have some hopes of attaining so as to encourage them constantly to make the effort?"

"A great craftsman," said Mencius, "does not put aside the plumb line
for the benefit of the clumsy carpenter. Yi [a famous archer] did not
compromise on his standards of drawing the bow for the sake of the
clumsy archer. A gentleman is full of eagerness when he has drawn
his bow, but before he lets fly the arrow, he stands in the middle of
the path, and those who are able to do so follow him."[26]

This passage reflects Mencius's rejection of a life of normal compromises
and adjustments. It also may manifest both a particular rhetorical strategy
and his disquiet about any position, like the Mohist one, that relies on
using the idea of personal benefits to motivate people.

But his position also reveals, I think, an important feature of the
logic of many traditional ethics that rest on ideas of virtue and thus of
human perfection. A very high standard is set when character not action is
the object of judgments, when purity of motivation provides a crucial criterion for such judgments, and when expressive as well as acquisitive
motives are thought to be valid. The idea of semblances of virtue somewhat softens this standard. But the loftiness of the ideal pursued still
remains a defining aspect of many traditional virtue theories, as our further examination of Mencius and Aquinas will show.

To sum up, Mencius shows a keen appreciation of the importance of
ways of life; and he believes a realm of injunctions exists. But he inconsis-
tently and unclearly articulates the relationship between the two realms.
This problem reflects both tensions within his thought and the absence of
a distinction between the obligatory and the supererogatory.

Aquinas, in contrast to Mencius, articulates well the distinctive characteristics of injunctions and underestimates the significance of differences
in ethos. Aquinas is acutely aware of how judgments must be fitted to circumstances. But he shows little awareness of how differences in ethos
might produce different judgments about the content of injunctions or
even of virtues. In common with most medieval thinkers his diet of possible counterexamples, of substantially different ways of life, is limited. (Rich
sources of examples, such as Islam or heretical Christian movements, usually are dealt with only as theological alternatives.) The key examples arise
mainly from accounts in the Hebrew Bible of different social practices,
such as polygamy, or from classical accounts, like Caesar's, that describe,
say, divergent ideas about the possession of property. Aquinas's analysis of
such examples shows that he does recognize the differences ways of life can
make. But that recognition is integrated only imperfectly into his thought;
he fails to examine their effects continuously and coherently.

He says remarkably little, for example, about how the first principles
of natural law are transformed into positive laws or rules. His usual analo-

gy is with the process whereby an architect takes a general form, say, a door, and makes it determinate, builds a particular door, by means of a set of choices. The analogy is evocative, but it fails to capture adequately the complicated procedures involved in relating judgments, especially about injunctions, to ways of life. Indeed, important features of Aquinas's work on the content and application of natural law become clearer when we see that he presumes there are no sharp divergences among ways of life.[27]

The limits on Aquinas's diet of examples helps to explain his position. But the failure to attend more closely to the examples he did have or easily could have obtained is more striking. It may arise from the continuing tension in his thought between an emphasis on reason and an emphasis on nature. That tension resembles in general form the tension in Mencius's thought between general human characteristics that could manifest themselves in different ways and the specific rules of the sages. With Aquinas, however, the tension is between natural characteristics that produce specific directives and rational judgments that will vary depending on the circumstances people encounter. We will discuss this issue in the next chapter (when we consider the relationship between reason and nature in Aquinas's theory of virtue) but now let us analyze his remarkably full examination of the realm of injunctions.

Aquinas argues that when people reflect on themselves as rational beings, they recognize they are obligated to do certain things. Moreover, they think the obligations constitute a system of laws or principles that bind all rational creatures. These principles are self-evident and indemonstrable; that is, they are not inferred but are known immediately and intuitively by the understanding (*intellectus*): "What is known in itself is like a principle, and is perceived immediately in the mind (*per se notum*)." The abstract first principles of ethics are, for Aquinas, self-evident. They enable people to judge, with little thought, that some actions are obligatory. Other actions that also are considered obligatory, however, can be made clear only through a detailed examination of various circumstances and a process of deduction that wise people alone can do well. As he says,

> For the moral character of some human actions is so evident that they can be assessed as good or bad in the light of these common first principles straightway with a minimum of reflection. Others, however, need a great deal of consideration of all the various circumstances, of which not everyone is capable, but only those endowed with wisdom.[28]

Aquinas's approach to injunctions exemplifies what Alan Donagan calls a *rationalist moral theory*. The formal characteristics of such theories — in which moral reasoning is taken to resemble legal reasoning — are five:

(1) they rest on a few fundamental principles, sometimes one, which are advanced as true without exception; (2) each of those principles lays down some condition upon all human action as being required by practical reason; (3) those principles do not constitute a set of axioms, from which all the remaining moral precepts of the theory can be deduced; but, rather, (4) the remaining moral precepts are deduced from the fundamental principles by way of additional premises specifying further the conditions those principles lay down as required of all human actions; and (5) both principles and additional premises are adopted on the basis of informal dialectical reasoning.[29]

The exact number and character of these self-evident moral principles (strangely to us) is not a major issue for Aquinas, or other medieval thinkers. Aquinas discuses them only when other issues are being examined. Indeed, his exact formulations always reflect the context; a formulation made in the context of natural law may differ substantially from one made in the context of the revealed Old Law.

Despite this ambiguity, or lacunae, Aquinas's general position on injunctions is relatively clear. The fundamental condition of an action is that good is to be done and pursued and evil shunned. More particularly, people should act so that fundamental human goods, whether present in themselves or in others, are promoted so far as possible and in no respect violated. That principle, for Aquinas, captures in philosophical form the meaning of the biblical idea that one should love one's neighbor as one loves oneself. (Aquinas's first principle probably can be formulated even better by utilizing Kant's notion of treating humans as ends not means: the crucial notion, then, would be that people ought to respect every human being, whether themselves or another, as a rational creature.) This principle, and others that Aquinas may think are of similar generality, then can be employed in informal, dialectical moral reasoning to produce specific directives. Vexing problems can arise in evaluating the directives produced, of course, but Aquinas believes wise people can always solve them. The directives, then, are absolutely binding, contain no contradictory guides, and can generate no real perplexity.[30]

For Aquinas the sphere of injunctions is clear and critical. But it also is narrow. Indeed, and especially important to us, Aquinas assumes that most human activity involves no unconditional obligations and therefore lies outside the sphere of injunctions. He never seriously entertains the idea that the immense panoply of possible human activity ought to be amalgamated into the realm of universal injunctions. To do so, he thinks, obviously would involve overlooking the evident differences among various kinds of human action; it would lead, in our terms, to confusing the three different realms of ethics. We must understand the integrity of injunctions, Aquinas thinks, but we also must recognize the limited area in which injunctions apply. Deciding what to do usually involves multiple considerations; the considerations that arise from injunctions will provide all the direction needed in only a few situations.

Humans operate for Aquinas, then, in a world where not only moral perfection but also intellectual, social, religious, aesthetic, and idiosyncratic personal perfections are of basic importance. The crucial issue people usually face is deciding which of the accomplishments that injunctions (or even ways of life) capture imperfectly, or what mix of them, lead to and manifest the flourishing of the species. Moreover, this situation is more true rather than less so because the final standard of human flourishing arises from the fullness of God's being. Humans, of course, mirror God only imperfectly. But they must realize that God's perfection is not restricted to moral perfection, and His actions as Creator have established both the limitations and possibilities within which people must operate. The immense variety of possible human perfection rests finally in God's being, then, as does the distinctive context within which that variety must be pursued. Most human activity for Aquinas, then, falls under the umbrella provided by ways of life and especially virtues. A few activities will arise from the realm of injunctions and many will arise from the ethos. Almost all of them, however, fall within the realm of virtue.[31]

Aquinas, also believes, as does Mencius, that injunctions will often provide directives for virtue. Moreover, like Mencius, he thinks that the list and ranking of virtues depends in substantial part on the way of life in which they are embedded. Mencius's articulation of the realm of injunctions is less clear than Aquinas's while Aquinas fails to grasp the importance of ways of life as clearly as Mencius. But both never cease to stress the significance of virtues. Virtues, for them, respond to the directives found both in the sphere of injunctions and ways of life and thereby enable people to manifest various kinds of excellence.

The discussion of this subject completes our treatment of the context for Mencius and Aquinas's theories of virtue and conceptions of courage. We began by examining issues in the interpretation of each figure. We then turned to Mencius and Aquinas's lists of virtues and the analytic procedures they manifest, and also examined how their lists compare. We ended by discussing their understanding of the relationship of the realms of injunctions and ways of life. Let us now, in the next chapter, turn to a detailed examination of their theories of virtue.

Chapter 3

Mencius and Aquinas's Theories of Virtue

I. Mencius and Aquinas: The General Conception of Virtue

We begin our analysis of Mencius and Aquinas's theories of virtue by discussing briefly the general notion of virtue that appears in each thinker. Turning then to their respective theories of virtue, we will focus on how they think reason interacts with natural inclinations to form emotions and dispositions and to enable them to distinguish semblances of virtues from virtues. We end by examining one topic where noteworthy differences appear, their understanding of failures to be virtuous, and another where noteworthy similarities appear, those features of their pictures of the self that affect basically their ideas about virtue.

I discussed various characteristics of virtue in the earlier, extended examination of the general conception of virtue. I argued, for example, that a virtue is a disposition to act, desire, and feel that involves the exercise of judgment, leads to a recognizable human excellence, and involves choosing virtue for itself and in light of some justifiable life plan. Moreover, I claimed virtues often employ expressive motives, have a corrective character, and can be divided into inclinational and preservative types. In that discussion, I drew the focal meaning of virtue, the distinctive and most characteristic meaning of the idea of virtue, from my understanding of contemporary English usage. The reason for and implications of this choice are many, and they will be discussed in the last chapter.[1] For now, however, we only need to note that the initial focal meaning of virtue I presented must differ in some ways from each thinker's usage. Moreover, the focal meaning, at least initially, almost always will be closer to Aquinas's terminology than to Mencius's, as I drew on a Western discourse. (Comparative analysis of course, will modify substantially the initially chosen focal meaning of any term, including virtue.) We now must investigate how Mencius and Aquinas actually use the concept of virtue, and to that task we turn.

Both thinkers believe the conception of virtue extends considerably beyond human action, a fact their secondary theories reflect. Their term covers more than the contemporary one, then, and it also may refer to human qualities we would not define as virtuous. Indeed, at a few times, and particularly in the case of Mencius, virtue as they use it may not always be the best equivalent for virtue as I have defined it. Nevertheless, their main concern, especially in their practical theories, is with those qualities that make people and their actions good, and this is the focus of our attention. This means we can confidently, if carefully, work from the notion of virtue discussed earlier. But we do need to examine closely the ways in which the term virtue is used by both Mencius and Aquinas.

The conception of virtue (*te*) operative in Mencius's time is a complex one that bears the marks of its long history. Although we need neither rehearse that history nor enter the scholarly debates that surround it, we can note several aspects of the history that illuminate Mencius's use of the idea. Originally the notion of virtue probably referred only to the sacred king. By at least the sixth century B.C.E., however, it signified a property that arises from a laudatory life or is given as a reward for one. It, furthermore, is a property that enables the holder to accomplish things that otherwise would be impossible. The idea of virtue, then, is thought of as a property tied to a commendable life. Moreover, the possession of virtuousness generates special abilities; indeed, "power" often is an appropriate translation for *te*. To possess virtue is to possess the ability to affect one's self, other people, and even the natural world.

Put abstractly, virtue is thought to be a quality, or perhaps more accurately a potency, that either generates the essential characteristics of something or makes that something adhere to those characteristics. Virtue also makes possible, however, the influencing of one thing by another; it manifests that "field of force" by means of which some things cause or inform the activities of others. To use the words coined by Peter Boodberg, virtue has both an "enrective" and an "arrective" component. The enrective aspect is the inner power or quality that gives strength and direction to a being. The *te* of water, for example, is its downward flow. The arrective aspect, in contrast, is the ability to arouse or cause the enrective component in another being to be animated. Virtue combines then the passive sense of an inherent quality with the active sense of the power to influence others.[2]

This power to affect others seems to have been conceptualized in three different ways in the times just prior to Mencius. One way refers to the ability of virtuous human models to draw and influence people by their "charisma." The virtuous model inspires loyalty, affection, a willing obedience, and an ongoing attempt to emulate the model's qualities. Another understanding of this power reflects a social process evident in any culture, like early China's, where reciprocal relationships are important. The bestowal of kindness or gifts engenders a response of gratitude in the person benefited; he or she feels a "gratitude credit" and thus a compulsion to do something for the benefactor. Such situations easily lead the party benefited to see an ethical force residing in the benefactor to which one must respond.

These two ways of conceptualizing virtue apply only to human activity. But another strand contains the idea that virtue manifests a principle operative in the whole world. Conceptualized this way in a secondary theory, virtue is a hypostatic entity, a "metaphysical" being or principle, some aspect of which a person or even object can possess. Virtue is what enables an object to possess a specific character and to interact with and influence other objects.

By Mencius's time many of the grander, more metaphysically charged aspects of the idea of virtue were being attacked by some and rethought by others. Although Mencius himself will speak of virtue as a single something, he often discusses it as a set of related qualities that make people good. He will claim, for example, that friendship must rest on virtue, on a person's good qualities; and he usually paints perfected people in terms of the good qualities or virtues they possess.

Nevertheless, a version of the idea that virtue can generate proper activity in other beings still operates in Mencius, even though he sometimes expresses doubts about just how effective it can be. His appreciation of the power of models or of "gratitude credit" explains some uses of the idea, but more than just that is involved. Significant residues remain of the idea that virtue's resonant causality can affect human actions and perhaps even nature's action. For example, he opposes the ideas of strength and virtue in terms of their ability to influence people: people may be temporarily subdued by strength, but they willingly submit themselves only to virtue. The power of virtuous kings, for Mencius, far exceeds just the appeal of their enlightened social policies to produce the kind of government that people will welcome. He consistently recounts dramatic myths about how people rush to a virtuous ruler's kingdom to become his subjects.

Moreover, Mencius does not limit virtue's productive powers to a king. He believes the ability to transform others is one of the distinguishing marks of a sage, and he quotes with approval Confucius's comment that "The gentleman's virtue (*te*) is like wind; the virtue (*te*) of the common people is like grass. Let the wind weep over the grass and the grass is sure to bend."[3] Such ideas reflect Mencius's acceptance of a version of the traditional notion that virtuousness connects one with powerful entities or forces. Evaluating the exact meaning and role in Mencius of these residues of traditional notions of virtue is difficult, however, given his apparent inconsistency when discussing them. (The inconsistencies often arise, as will be discussed, from tensions between his practical and secondary theories.) But Mencius does believe that virtuousness connects people to forces that can energize them. Most notably, it manifests Heaven's (*T'ien*) presence, helps release psychophysical energy (*ch'i*), and even apparently links one to the force of the daimonic (*shen*). Furthermore, these beliefs at times affect his response to important questions. As we will see, they affect, for example, his response to questions about why humans fail, about whether virtues always are beneficial, and about whether virtue is a hypostatized entity that causes behavior. Mencius's conception of virtue, then, refers mainly to qualities that make a person good, but it also extends considerably beyond the realm of simply human activity.

Aquinas also thinks the conception of virtue refers to more than just human action. But virtue for him is not, as in parts of Mencius, a separate power the possession of which generates separate abilities. Rather, it is a conception that is general enough to be used to analyze almost all activities or beings. In its most extended sense, virtue (*virtus*) in Aquinas usually can be translated by either power or excellence, by either strength or perfection. It signifies whatever excellence or strength appears in the performance of a being. (In the phrase of Aristotle that Aquinas often quotes, "virtue is what makes its possessor good and renders his operation good.") In the widest sense, then, virtue refers to the perfection of any capacity or potency (*potentia*) and signifies the excellence present in the natural functioning of anything. As Aquinas says, "the virtue of a horse makes it be a good horse, run well, and carry his rider well — which is the work of a horse." Therefore, "the virtue of a horse is what makes it and its work good. A similar situation holds for the virtue of a rock, or a man, or any other thing."[4]

Although the conception of virtue helps us explain almost anything, Aquinas thinks its *more proper* use appears with potencies that are both active and passive. These kinds of potencies, which can both initiate and be moved to action, do not produce only one specific kind of action. Therefore, we need to add the conception of dispositions if we are to explain uniformity in activity, ready performance, and, in many cases, accompanying pleasure. Virtue's *most proper* use, however, occurs when we add not just the notion of dispositions but also the notion of rational direction. That is, the notion of virtue belongs in a distinctive, focal fashion only to specific activities: those activities called good not just because they manifest a natural functioning but because they manifest agency, a person who moves to goods perceived as goods. Virtue's focal meaning, then, appears with human dispositions where the exercise of will and thus rationality is the crucial defining mark.

Aquinas uses the concept of virtue to describe many items that most moderns do not gather under the idea of virtue: human excellence, such as strength or beauty, and even the nonhuman perfection that can appear in rocks or horses. But the focal meaning of virtue refers to rationally informed human actions and its secondary meanings cover other human or nonhuman excellence. Aquinas carefully distinguishes among the focal and secondary meanings of virtue. Indeed, as discussed, the examination of analogy, of the multisignification of language, lies at the heart of his analysis. He constantly distinguishes between the focal meaning and the secondary meaning of terms or sentences, between, for example, *x simpliciter* or *vere x* and *x secundum quid* or *x secundum aliquem modum.*[5]

Moreover, this procedure underlies Aquinas's insistence that the concept of virtue should not be reified. As he says, "virtue is called good because by it something is good." Virtues are not substantial somethings and ought not be hypostasized; they are defined by their exercise, they do not account for it. Virtues, then, are good operative dispositions that strengthen a power and thereby give a being an inclination toward, or aptness for, the realization of its fullest activity. Humans need virtues and thus dispositions "because the [human] soul is not restricted to a single activity but is capable of many and this . . . is just the situation in which dispositions are necessary."[6]

With beings directed to a single goal, the conception of disposition is used only analogically. But with human beings it is the crucial middle term that bridges the gap between the existence of multiple capacities and any particular result that occurs. The normal acorn, barring external problems, will grow to be an oak. But the normal human will need a disposition to benevolence if the capacity for it is to flower. More than just a simple disposition is needed, however, for Aquinas, if true human virtue is to appear. Most crucial is the presence of the kind of rationality that can guide and inform those dispositions.

In fact, both Mencius and Aquinas think the defining mark of human virtue is the presence of a guiding, informing intelligence. That presence is a necessary if not sufficient condition for the occurrence of real virtue. The relationship between the needed intelligence and both natural inclinations and acquired propensities presents a set of knotty problems that are at the center of each thinker's theory of virtue. Let us, then, turn to those theories, beginning with Mencius's account and focusing on two related topics. The first is how each thinks reason and natural inclinations interact to form emotions and dispositions. The second is how each thinks that interaction allows them to distinguish virtues from their semblances.

In examining these two topics, I will present Mencius and Aquinas's ideas chiefly in their own terms and rarely compare them. However, I then will compare their positions on two subjects. One is the human propensity to fail to be virtuous, the other is the general picture of the self that underlies both thinkers' theories of virtue, especially the character and relationship of reason, emotions, and dispositions. In examining their respective understanding of human failures, we see some surprising similarities but most important are several critical differences. In examining their respective pictures of the self we see mainly similarities, a situation that also leads me to argue, in constructive fashion, for the cogency of their ideas. Let us turn, then, to our next task, the explication of each thinker's theory of virtue.

II. Mencius: Human Nature's Fundamental Inclinations as a Basis of Virtue

Mencius's theory of virtue rests on his ideas about human nature's basic character and reason's ability to develop that character. He argues that virtue's cognitive elements join with appropriately developed dispositions to determine a person's character, actions, and emotional responses. He shares this abstract model of virtue with Aquinas, but he develops it in terms of his own ideas and the conflicts he faces.

Various intellectual options existed in Mencius's time, but he found two movements especially important opponents. One, found in the followers of Yang Chu, is a form of philosophic hedonism. Proponents of this position probably embraced a relatively sophisticated skepticism about ethical judgments; they surely counseled people to protect themselves and pursue those individual pleasures that come from satisfying natural inclinations. The other position, found in the followers of Mo Tzu, is a proto-utilitarianism. Its proponents wanted to replace most traditional norms with rational judgments about what would materially benefit the most people. The one position, then, emphasizes reason, the other natural action. Mencius attempts to show the superiority of Confucianism to the two approaches by articulating a theory of human virtue or excellence. Our examination of that theory will begin by analyzing briefly his ideas on the basic character of human nature. We then turn to his conception of ethical reasoning and the three interlocking notions it contains: extension (usually *t'ui* or *ta*), attention (*ssu*), and intelligent awareness (*chih*). This conception underlies his depiction of true virtue and its semblances.[7]

What can be called a *biological framework* informs Mencius's ideas on human nature and its characteristic successes and failures. (A somewhat similar framework is present in Aquinas, as we shall see.) To speak of the nature of something within such a framework is to refer to some innate constitution that manifests itself in patterns of growth and culminates in specifiable forms. These forms display characteristic, regularly repeated kinds of activity, and these activities reveal the normal or natural functioning that represents the excellence of the particular species. Achieving such excellence depends upon the environment in which the organism grows. As Mencius says:

> Take the barley for example. Sow the seeds and cover them with soil. The place is the same and the sowing is also the same. The plants shoot up and by the summer solstice they all ripen. If there is any unevenness, it is because the soil varies in richness and there is no uniformity in the fall of rain and dew and the amount of human effort devoted to tending it.[8]

Mencius thinks, then, fulfillment occurs only if an organism is both *uninjured* and properly *nurtured*. Differences in the final state of a growing plant, for example, result from injury done to them — such as animals chewing on them — and from failures in nurture — such as irregular watering.

Mencius's ideas rest on a relatively simple conceptual model. A basic set of capacities exist and their unhindered, nurtured development generates qualities that lead to specifiable actions or characteristic forms. Barley seeds, for example, have the capacity to grow at an identifiable pace and to reach specifiable forms, and they will do so if circumstances are favorable. Similarly, a frog's capacity to live six years and to jump well engenders, if the frog is uninjured and properly nurtured, qualities that leads to jumping and death at age six. These actions provide observers with a standard that allows them to determine a being's nature. They can then judge whether any specific action of a creature represents its nature in normal, exemplary, or defective fashion.

Notorious problems arise in applying this model to the description and evaluation of human behavior. The model is usually the product of a metaphysical teleology or biology, and even those, like MacIntyre, who try to revive a version of it make substantial changes in it.[9] However, neither Mencius nor Aquinas, at their most sophisticated, adopts a simple version of the model. As we will see, this introduces both significant tensions and productive possibilities into their accounts. Most important here, however, is another issue: the distinction between a development model and a discovery model of human nature and virtue.

Virtue theories of the kind Mencius and Aquinas propound can rest on either a *development* or a *discovery* model. Both Mencius and Aquinas utilize a development model, although Aquinas modifies it in substantial ways. (Their successors, however, often employ a discovery model and use it to interpret Mencius and Aquinas; as noted, this is one crucial reason why many Neo-Confucian and some Christian commentators produce powerful but misleading interpretations.) Mencius's model is developmental because capacities produce proper dispositions and actions only if they are nurtured and uninjured. If improperly developed, capacities either attain only a truncated form or become so weak that animating them becomes virtually impossible.

In a discovery model, however, human nature exists as a permanent set of dispositions that are obscured but that can be contacted or discovered. People do not cultivate inchoate capacities. Rather they discover a hidden ontological reality that defines them. The discovery model reflects, then, ontological rather than biological notions. An ontological reality, the true self, always is present no matter what specific humans, particular instances of it, are or do. Biological growth does not provide the appropriate images by which to understand the human situation. The appropriate images, rather, are those of people obscuring a fundamental, unchangeable, and "apersonal" reality, of people covering it over with defilements such as errant passions or misguided perceptions. Moreover, the goal sought resembles not the flourishing of a plant after a slow process of growth but the attainment of a state where people touch, often immediately, the fundamental nature that controls all their actions.[10]

Mencius's employment of a developmental model means that when he declares human nature is good he refers not to a hidden ontological reality but to the capacities humans possess. Goodness, then, equals the presence of those four sprouts that can grow into the basic virtues that define the distinctively human. As he says: "As far as what is genuinely (ch'ing) in him is concerned, a man is capable of becoming good. . . .This is what I mean by good. As for his becoming bad, that is not the fault of his native endowment."[11]

Various issues circle around this claim, and it has been much discussed by both traditional commentators and modern scholars. Most important to us, however, is Mencius's understanding of how people develop their basic capacities into virtues; that is, how people direct or cultivate the proper dispositions.

We will examine some features of Mencius's position in discussing his ideas about human beings' propensities to fail to be virtuous. Most notable are his ideas on the role of ethical leadership and correct social arrangements in the development, over time, of correct virtues. Here, however, I want to focus on his critical and distinctive ideas about the direct, personal cultivation of virtue. Mencius stresses the need for gradual self-cultivation. For example, when discussing the problem of developing virtues, especially righteousness, he declares that:

> One must be concerned about it, but not correct it. Let the heart not ignore it, but not help it grow. Be not like the man of Sung. Among the people of Sung there was one who pulled on his grain sprouts because he was worried they would not grow. Having absorbed himself in doing so he returned home and told his family, "Today I exhausted myself helping the sprouts grow." His son ran by leaps to see them. By the time he got there the sprouts had withered. Few are those in the world who do not help their sprouts grow. Those who take it to be of no benefit and cast it aside are those who do not keep weeds from their grain sprouts. Those who help it grow are like those who pull on their grain sprouts. Not only is this of no benefit but it harms them.[12]

The evocative image of the man of Sung miscultivating his field presents well that view of gradual self-cultivation that proponents of a developmental model must propose. (The image also raises but leaves unanswered the vexing question, noted in the discussion of supererogation, of whether people ought to forgo some obligatory actions if they threaten to harm their cultivation.)

A theoretical account of the process Mencius proposes exists in the much discussed lines that preface the story. They say, in a different translation, "There has to be practice, but one must not aim at it; the mind should not forget it, but one must not (forcibly) help it to grow (*pi yu shih yen, erh wu cheng; hsin wu wang, wu chu chang yeh*)."[13] Mencius's point here resembles, I think, the one discussed earlier in distinguishing the role of first-person reflection and third-person ascription in the case of the virtuous person. People must constantly cultivate virtue, but (at least with most virtues) their actions ought not be motivated by the desire to possess or manifest the virtue. An action is not fully benevolent, for example, if it is motivated by the desire to appear to be benevolent or to gain benevolence. Nevertheless, people must keep benevolence in mind as they cultivate themselves. They must possess a second-order volition to become a particular sort of person. A kind of executive control always must be present, even though people will not aim solely to become benevolent or manifest the trait, the benevolence, they want to attain.

A fuller picture of Mencius's ideas about cultivation and virtuous actions emerges when we examine three closely related notions, three critical terms of art, in his practical theory about what virtue is. The three are extension (*t'ui* or *ta*), attention (*ssu*), and intelligent awareness (*chih*). Mencius thinks people actualize virtue when they learn to extend knowledge and feelings from situations where correct action is clear and motivation is strong to analogous situations where correct action is unclear and motivation absent. He presumes that in some situations we both understand what we ought to do and possess the motivation to do it. This occurs because in those situations we contact the sprouts (*tuan*), the defining potentials, of our nature.

His most famous example of such a situation is the "baby at the well."

> My reason for saying that no man is devoid of a heart sensitive to the suffering of others is this. Suppose a man were, all of a sudden, to see a young child on the verge of falling into a well. He would certainly be moved to compassion, not because he wanted to get in the good graces of the parents, nor because he wished to win the praise of his fellow villagers or friends, nor yet because he disliked the cry of the child.[14]

Neither a desire for the profit represented by the parents' good will or other people's praise, nor a desire motivated by discomfort at the child's cry moves people in such a case. Rather they move from a sympathy that is understood to define both themselves and all other humans. They both know what to do in such paradigmatic situations and have the motivation to do it.

Given this, all that remains for people to do is always to be able to contact such reactions and always to be able to extend them in an appropriate way to other situations. This process, which relies on people's ability to attend and extend in a way that utilizes intelligent awareness, undergirds virtuous action and virtuous character. It therefore also is what allows people to overcome their propensity to fail. Examining this process allows us, then, to see Mencius's vision of virtue at its most voluntaristic and most grand. He presents here, in uncompromising fashion, his vision of why humans need not fail to flourish. It, in fact, is a lofty and dramatic enough vision of human possibility to take its place with any of humanity's most noble religious ideals.

III. Mencius: True Virtue as a Product of Ethical Reasoning's Use of Extension, Attention, and the Understanding of Resemblances

The idea of extending (usually *t'ui* or *ta*) covers an operation that Mencius names or describes in various ways, but the basic process is relatively clear. To extend knowledge is to see that one situation resembles another situation. To extend feelings is to have feelings that clearly manifest themselves in one situation break through in another situation

Mencius discusses these notions graphically when he talks with King Hsüan. The king has displayed compassion by saving an animal that was about to be sacrificed, but he says he lacks the ability to care for his people. Mencius declares the king must merely extend the compassion he already has displayed.

> Hence one who extends his compassion (*t'ui en*) can take care of all people within the Four Seas. One who does not cannot even care for his own family. There is just one thing in which the ancients greatly surpassed others, and that was in being good at extending what they did (*t'ui chi's so wei*). Why is it then your compassion is sufficient to reach animals yet you do no good acts that reach the people. . . . So the reason why you do not become the real king is because you do not do it, not because you cannot.[15]

Mencius claims that people have the same freedom to focus their attention on specific objects of knowledge and emotion as they have to focus on specific external objects. If I see a person in psychological or physical pain, I either may be unsure about what to do or feel no real desire to help. But I can focus attention on the knowing and feeling that I would have if the person were a close friend and thereby gain the knowledge and power to act. People, then, are predisposed to act in appropriate ways, but they must be in contact with those predispositions. That contact occurs when they focus on actions where those predispositions are clear. They then can proceed to apply them to the relevant situations.

The specific capacity of the mind that underlies one crucial part of this process is the ability to attend (*ssu*). Mencius thinks the senses of hearing and seeing cannot attend; they are passive and drawn automatically to their objects. But the mind can choose to attend to one or another of the various movements within the self that can or have arisen. This capacity to focus, say, on the movements if a sprout seems close to (or at least is modeled on) what occurs when people direct their attention to the observation of concrete objects. *Ssu*'s action might best be pictured, then, as an inner ability to focus attention in a selective but concrete fashion. (The picture is misleading, however, insofar as it simplifies both the connection between outer events and inner responses and the processes of identifying the movements of dispositions.)

Mencius believes that people can grasp what they need to know through an inner perception of their defining characteristics rather than through a kind of "linear" reasoning. The capacity to do this both undergirds correct action and allows people to identify what truly constitutes their natures. Indeed, to think that the four virtues are unnatural, are welded on from without, is to not attend (*fu ssu*). Similarly, failures in attention underline misdirections of self-cultivation and misunderstandings about what is truly exalted within one's self. This means that neither linear reasoning, the application of rules, nor the intervention of truly transcendent forces is required for people to obtain all they need to avoid the failure to achieve full human flourishing. If people attend, all that is necessary is within their reach. As he says, "if one attends (*ssu*) one gets it (*te chih*) if one does not (*pu ssu*) one does not."[16]

People also, however, must be able to extend that to which they have attended. The clearest theoretical development of the idea of extension occurs when Mencius examines the understanding that takes place when people grasp what they will not do. He claims that extending what is grasped in such situations solves the problems both of knowing what to do and having the correct motivation to do it. It, then, underlies his version of the belief that to know the good is to do the good, just as it undergirds the knowledge and motivation that inform fully virtuous actions.

> For every man there are things he does not endure. Getting this to break through (*ta*) to what he does endure results in benevolence (*jen*). For this to break through to what he does results in rightness (*yi*). If a man can fully develop (*ch'ung*) his disposition ("heart," *hsin*) not to desire to injure others, his benevolence will be more than he can use. If he can fully develop his disposition not to bore through or jump over [a wall], his rightness will be more than he can use. If he can fully develop the actuality (*shih*) [in himself] of refusing to accept the informal "thee" and "thou" [when people address him], then in whatever he sets out to do he will not do anything that is not right. If you say something to a gentleman that you ought not to say, this is flattering him with speech. If you do not say something to him that you ought to say, this is flattering him with silence. Both are in the category (*lei*) of boring through and jumping over [walls — i.e. to seize one's neighbor's daughter as a wife].[17]

We all, Mencius thinks, encounter or can imagine situations in which we can neither undertake an action nor allow others to undertake it. I cannot imagine myself, for example, heedlessly allowing a baby to fall down a well, seizing someone as a spouse, or accepting some demeaning forms of address. The abhorrence can arise, then, in cases where the issue concerns benevolence, righteousness, or propriety. The recognition that the acts I abhor fall into general categories leads me also to recognize that other actions, to which I do not initially react so strongly, share the features of the acts I abhor. I will then respond to those other actions in a similar way. Moreover, understanding that my negative response implies certain positive reactions leads me to act on those virtues that define me.

The process Mencius describes is a complex one, and we may question some steps within it. Mencius seems not to be troubled by what seems to us to be significant differences among being addressed improperly, seeing a baby about to die, and seizing a wife against her family's will. As we discussed, directives arising from injunctions and from ways of life fit together more closely for him than they do for us. Moreover, he does not examine (at least in this and most other contexts) the difficulties that arise when we try to fit specific actions within general categories to decide what to do. Finally, the movement from a negative judgment to a positive action can seem to us to contain motivational and cognitive problems that he fails to address fully.

Nevertheless, Mencius's picture of ethical thinking illustrates the emphasis on the perception of salient characteristics that also underlies Aquinas's position and this general kind of theory of virtue. Mencius, however, develops the idea in a distinctive way. He conceives of ethical reasoning as a process that depends on perceiving clearly and then identifying correspondences or affinities. He especially opposes the idea found in Mohism (and also, of course, evident in the contemporary world) that ethical reasoning mainly involves the application of rules or principles. The view he opposes need not embrace a simple or mechanical idea about how people know and apply rules. Rules, for instance, may become apparent to people either only after careful reflection or only in situations where duress forces them to make a thorough assessment. But a style of thinking that operates from rules differs from one that moves from concrete cases where the perception of salient characteristics is clear to other concrete cases where it is not clear.

The most significant difference between the two points of view probably lies in the importance given to the true description of a situation, and thus to the intelligent awareness that produces the description. To gather a situation under a rule, a person must describe the situation. If I am to decide whether certain rules apply I must know the person before me is a brother rather than a friend or a distant acquaintance. But such descriptions are hardly as textured as those that occur when I try to see if correspondences or affinities fit. In those situations, I must carefully appraise all the relevant aspects of the apparent correspondences, including my relationship to both cases. Indeed, in cases where correspondences seem to fail, I may need to try out different descriptions to see if a change in description displays a correspondence that previously was obscured.[18]

Take the case, for example, where I move from feelings of compassion about by brother's psychic pain at an important loss to the similar pain a friend feels. I will have to describe as accurately as possible the character of the loss each feels, and that involves understanding both the character of what is lost and the relationship each person has to the loss. Both may have lost a spouse or a job, but understanding exactly the character of the spouse or job and how it functioned in their respective lives demands very textured descriptions. To my surprise, I may discover my brother's spouse meant relatively little to him and his job a great deal, even though I had previously thought the reverse was true. Furthermore, I also must have a textured description of my feelings toward my brother as a person, as a family member, as one with whom I share a rich history, and as one toward whom I may have some deeply ambivalent feelings. Similarly, I will need to describe carefully a whole set of my attitudes toward my friend. Only by doing this can I both perceive the real resemblances and gain the needed motivation.

The descriptions must, then, be thickly textured because only that thickness gives me both the needed knowledge and the necessary emotional impetus. "Brother" as an abstract category has little emotional impact for me. But the term *brother* as signifying the one who first taught me about sexuality, saved me from neighborhood bullies, infuriated me with his adolescent disregard, and consoled me during my first failed love affair has considerable impact. Ethical thinking that relies on resemblances or affinities demands what John Henry Newman calls real apprehension, a contact with complex particulars, rather than just notional apprehension, an abstract understanding of something's general character. It calls for that kind of attention to nuanced, complex particulars that Iris Murdoch so powerfully has portrayed.[19]

Perhaps the clearest example in Mencius of how this reasoning differs from the application of principles occurs when he is questioned about whether one ought to take the hand of a drowning sister-in-law even though propriety forbids one touching her. He replies: "Not to help a sister-in-law who is drowning is to be a brute. It is prescribed by the rites that in giving and receiving, man and woman should not touch each other, but in stretching out a helping hand to the drowning sister-in-law one uses one's discretion."[20] One might argue that in this case Mencius uses a higher ethical principle about care for life to overrule a lesser ethical principle about concern for social rules. But Mencius, I think, is saying that of the two relevant descriptions of the woman, sister-in-law and person in mortal danger, the latter must take precedence. Moreover, recognizing which description applies makes people's judgment easy and their acts spontaneous.

For Mencius, therefore, once truly virtuous people attend to their natures, decide in what category an event belongs, and describe it truly, the appropriate extension follows easily. The moral judgment becomes virtually a true description, and the proper action follows spontaneously. The cognitive elements in virtue, the ability to attend, to give true descriptions, and to see real correspondences (and thus, as we will discuss, to form emotions) resolves all the problems of motivation. A virtuous person knows what is good and effortlessly does it.

IV. Mencius: Virtues, Their Semblances, and the Role of Intelligent Awareness

This approach to ethical reasoning also allows Mencius to differentiate levels in apparently similar actions; that is, to identify virtues and their semblances. Proper ethical reasoning generates appropriate motivation. The presence of such motivation, in turn, differentiates apparently or partially good actions from really virtuous actions. Actions that flow from intelligently activated dispositions are fully virtuous acts, then, but people often do the right act but lack the proper motivation for it.

Distinguishing virtue's true forms from their semblances is an especially important task for Mencius. The Confucian emphasis on propriety (*li*) makes it likely that a mindless following of convention can pass for virtuousness. Moreover, this misidentification is very dangerous; it leads people either to feel content when they ought not or to undertake harmful forms of self-cultivation.

Mencius highlights these problems when he contrasts the man of virtue with the "village honest man" (*hsiang-yüan*),what one translator calls the "Bourgeois Righteous [who] are simulators of Excellence." The village honest man is one who thinks that:

> "Being in this world, one must behave in a manner pleasing to this world. So long as one is good [at such pleasing], it is all right." He tries in this way cringingly to please the world. . . .
> If you want to censure him, you cannot find anything; if you want to find fault with him, you cannot find anything either. He shares with others the practices of the day and is in harmony with the sordid world. He pursues such a policy and appears to be conscientious and faithful, and to show integrity in his conduct. He is liked by the multitude and is self-righteous. It is impossible to embark on the way of Yao and Shun [two sages] with such a man. Hence the name, "enemy of virtue." Confucius said, "I dislike what is specious. . . . I dislike the village honest man for fear he might be confused with the virtuous."[21]

The category of the village honest man, I think, contains two kinds of people, although they may not be clearly distinguished in this passage. The first, less interesting kind are those who harmonize easily with a sordid world, often desire only to win people's praise, and act for selfish personal profit. The faults of such people can be identified relatively easily, although stopping the harm they do themselves and others may be difficult.

The second, more complicated kind of people who fit within the category are more important to us. Most observers find nothing to censure in these people; they seem to be conscientious and to show integrity. Mencius, in contrast, thinks that these "righteous bourgeoisie" serve as beacons that lead others (and themselves) in errant directions. He understands, however, that identifying the problem with them is difficult and utilizes the idea of virtue and its semblances to show what the problem is.

The idea that virtues can be differentiated from their semblances rests, as we discussed, on the idea that modes of action can be distinguished. I think we can say that, put schematically, Mencius identifies four kinds of human action, and thus character, with the differences among them arising from differences in motivation. According to Mencius, only one kind manifests virtuous behavior and character; the other three are either counterfeits or semblances of virtue. The four can be classified as actions that arise from a *desire for gain*, actions that arise from *habitual responses*, actions that arise from following *rules*, and actions that arise from *extension*. At the lowest level, people are motivated by personal profit. (If profit for the whole community motivates people, as is the case with the Mohists, their pursuit fits within the category of actions that follows a rule.) Actions aimed only at selfish profit usually are counterfeits not semblances of virtue. Although Mencius at times despairs of changing people who act in this way, he also believes most can recognize their subterfuges and consequently will not be tempted by their approach to life.[22]

At the second level, people act from habit rather than from intelligently activated dispositions. Their responses simulate those found in extension, but they produce only untextured, rote actions because neither attention nor intelligent awareness inform them. (The unreflective follower of propriety who is also inattentive to the nuances of situations belongs at this level.) The actions of these people neither arise from accurate perception nor involve the full activation of a human beings defining characteristics.

At the third level, people act from adherence to rules. The rules can be very specific (e.g., one ought to treat a specific kind of official in a particular way) or very general (e.g., one ought to act in ways that will most benefit the most people). The agent has a positive attitude toward the obligations that arise from the rule, but some conflict about following the rule also is present. To use Mencius's language, the rule is external. That is, the action the rule commands differs in some ways from the agent's internal inclination, else no rule would be needed or accepted.

At the level of truly virtuous action, people act from dispositions they have freely chosen and maneuvered into position, either at the moment of action or as the result of a long process of cultivation. At this level, they resemble the sage Shun who, as Mencius tersely puts it, "acted through benevolence and rightness. It was not that he put into action benevolence and rightness [*yu jen yi hsing, fei hsing jen yeh*]."[23] Such a person "acts out of *jen yi*, rather than [just] practices *jen yi* "; he acts ethically rather than doing ethical acts. He does not do something "because it is ethical" in the purposive sense of because. Rather he does it "because I am ethical" in the causitive sense of because. (To use our earlier terminology, the first-person deliberation differs markedly from any third-person description, especially when expressive motives are in action.) Actions at this level arise from those inclinations that a person's intelligent dispositions produce in response to specific situations.

Although these actions manifest true virtue, they may appear to violate common standards of propriety and righteousness. Nevertheless, fully virtuous people's actions never violate the spirit of propriety or righteousness. This is true even if their actions seem to differ from what most think the rules of propriety and righteousness demand. As Mencius says, in all of its cryptic literalness: "The propriety (*li*) that is not propriety, the right (*yi*) that is not right — these things the great man does not do." Mencius's point here surely reflects his insistence that rules be applied in ways that are sensitive to situations. However, more than just this is involved, I think, and it appears in striking form in an apparently dark saying of Mencius. The great man, he declares, "does not make a point of being true to his word or carrying through his acts[;] he simply aims at what is right [*ta jen che yen pu pi hsin, hsing pu pi kuo, wei yi so tsai*]."[24] Mencius thinks some guidelines or injunctions bind everyone, as we discussed. But the great person apparently can legitimately either violate promises (perhaps even lie) or fail to complete expected courses of action. All that matters is that he aims at the right; that is, acts from inclinations to righteousness.

Although this kind of idea may seem to fit uneasily into Mencius's general perspective, the internal logic of his position clearly leads to it. Various notions in him all point to a position where the fully virtuous person is not guided by rules and therefore may violate what many think are the correct standards of behavior. For example, he emphasizes the difference between acting on rules and acting on extended reactions; he focuses on the overwhelming significance of grasping the salient characteristics of changing situations; and he believes we can grasp through attention the defining, Heaven-given movements of our nature. We see few antinomian tendencies in Mencius himself, in the incidents in the *Mencius*, or in the spirit of the book. (The atmosphere differs markedly from what appears, for example, with certain followers of Wang Yang-ming.) Moreover, we see no indication that Mencius thinks that injunctions, correctly understood, can be violated. Nevertheless, an unconventional, even subversive side does exist in the *Mencius*.

That side resembles certain Taoist ideas of roughly his time, such as the one that opens the second half of the *Tao Te Ching*: "A man of the highest virtue does not keep to virtue and that is why he has virtue. A man of the lowest virtue never strays from virtue and that is why he is without virtue."[25] The exact meaning of ideas like this can differ remarkably depending on who develops their implications. In some hands, such as in the first seven chapters of the *Chuang Tzu*, they generate a radical break from almost all accepted notions of behavior. In other hands, such as in most of the rest of the *Chuang Tzu*, they signal only a freedom from conventional forms of behavior and a diminished attachment to normal expectations. Mencius never even flirts with the more radical form of these ideas, but their more modest versions appear in his ideas about virtues and their semblances. He does not reject conventional, rule-governed ideas of behavior, but he places them within a hierarchy of kinds of action.

Truly virtuous activity, for Mencius, differs markedly from the semblances that constitute each of the three lesser levels of action. The difference from actions done for personal profit is most clear, especially as many such actions are only counterfeits of virtue. Despite this, one significant characteristic is shared by virtuous action and action for profit. Both lack the regularity that marks actions arising from either habit or the following of rules, and therefore both can diverge from expected standards of behavior. (This similarity helps explain why conventional people can think virtuous people's actions, at times, are unethical.)

Most important here, truly virtuous action differs from actions that arise either from habits or rules. Virtuous people act from extended inclinations not from accepted rules. Moreover, their actions display not just habitual responses to stimuli but textured responses to varying circumstances. With virtuous actions, then, variations occur that may seem to be mysterious — and even unethical — to the untrained eye. Exactly these variations, however, manifest the presence of intelligent awareness (*chih*). Just because such actions arise from a perception of salient characteristics and involve the intelligent activation of dispositions, they cannot fit into specific act types. As the free responses of individuals to the specifics of situations, they differ from the predictable reactions that occur with either habitual responses or the following of rules.

Mencius highlights the significance of intelligent awareness when he distinguishes the excellence Confucius showed from that observed in three other sages. All four figures display benevolence and at least the most major forms of righteousness. Confucius surpasses them all, however, through the quality of his intelligent awareness. Each of the other three has a rule he follows. Lui Hsia Hui, for example, will serve a tarnished prince or accept a modest post; Po Yi will not stay with a prince or even a villager who is in the wrong; and Yi Yin will take office whether order exists or not.

Confucius's excellence surpasses that found in these sages because he follows no rule; he is "timely," he alone does "all according to circumstance." (Indeed, Mencius declares that "ever since man came into this world, there has never been another Confucius.") As Mencius says, "Po Yi was the sage who was unsullied; Yi Yin was the sage who accepted responsibility; Lui Hsia Hui was the sage who was easygoing; Confucius was the sage whose actions were timely."[26] People who fully manifest intelligent awareness operate neither from rules, habits, nor temperamental dispositions. Rather they operate from a delicate appreciation of and judgment upon the particular circumstances they face. That appreciation and judgment is particularly important, Mencius thinks, because people must work with organically related dyads, such as benevolence and propriety or benevolence and righteousness. These must always be applied in situations where one or the other may need to take precedence, to be highlighted, or to be given its due. Indeed, the role of intelligent awareness makes clear that Mencius, like Aquinas, employs what we earlier labeled the *good person criterion*. Except for those few actions covered by injunctions, the ultimate standard of evaluation is that the sage would do that particular action in that particular situation.

The place of intelligent awareness in Mencius's theory of virtue can be formulated in a revealing, if also speculative, way by focusing on how he argues that Confucianism mediates between the extreme positions represented in Yang Chu and Mo Tzu. On the one side are proto-Taoists who see appropriate action in terms of the spontaneous expressions of a human nature unfettered by reason. On the other side are Mohists who think people should rely on rational calculations about both goals and the means to those goals. The reliance on intelligent awareness that Mencius commends mediates between these two positions. That is, intelligence should guide spontaneous movements, but it fits natural impulses to circumstances in a way that cannot be codified into rules or fixed procedures.

Consummate virtue may seem to resemble most closely the naturalness of the proto-Taoists, given that actions may appear spontaneous to both the agent and an observer. Indeed, Mencius declares that those who desert Mohism will turn to Yang and those who desert Yang will turn to Confucius, thereby implying that an emphasis on nature rather than calculation moves one closer to Confucianism. Nevertheless, the intelligent guidance of natural movements remains central for Mencius. In even the most apparently spontaneous movements of true virtue, the perfected agent can reconstruct the activity of intelligent awareness and present a justification of its judgments. Moreover, both the cultivation that moves

people toward complete virtue and many actions of most people must utilize rational judgments. Deliberative modes, intentional acts, and self-cultivation are necessary. They connect people with "the inertial tendency
toward goodness" that defines them, with the natural tendency to expression that can be blocked off. Perfected people, the sages or the daimonic
(*shen*), may never lose touch with their true hearts. But those who have
not attained this level, at times at least, must exercise the abilities that are
manifested in attention, intelligent awareness, and extension.[27]

To focus too much on self-conscious processes, however, is to make
the fundamental mistake of overlooking both the natural movements within
humans and the significance of nuanced descriptions of situations. This
approach misreads what is truly significant in the self and in situations.
Moreover, it leads people to focus on profit (*li*) in a way that, Mencius
thinks, will lead them to value selfish or superficial desires too much. This is
especially true if such a focus ever becomes more than a feature of a cultivation process aimed at making unnecessary most self-conscious forms of
deliberation.

The presence of intelligent awareness, attention, extension, and ethical reasoning based on resemblances underlie, indeed define, Mencius's
picture of the distinction between virtue and its semblances, between the
village honest man and the truly virtuous person. They also illuminate,
from another angle, his understanding both of the relationship of reason
and nature and of reason's formation of emotions and dispositions. Let us
now turn to Aquinas's analysis of these topics in his theory of virtue.

V. Aquinas: Reason and Nature

Our main concern here is with Aquinas's notion that reason rather
than nature underlies human virtuousness. But to analyze this idea we
need to examine briefly his understanding of the structure of the human
self. That understanding appears to differ markedly from Mencius's
understanding of the self. As we will discuss, however, the two views of
the self actually share fundamentally similar notions about the character
of and relationships among practical reason, emotions, and dispositions.

To grasp these resemblances, as well as Aquinas's own position, we need
to recognize that although Aquinas employs a "faculty psychology" in his
analysis, he does not divide the self into various semiautonomous agencies.
The divisions are used only for analysis or convenience. Statements about
what a power does always can be reformulated as statements about what
human beings as possessors of a power do or can do. (For example, he meets

the objection that the will cannot understand a command by saying "a man enjoins an act of will on himself inasmuch as he understands and wills.")[28]

Humans, for Aquinas, have both a rational soul and an irrational soul, the soul being the "that by which" activities occur, the functional power that makes something what it it. The rational soul has both theoretical and deliberative powers, and they can function in more or less excellent ways and therefore be spoken of as more or less virtuous. The irrational soul has two aspects which can be distinguished by whether reason can form them. Our main concern will be with how the rational soul's deliberative capacities can inform one aspect of the irrational soul. We need to sketch out the features that characterize each soul, however, especially as some of them will become important in our later analyses.

The rational soul, according to Aquinas, divides into a theoretical or contemplative mentality that generates conclusions, and a practical or deliberative mentality that generates decisions, resolutions, and actions. The former, which has no clear equivalent in Mencius, deals with the unchanging, produces "truth," and exhibits a kind of passivity or receptiveness. The latter, in contrast, deals with judgments about the changing world, aims to produce a product, either an act or artifact, and usually involves some obvious activity.

Further distinctions are made within each of the two realms. Within the theoretical realm, three powers are distinguished: the ability to grasp immediately the truth of some idea, such as that humans are mortal (*intellectus*); the ability to deduce conclusions from premises, to gain new knowledge from knowledge already possessed, such as that I am mortal (*scientia*); and the ability to use these two powers in harmonious concert (*sapientia*). (Many people, of course, do not think mortality is the last word in human affairs, but the point here is that they must think it is the first word — that it provides the context for thinking — if any words are to have meaning.) For Aristotle, from whom Aquinas draws these distinctions, full assent, then, must rest on self-evidence, reasons, or a harmonious combination of the two. The states of doubt, manifested in withholding assent, and of opinion, manifested in tentative assent that allows for the possibility of error, fill out Aristotle's picture. Aquinas, however, adds the theological virtue of faith, an unquestioning assent where neither self-evidence nor universally compelling reasons are present, that rests on love and hope. This leads him (as we will discuss in examining courage) to focus on how certain levels of understanding involve trust and unformalizable kinds of sensitivity, and on how love — or even hope — produces contact with religious realities that can be reached in no other way.

In Aquinas's view, the practical or deliberative powers divide into excellences of doing and making (*intellectus practicus, ars*). Excellences of doing guide judgments about and action in the world, those of making guide judgments that aim to create a product. The line separating the two can be sinuous and in so far as it informs the distinction between virtues and skills consideration of it is important, as we shall discuss. In many cases, however, the separation is clear. Obvious features, for example, differentiate my thinking about and deciding to be stern with a recalcitrant child and my thinking about and deciding to make a chair from the planks of wood that confront me. The theoretical and practical mentalities interact with each other in various ways (some of which will be examined later), but our major concern here is with the practical not theoretical mentality and its power to act rather than produce.

The power to act operates by interacting with those parts of the irrational soul that reason can affect. The more biological aspects of the irrational soul, such as reflex actions or the digestive system, cannot be directly affected by reason. But the irrational soul contains two processes that practical rationality can form. One is the simple attractions to a good object that easily can be attained or simple repulsions from a bad object that easily can be avoided. These are impulse, affective, or concupiscient movements (*concupiscentia*). The other process occurs when an agent encounters some difficulty that will take a determined effort to overcome. These are contending, spirited, or irascible movements (*irascibilis*). (Impulse movements underlie what we called *inclinational virtues* and contending movements inform what we called *preservative virtues*.) I have an impulse movement, an affective desire, to save a baby about to fall down a well. But if a sinister person stands between me and the baby, the action involves contending movements. To reach the desired good, I must now overcome my fear of confronting the sinister person.

If these movements of the irrational soul are formed by reason, will (*voluntas*) appears. Will, for Aquinas, arises whenever reason judges that something is a good to be pursued. (His use of *will* is considerably wider than our normal, contemporary use of the term.) The power of the will is directed to an object only in as much as it is taken to be good (*sub ratione boni*); indeed, "will means rational appetite." Freedom appears with will, then, and therefore the whole realm of distinctively human action emerges. Aquinas's nuanced analysis of human action breaks it down into various steps, such as intending, deliberating, and choosing, but most important here is a more general point. He argues people are necessarily drawn to certain sense objects, as in Mencius's account, but that no such necessity occurs when reason judges whether an object is good and then decides about pursuing it. For Aquinas as for Aristotle "only the bare commitment to pursue the Good itself lies outside deliberation."[29] Lacking any inexorable movement to a specific object, people must choose whether and how to pursue any particular good.

People, then, can choose freely both the goal to be pursued and the means to reach it. This situation produces what, for Aquinas, are the two major human difficulties. One is the misidentification of goods, a failure of knowledge, and the other is the subsequent misdirection of the self to inappropriate goods, a failure of the will. The failure to recognize the distinctions between real and apparent goods (*bonum apparens*) and the failure to act on that recognition are the crucial human problems. These problems raise important and complicated issues that we will discuss at length later when we compare Mencius and Aquinas's understanding of people's failures to be virtuous. For now, however, we can turn from outlining Aquinas's picture of the soul to examining his views on the relationship of reason and nature.

Aquinas's ideas about the soul underlie his belief that following human nature's inclinations is of secondary importance. People, instead, should commend actions or states because they accord with a correct understanding and pursuit of some not yet realized human activity that is good and obtainable. That is, Aquinas thinks the notion of the good coheres more basically with "reason" than it does with "nature." (Aquinas's perspective on this issue resembles Mencius's then, as we shall see, but with important differences as well as similarities.) Conformity either to nature or to some superior moving force perceived within the self, for him, is not the most critical factor in the guidance and evaluation of activity. Most important here, Aquinas's position differs from what I will call a *Stoic* position, with which it can be easily confused. Indeed, an influential tradition of commentators on Aquinas usually interpreted aspects of his thought in a way that reflects a Stoic position.

In a Stoic position, to be virtuous is to live according to reason as it is guided by nature. Nature's guides are discovered when a person focuses on those inclinations that define human nature. Reason's role is both to follow those inclinations and to make inferences from them. Proponents of a Stoic position presume, then, that human nature either harmonizes with or manifests the universal reason present in the whole cosmos; indeed, that notion underlies any justification of their position. It also leads them to assert that no fundamental difference exists between practical and theoretical reason. They argue that to distinguish them by means of the indeterminacy of the sphere in which practical reason operates is to misunderstand the character of reason. Moreover, they believe that to be concerned with specific practical goods is to live an imperfect life.

The broad outlines of the Stoic position resemble the rationalist moral theory that Donagan describes, and that we discussed in examining Aquinas's ideas on injunctions. But the Stoic thinks such a theory applies not only to the realm of injunctions (where Aquinas would agree it does apply) but also to all important human activities (where Aquinas thinks it does not apply). Subtle controversies surround the interpretation of Aquinas's ideas on these matters, but we need to examine briefly several key distinctions between Aquinas and the Stoic position. That examination illuminates Aquinas's view on the relationship between reason and nature, and it also will help us to compare Aquinas with Mencius, aspects of whose ideas may seem to fit a Stoic position. Moreover, the examination enables us to specify an important strength and weakness in Aquinas's approach. We can see why he is untouched by critics who argue he misunderstood the need to separate fact and value. But we also can see why he can be criticized for his insensitivity to the acceptable variety that some kinds of ethical judgments can display, an insensitivity that arises from his limited understanding of the role of ethos in ethics.[30]

Aquinas assumes (as do Stoics) that any activity has a natural goal or end, and that the end manifests the maturity characteristic of a species. But, unlike Stoics, he also think the actualization of human rationality, itself a natural goal, may lead to justifiable interferences with other natural human goals. The legitimacy of these interferences with a natural end can be judged only by reason. We can judge, for example, that inducing vomiting to be able to continue to gorge oneself or remain slim is wrong because it interferes with the natural end of eating. But we also can declare that lying is justified in some cases, even though it thwarts the natural end of speech, which is to communicate truthfully. When an enraged person demands you return the gun she loaned you, lying enables you to avoid contributing to the horrible goal of helping someone use another person, the one who will be shot, as a means rather than an end. Natural ends can be interfered with, then, but the cogency of any interference must be judged by reason. This position leads Aquinas to think that practical wisdom's role is crucial because it, rather than adherence to nature, will determine the value of actions. Only people's rational appropriation of ideas about nature can rightfully lead them to judge that some acts either are correct or better than other acts. As he says, all sinful acts involve a drawing back from reason because all such acts cause one to become less than fully human.[31]

Aquinas's views on conscience illustrate this crucial distinction between his position and a Stoic position. Conscience for Aquinas is a disposition to understand and apply the principles presented by *synderesis*, the cognitive disposition to recognize the first principles of the ethical order. Conscience is an act not a power, as in a Stoic position. It is practical wisdom's application of ethical understanding to conduct, rather than reason's application of a crystalized, specific moral directive. (Again, when only the realm of injunctions is involved, Aquinas's position resembles the Stoic position.) Conscience, then, is not a separate faculty from, say, reason and desire. It is not a higher force or actuality that people contact to know what to do in all cases or almost all cases. Rather conscience connects people to general principles and points up the necessity of some means to an end or object that is thought to be good.[32]

Put in schematic, almost formulaic, terms, Aquinas's position on the relationship of reason and nature is as follows. He assumes that "good and bad in actions should be discussed like good and bad in things, since action springs from each thing according to the sort of thing it is." But he also believes that "when we speak of 'good' and 'evil' in human acts we take the reasonable as our standard of reference (*per comparationem ad rationem*)." Good then equals "what benefits the reasonable order of life. . . [and bad what] is out of keeping with such order." This approach leads him to develop a hierarchy of ethical terms that starts from the widest category, the natural, and proceeds down to the far narrower category of the rational. The process he employs, then, resembles the process he uses (and we discussed) in examining virtue. Human activity provides the focal meaning, but the term's secondary meanings extend considerably beyond the human realm. Just as good (*bonum*) is wider than right (*rectum*), evil (*malum*) is wider than sin or failure (*peccatum*). Failure, in turn, is wider than culpable fault (*culpa*), which involves only voluntary activity and therefore arises from choice and thus reason. The nonethical good or evil found in nature is the widest of categories. But failure and especially culpable fault characterize fully human activity, and they occur only if practical wisdom is present.[33]

Practical wisdom, then, is central. But the procedures it follows and the judgments it makes depend on whether it operates in the realm of injunctions or of virtues. Within the realm of injunctions, practical wisdom reflects on human beings as rational creatures and thus as ends in themselves. Within the realm of virtue, practical wisdom judges whether an object is a good or is a more worthy good than some other good. The idea of nature operates in both realms. Our nature as rational beings operates in the first. Our nature as beings who incline to activities that we think fulfill us operates in the second. But with universal injunctions the idea of nature provides clear, if general, directives: the foundation nature provides resembles that found in a Stoic position. With virtues, however, the directives are less clear. The notion of the maturity characteristic of a species — that is, the kinds of activity that will fulfill human beings — is much more murky than is the notion of injunctions. Considerable indeterminacy, then, informs Aquinas's idea of the fully human good. This is true even though at times he so underestimates the significance of ways of life that he writes as if the character of all real human goods was fully evident.

Determinate elements, of course, are present. He believes the general human good is fixed in so far as human beings are created by God to have a specific nature and an evident end, the beatific vision. These determinate elements are extremely important, but they can provide firm guidance to people only in limited areas or ways. A second element, revelation, also might seem to give clear guidance, and Aquinas surely does believe it provides invaluable aids to people. But revelation, for him, cannot cover all or virtually all actions. To claim he thinks it does would be to overlook his emphasis on practical wisdom. Furthermore, the claim does not account for the fact that he thinks much of what revelation most clearly shows in ethics also is shown by injunctions. Finally, such a claim fails to take seriously enough his complex picture of what it means to interpret the guidelines that revelation does give.³⁴

Aquinas believes that the human good manifest in universal injunctions is determinate, however. When injunctions are the subject, considerable rational clarity and even motivational ability normally are present. Most people can rightfully feel secure about their knowledge of the contents of injunctions and even about their mastery of the procedures of the needed, informal dialectical reasoning. Moreover, they can rightfully believe that they in fact will act on the narrowly defined directive injunctions give.

When the goods virtue pursues are the subject, however, the situation changes. All that is determinate is a revelation that must be interpreted, a nature whose specific characteristics never are clearly knowable, a general inclination to an ultimate good, and the need to choose freely and rationally the means (or subsidiary goods) that move one toward it. Aquinas thinks, then, that people cannot know human nature's specific characteristics in a way that always will clearly guide their actions. Humans are finite, free, and sinful. Their pursuit of the good involves choices made in situations where the good's character never is entirely clear, the proper mode to realize it never is completely evident, and the ability to follow reason never is sure.

Indeed, this situation illustrates why human and nonhuman goods differ radically. If circumstances are appropriate, an acorn will move inexorably to its fulfillment, and that movement allows us to establish clear criteria for what constitutes a "good" oak tree. But no similar process is evident when most human goods are the subject. The role of practical reason is crucial, then, in the attainment and maintenance of human excellence or virtue.

Let us turn now to examine more closely Aquinas's ideas on how reason actually operates in virtuous activity. I will begin by discussing briefly his modified developmental model of human nature. That model can help us grasp his understanding of our main subject: reason's relationship to both inclinations and to emotions, and the picture of virtue and semblances of virtue that emerges from it.

VI. Aquinas: Reason's Relationship to Inclinations and Emotions and the Resulting Understanding of the Semblances of Virtue

Aquinas's understanding of virtuous activity ill fits a discovery model of human nature, many features of which fit the Stoic position. Virtues for him are not within people in their perfected form; they are within people only in the sense that people have the ability over time to aquire them. As he says, all natural virtues "are in us by nature as aptitudes and beginnings but not as perfections."[35] Nevertheless, Aquinas cannot embrace a pure developmental model. God must act if humans are to realize even aquired virtues and must transform humans if they are to attain the needed infused virtues. Moreover, God creates human nature and ensures that some of its capacities will never be lost; most notably, the aptitude for virtue and the ability to know the first principle of ethics.

Aquinas believes, then, that although few ever possess the virtues in their full flower, the embryonic seeds are present in every person: "certain seeds (*semina*) or beginnings of aquired virtue pre-exist in us by nature." These seeds provide a standard that leads all people both to judge themselves and others and to be attracted to or repelled by their own or other's activities. As Aquinas says, "even though one is not virtuous oneself, one loves the person who is, as measuring up to the standards demanded by one's own reason."[36] (Interestingly enough, Aquinas presents this as an alternative explanation to one that appeals to many today, viz. that the ungenerous love the generous and inconstant the constant in order to get something they want.)

Aquinas's modified version of a developmental model of human nature leads him to view virtues and their semblances in terms of reason's relationship to inclinations, emotions, and dispositions. (As we will see, an account of these relationships that resembles Aquinas's also appears in Mencius.) For Aquinas, a person's natural inclinations can never fully constitute virtue. They can provide an aid to real virtue or a starting point for it, but real human virtue rises only from dispositions that manifest rationality. Virtue can coexist with natural propensities: it does not "contradict the notion of virtue if someone has a natural tendency towards it because of his natural characteristics." Nevertheless, rationally informed dispositions are necessary. In fact, inclinations to virtue can be dangerous. As Aquinas writes:

> The natural inclination to the good of virtue is a kind of beginning of virtue, but it is not perfect virtue. In fact, the stronger the inclination

is the more perilous can it prove to be, unless it be governed by right
reason . . . just as, if a running horse be blind, the faster it runs the
more heavily will it fall, and the more grievously be hurt.[37]

Aquinas believes that acts arising from laudable inclinations may lead
to errant results if rationality is missing. An inclination to kindness when
sternness is needed, for example, or to reflectiveness when immediate
action is required can generate inappropriate actions. Reflection, then,
constantly must inform even generally praiseworthy dispositions. A benevolent act aimed at one person can involve, when all relevant circumstances
are understood, harmful and thus unbenevolent actions either toward
other people or even toward the recipient's own long-term good. My
benevolence toward a distressed student unable to complete an assignment
may harm other students struggling to discover what is required of them
and impede the distressed student's attempt to grasp the character of the
educational process. Furthermore, only the presence of rationality can
guard against the tendency of virtues, as discussed, to promote or even create situations in which the virtue can be expressed. Rational reflection is
what allows me to curb, for example, the tendency of my courage constantly to see difficulties I must confront when, in some cases, a more
appropriate response is to view matters with ironic detachment. Virtuous
dispositions in humans, in short, always must include practical wisdom.

Indeed, the presence of practical wisdom differentiates a real virtue from
a semblance of virtue. As Aquinas says, an incomplete or an "imperfect moral
virtue . . . is no more than a leaning by nature or by habituation towards a type
of acting that is in fact good." Those good deeds that arise from what Aquinas
calls "natural temperament or by some sort of routine" can be only semblances
of virtue because they lack practical wisdom's full presence. Natural tendencies
and routinized reactions may help a virtue operate. But they may also impede
or even destroy it, if practical wisdom is not present.[38]

Specifying exactly what is meant by the "presence" of practical wisdom underlies, then, any understanding of semblances of virtue. In any
given case, that specification involves examining the circumstances surrounding an act, a specific person's state of mind, and the way in which
semblances vary in form from virtue to virtue. In analyzing courage, we
will see how Aquinas presents such a textured account. Here, however, we
will only note the general guidelines he uses, guidelines that resemble in
instructive ways those found in Mencius.

Practical wisdom for him functions in three areas: *deliberations* about
what to do, a *decision* to do one rather than another act, and the *formation* of
the self that actually produces the action. Semblances of virtue appear when

malfunctions occur in any or all of the three areas. Failures in deliberation or decision concern problems in a person's thought about both ends and means to an end. Failures in informing the self concern problems in a person's thought about both ends and means to an end. Failures in informing the self concern problems that arise when a person puts a decision into action. One typical semblance of practical wisdom, then, will be a failure to specify a legitimate good, either as an end or as part of the means to an end. Another is a failure effectively to translate the decision into action. A third is a failure to specify a universal enough good.

The more radical permutations of all these failures will be discussed when we compare Mencius and Aquinas's accounts of human failures to be virtuous. Here, however, let us examine, if briefly, Aquinas's ideas about the need to reflect on general goods, because it underlies his claim that to pursue a limited end is to manifest only a semblance of virtue. We then can analyze at greater length his understanding of the failure either to turn decisions into action or to do so in a fully appropriate way, an account that rests on his ideas about how reason forms emotions. (The failure to specify particular legitimate goods, the misidentification of goods that Aquinas thinks haunts human life, already has been discussed.)

Aquinas presumes that practical wisdom must concern itself with a human being's overall good, with what plan of life leads to full flourishing. This kind of general reflection takes two forms. The rarer one appears when I think explicitly about who I am or want to be, about how my whole life plan fits into a justifiable picture of what a human being ought to be. The more common form manifests itself when I evaluate particular goals in light of general considerations about the human good. When, for example, I think about my actions toward a child or a friend in terms of my ideals about being a parent or a friend, I recognize that those ideals help constitute my general sense of what a good human life contains. In Aquinas's view, then, the judgments of practical wisdom must always contain, however implicitly, second-order reflections on what constitutes human flourishing. Moreover, those reflections will also affect decisions about whether the means to an end are appropriate. My belief, for example, about an end's importance may justify what I would otherwise think were inappropriate means. As Aquinas says, "cunning" (*astutia*, an adroitness and dexterity that uses guile and stratagems) normally is wrong, but it may be justified if the goal is significant and the circumstances appropriate.[39]

Aquinas does stress rationality's role in virtuous action, but that does not preclude him from also focusing on emotional states. These states, for him, are a critical part of most virtuous behavior. Many outright failures to act correctly and most semblances of virtue arise in significant part from reason's imperfect formation of emotion. The importance of the emotional component in virtue, however, depends on the character of the virtue. With some virtues, notably forms of justice, only the act is really critical. If I begrudgingly honor a contract the just act is diminished, but the critical fact is that I honor the contract. But with most virtues the person's emotional state is important and with some it is crucial. The emotional state is crucial with courage, for instance, but only important with beneficence. The exact praiseworthiness of my beneficent actions depends on my emotional state. I am beneficient if I help an aged person out of a sense of sympathy, but just how praiseworthy I am will turn on how vague or acute is my sense of sympathy. With courage, in contrast, the entire evaluation of my action can rest on the character of my emotions. Whether I am called rash or courageous depends largely on an evaluation of my emotional state.[40]

Furthermore, when we judge not simply the act but also the agent, the emotional state almost always is of great significance. Even with justice, we normally are uneasy labeling someone just who behaves justly but clearly feels no desire to render others what is due them. Similarly we call people beneficent only if they act from strong sympathetic reactions, and our focus on a person's emotional state is even more pronounced when courage is the virtue in question. If I feel great anger at a trivial slight but seek neither revenge nor even confrontation, we will judge my refusal to act to be correct but my character to be flawed.

In all those virtuous actions where emotions are important, Aquinas thinks reason forms rather than commands or weighs the emotions. (Following Aristotle, he also thinks, as we will examine in considering courage, that the aptness of the formation can be defined in terms of a right amount, a mean, and the poles of excess and deficiency.) Moreover, he believes the contending and impulse appetites have their own proper movement. Indeed, those appetites usually reflect cognitive judgments that, at times, properly can interfere with other forms of rational judgment. My judgment that justice demands I punish my child may legitimately be overruled, for example, by the attachment to the child I feel. A kind of rationality informs my sense of attachment, it is not simply an expression of my biological connection. The emotions arising from the attachment therefore can justifiably take precedence over the clearer, simpler rational judgment that punishment is due.

Reason's relationship to the emotions, then, must be characterized by a kind of political control. Reason "rules [them] . . . with a political control, as free men are ruled who have in some matters a will (*voluntatem*) of their own. This is why virtues [i.e., dispositions] are required in these powers, so that they may be well fitted for operation."[41] Political control, for

Aquinas, exemplifies that harmonious operation found in all appropriate dispositions. The essential characteristics of the organism's different parts are both respected and harnessed in a way that enables them to serve the organism's highest purposes. This position leads Aquinas to oppose proponents of "Stoic equanimity" or of harsh asceticism; he emphasizes that reason must not attempt to extirpate the emotions or even to overrule or radically change their nature. Emotions for him have an integrity, they manifest a kind of judgment. Practical wisdom therefore must respect and structure them, and at times even follow them. Only in this way can it produce the full harmony that real virtue manifests.

Ease rather than conflict, then, is the final criterion for the full operation of a virtue. Aspects of this are summed up in two formulaic statements, drawn from Aristotle, that Aquinas often repeats. One is that by "its nature virtue is concerned with the good rather than the difficult"; the other is that "the nature of virtue . . . requires that by it we should not only do what is good, but also that we should do it well." Virtue both makes it possible for people to do appropriate things and confers on them the propensity to do such things easily and well. Virtue confers, as he says, "not only the aptness to act well, but also ensures that this is brought to bear rightly." What he calls power, the ability to do something, is a lesser state of virtue than excellence, that state in which the occurrence of good actions is very likely.[42]

These general characteristics of virtue underlie Aquinas's distinction between virtuous people and people who possess only semblances of virtue. Moreover, his depiction of these distinctions often resembles Mencius's depiction. People who act from habitual responses or from rules fail to utilize fully practical wisdom's ability to activate intelligently their dispositions and form their emotions.

Let us now examine more closely the similarities and differences between Mencius and Aquinas's accounts of these distinctions as well as their general theories of virtue. I will discuss two topics, and normally use language (especially with the second topic) that enable us to compare the two thinkers, even if it therefore mirrors imperfectly the language of either thinker. One topic is their understanding of the human propensity to fail to be virtuous, the other topic their understanding of the self, especially the character and relationship of reason, emotions, and dispositions. The topics often relate closely, and therefore each analysis builds on the other or refers to it. Although differences and similarities between their accounts appear in each topic, the differences are more pronounced with the first topic and the similarities with the second. That situation leads me to argue in a constructive fashion for the cogency of their understanding of the self. Let us start, then, with their often differing views on the propensity of human beings to fail to be virtuous.

VII. The Understanding of Human Failures to Be Virtuous in Mencius and Aquinas

The question of why humans fail to be virtuous needs to be distinguished from several other questions. One only distant relative is the question of why evil is present in the world. I am not concerned here with either explanations of specific events, such as the death by cancer of a child, or general explanations of why the world contains such events. (Indeed, although these problems are important to Aquinas, they are difficult even to formulate in Mencius's organismic cosmology.) Two more closely related questions are why people fail to follow injunctions and why they manifest semblances of virtue rather than real virtues. Each fits within our more general question. The failure to follow injunctions represents an especially egregious fault that in virtually every case will be just a particularly pronounced instance of the more artful failures that are our main concern. The propensity to embrace semblances of virtue, in contrast, represents the most subtle kind of failure. Explaining why each thinker believes they occur rather than, as in the previous examinations, how each differentiates them from real virtues will be a substantial part of our concern. Our subject, then, is each thinker's understanding of people's apparent proneness to fail to reach full human flourishing. Put one way, it is the theory of error that any adequate theory must have, the explanation of why what apparently should happen, does not. In examining it, we find, I think, several important and surprising similarities in Mencius and Aquinas's accounts and three basic differences.[43]

Focused narrowly, and in terms of separate virtues, our question is why Aquinas develops and highlights certain virtues that Mencius does not. Especially important are three kinds of virtue. One kind are those that master errant forces, such as the virtue of moderation, one of Aquinas's four cardinal virtues. Another are those virtues that confront major deficiencies, such as all those infused virtues that transform people's natural abilities. A third are those virtues that reflect people's need to deal with their inevitable failures. Examples of these are the virtues of regret or remorse, like humility or penance, that should pervade the whole character. These three kinds of virtue reflect Aquinas's belief that examining humanity's normal inclinations leads us to a sobering recognition. People need always to control some of their inclinations, radically to change many of them, and to express regret about most of them.

Analogues to these virtues are present in Mencius; for instance, the aspect of righteousness that rests on shame and the aspect of courage that overcomes improper fears. In comparison with Aquinas, however, Mencius discusses few such virtues and almost all of them are relatively unimportant. Indeed, his crucial virtues usually fit within the category of inclinational not preservative virtues. Moreover, he highlights no excellences that manifest people's need to express remorse for their actions or aspects of their character. These omissions occur despite the loftiness of his ethical ideal and the lack of a concept like supererogation to ameliorate failures.

Focused more abstractly, our question concerns the seeming disagreement between Mencius and Aquinas about whether major impediments to goodness exist within people. To use common labels or formulaic designations (which obviously are too simple for thinkers this subtle), Mencius thinks human nature is good and Aquinas thinks human nature is sinful. The idea of human goodness informs Mencius's theory of virtue and list of virtues just as the idea of original sin informs Aquinas's theory and list. Activating one's naturally good character is the goal for Mencius, and overcoming original sin to reach a new state is the goal for Aquinas.

Such stark distinctions often have been seen as basic to any comparison between traditional Christians and at least those Confucians who fit within the Mencian stream of Confucianism. Moreover, some have said that these distinctions resemble closely the key distinctions between traditional Christian and classical Greek thinkers. We should be suspicious, however, about such a resemblance and the implications drawn from it. Homologizing classical Greek and Confucian ideas is risky. It well may be true that Christianity introduces into a classical Greek perspective both a new goal, full union with a personal God, and a new difficulty, a propensity to sinfulness, to a vicious deformation of the human. Our case is considerably more complicated. Mencius may lack, for example, the ideas of theoretical reason and of a fully personal God that underlie Aquinas's picture of humanity's goal. But aspects of his ideal of fulfillment relate closely to Aquinas's ideal. More important to consider here, their understandings of the character of impediments to human flourishing resemble only in part those that differentiate classical Greeks and traditional Christians.

The apparent distinction between the two on this issue is put in clear form (if also, at times, in off-putting form) by James Legge, the nineteenth-century translator of Mencius who was a Protestant missionary. He says:

> Mencius is not be blamed for his ignorance of what is to us The Doctrine of the Fall. He had no means of becoming acquainted with it. We have to regret, however, that his study of human nature produced in him no deep *feeling* on account of man's proneness to go astray. He never betrays any consciousness of his own weakness. In this respect he is again inferior to Confucius.

His glance is searching and his penetration deep; but there is
wanting that moral sensibility which would draw us to him, in our
best moments, as a man of like passions with ourselves. The absence
of humility is naturally accompanied with a lack of *sympathy*. There is
a hardness about his teaching. He is the professor, performing an
operation in the classroom, amid a throng of pupils who are admiring
his science and dexterity, and who forgets in the triumph of his skill
the suffering of the patient. The transgressors of their nature are to
Mencius "the tyrants of themselves" or the "self abandoned." The
utmost stretch of his commiseration is a contemptuous "Alas for
them." The radical defect of the orthodox moral school of China,
that there only needs a knowledge of duty to insure its performance,
is in him exceedingly apparent.[44]

Legge's comments may initially seem to be heavy-handed or even crude.
We should note, however, that he declares Mencius's attitude to be inferi-
or not just to Christian ideas but also to Confucius's ideas; he makes a
telling comparison within the Confucian tradition itself.

More important, Legge presents several ideas that are well worth
considering. He links Mencius to thinkers in the Western tradition, starting with Socrates, who argue that to know the good is also to do the good.
As we will discuss later, this connection reveals much about both Mencius
and his relationship to Aquinas, who also accepts a version of that idea.
Moreover, we need to consider Legge's argument that Mencius's lack of
sympathy (especially important given Mencius's emphasis on benevolence)
arises from his failure to recognize the proneness of people to go astray
and to be conscious of his own weakness. Mencius's attitude may arise, in
part, from the rhetorical posture he takes, from his desire to exemplify personally the availability of all that is necessary. But we must remember
Legge's contention when we probe Mencius's ideas on human failures, as
well as his ideal of equanimity. Legge's comments, then, raise important
issues to which we will return. Let us now, however, treat briefly a subject
that sets the stage for our comparison of Mencius and Aquinas's positions.

The subject is Aquinas's complex understanding of people's propensity
to sin: I begin with his enumeration of basic sins and then turn to his analysis
of original sin. Aquinas follows his tradition in highlighting the "seven deadly sins." These seven sins are capital sins in that they give rise to other sins as
final causes. They, however, are not the only causes of sin. Aquinas enumer-
ates many other sins when he examines the excessive and deficient deformations of virtue, and he specifies several other especially potent sources of sin,
such as stark hatred (*odium*) of God and his creatures, malice (*malitia*), a disposition to ethical evil, and resolute malice (*certa malitia*), a love of evil for its

own sake. Indeed, the seven sins are less central to his analysis than they are to the analysis of many other theologians and to almost all who used them in artistic or devotional ways. Moreover, he is most interested in those among the seven, such as envy, that distort higher human states, and this will become significant when we compare him with Mencius.[45]

Nevertheless, the seven deadly sins are important enough to Aquinas's understanding of the propensity to fail to discuss them briefly and simply. Vanity or vainglory (*inanis gloria*) is the pursuit of recognition or honor from unworthy people or for unworthy objects. Envy (*invidia*) is a resentment about the good that others possess that often combines with the desire to destroy what is envied. Anger (*ira*) is a rage that, when unformed by reason, attempts to wreak revenge on what has produced pain. *Acedia*, "spiritual sloth or insensitivity," is a kind of dejection or sadness about the highest goods that combines with a sense of their desirableness. Avarice (*avarita*) is a greed or rapaciousness that aims mainly at amassing material goods. Gluttony (*gula*) is immoderate eating and drinking that arises from an inordinate desire for the pleasures they bring. Lust (*luxuria*) or lechery is the disordered desire for sexual pleasure. A more general sin than any of these seven but a support for all of them is pride (*superbia*). It is an inordinate appetite for one's own superiority that, unlike simple vanity, appears in many guises. For example, it often manifests itself in a self-centered satisfaction with one's natural endowments and a pursuit of their fulfillment, and it can produce uppishness, blind autonomy, or even self-complacency.[46]

These sins all have the power they do because of that fundamental deformation of human nature captured for Aquinas in the idea of original sin. Aquinas defines original sin in various ways, but most illuminating for our purposes is the definition that sets it in terms of the possible goods that might be found in human nature. Those goods are threefold. First are the principles of that nature and the properties derived from them; for example, powers of the soul. Second is the inclination or bent (*inclinatio*) to virtue contained in that nature. Third is the "gift of original justice," the harmonious operation of all the elements in human nature found in Adam and Eve before they fell. Original sin affects each of the three goods differently. The presence of the first, the principles, is neither destroyed nor diminished. The second, the inclination to virtue, remains but is diminished in strength. The third, original justice, is totally destroyed.[47]

Mencius, even in his retelling of myths, never speaks of anything like original justice. (Aspects of his past, perfect society resemble it faintly an portraits of sages resemble it more closely, but the differences still are pronounced.) Apart from this, however, the general similarities between

Aquinas's account and Mencius's account are striking. Mencius defines human nature as good, but by that definition, as discussed, he means that humans are capable of becoming good. In his developmental model, the capacities for goodness are present within people, can be developed, and constitute what is distinctively human. Mencius, then, recognizes that some people constantly do bad things and even that good people can fail always to do good. But he believes that capacities for good define the fully human, and that if they are nurtured and uninjured they will always produce good characters and actions.

Both Mencius and Aquinas agree, then, that the basic principles and properties that make humans human are intact. Both also agree that given, fundamental inclinations toward the good remain, even if the force of those inclinations is diminished in almost all people. Their disagreement occurs on two subjects. The first is the exact character of the diminishment; the second is on the possibility of overcoming it. The distinctions between them on these subjects are subtle. The contexts in which these subtle distinctions live, however, are immensely different.

The subject matter and conclusions of each thinker's secondary theories and of their more "historical" inquiries differ enormously. Mencius, for example, presents and relies on detailed examinations of a recent and mythic history that resemble nothing with which Aquinas deals. Aquinas, in contrast, treats a variety of abstruse theological questions such as the character of the pre-Fall state of Adam and Eve and the transmission of original sin. Moreover, he examines issues that Mencius (happily some might say) neither touches on nor probably could imagine. In answering the question of how the devil and demons tempt people, for instance, he analyzes how they modify the physical preconditions of fantasy and feeling indirectly to change a person's emotion-toned attitudes and dreams.[48]

In considering their treatment of human failure we must always remember just how substantial are the differences in the contexts within which each thinker works. Most important to us, however, are their more concrete examinations of how propensities toward fulfillment and deformation operate in human beings. We are, to use my earlier terminology, interested in their practical not secondary or primary theories. Their practical inquiries can be highly theoretical; they are not simply versions of primary theory. They concern, for instance, their understanding of human beings' fundamental leanings, of those diminished inclinations that rest on the undestroyed and undiminished principles and properties of humans. But the inquiries on which we will focus normally do not utilize the special terms or concentrate on the subjects that are part of their secondary theories; for example, in Mencius the power (te) of a sacred king to affect monumental changes or in Aquinas the exact vehicle by which original sin is transmitted.

Some of these subjects and terms, of course, affect the analyses we will examine. One reason that Mencius pursues issues of statecraft and leadership as the means by which to solve deep human problems, in a way that Aquinas never does, is because of his ideas about the power of sacred kings. One reason that Aquinas treats some distortions as inevitable, in a way Mencius never does, is because of his ideas on original sin's transmission. Nevertheless, we can separate out their different kinds of theorizing in a way that helps us understand and, especially, compare the two thinkers. In undertaking that task, I will begin with Aquinas and then examine how his account both resembles and differs from Mencius's.

Aquinas believes inclinations to virtuous states remain but they also coexist with, and even connect to, powerful inclinations to bad states. Present human capacities, then, point in various directions. They move to compassion but also to envy, to justice but also to avarice. Indeed, Aquinas claims coherence and integrity characterize the virtuous life and chaos and fragmentation the unvirtuous life. This situation occurs because bad people, unlike good people, are pulled in various, often conflicting directions. (His picture resembles, as we shall see, Mencius's account of the equilibrium and equanimity that characterizes the truly virtuous.)[49]

In examining the often divided leanings that define most people, Aquinas focuses his attention not on crude sins, like lust and gluttony, but on more complex and subtle sins, like envy, vanity, and spiritual apathy. He attends to these sins for three reasons. Subtle sins are especially important because they feed on higher human states. The subject of vanity, for example, is the legitimate desire to receive appropriate regard from others. Crude sins, in contrast, work from those inclinations, such as the desire for simple nourishment or raw sexual expression, that humans share with animals. Sins involving these more animal like states may connect to subtle sins, but in those cases Aquinas normally concentrates on the subtle sin. (As with most great Christian theologians, he is a connoisseur of the will's permutations.) If sexual desire involves a person in jealousy or revenge, Aquinas thinks envy or anger is more critical than lust.

Most important, Aquinas focuses on subtle sins because they are considerably more dangerous than crude sins. Just because they distort higher human states, they can more consistently pervade the whole personality. Subtle sins, then, can poison all of a person's activities. In fact, these sins make especially clear why vices, like virtues, should be thought of not in terms of individual acts but in terms of those dispositions that produce such acts. The characteristics of the actions produced can differ from, or even oppose, the characteristics of the dispositions that produce them. Spiritual apathy, for example, can produce frantic activity. The apathetic disposition, like Kierkegaard's despair, can generate intense curiosity, bodily agitation, and mindless chatter.[50]

A final reason why Aquinas concentrates on these sins is that they reveal especially clearly how all sins are finally sins against charity. All sins are violations of humans' need to move toward, lean on, and delight in the omnipresent goods that surround them. Those goods often may be only faintly evident in the world, and therefore sorrow must coexist with joy as it does in the infused virtue of patience. But they clearly are evident in the friendship with God, the highest good, that is charity. Envy, the inability to find joy in the goods that others possess, is probably the clearest instance of such a failure to love. All sins show it in some way, however; even gluttony involves the failure to actualize those goods eating and drinking can contain.

Aquinas's belief that all sins deform charity leads him also to believe that human fulfillment involves recognizing goods and delighting in them, not following rules. Rules will have a place, of course, but they represent a necessary accommodation to human frailty. A muted version of Augustine's famous dictum to love and do what you will operates in Aquinas. Like Augustine, he thinks that we best understand people by seeing what they love, what they spontaneously are drawn to be and do. In Aquinas's terminology, the Old Law has been superseded by the New Law; that new "law" inclines people to a connatural understanding of real goods and thus a full attachment to them.

Aquinas's understanding of the goals humans should pursue and the deformations in them that impede their pursuit resembles important parts of Mencius's account. Both see the goods that should be pursued as omnipresent, and both believe people should lean on and delight in them. Both think this pursuit produces personal coherence, ease of action, and integrity of being in virtuous people and believe incoherence, conflict, and fragmentariness characterize unvirtuous people. Both also think following rules at best is a lesser human state and at worst a fundamental deformation. Indeed, both agree, in the abstract at least, that social forms should be modified or abandoned if they fail to allow for the fullest manifestations of human flourishing, although those forms do provide necessary channels for people's actions and may even have sacred sanction.

Noteworthy differences, of course, also characterize their accounts. As discussed, the conclusions and even subject matter of their secondary theories and historical inquiries are immensely different. Most important to us, however, are three differences in their views about people's propensities toward fulfillment and deformation. The first concerns their views on *the role of more subtle deformations* or sins. The second concerns their position on the principle that *to know the good is to do the good*. The third concerns their notion of what is involved in *changing acquired inclinations*. Each reveals something important about general similarities and differences between the two thinkers, and we therefore need to examine them with care.

Aquinas's concern with the more complex and subtle sins, such as envy or vanity, usually is not reflected in Mencius. Mencius especially in his more theoretical accounts of people's failures, tends to concentrate on inclinations that arise largely from people's bodily states. Major human problems, for Mencius, arise because people are drawn automatically, through hearing and seeing, toward some objects. (That is, he focuses on matters that Aquinas would treat as instances of, say, lust or gluttony.) More subtle deformations are depicted by him, most notably when he advises kings, especially King Hsüan. In such cases, the issue does not seem to be just the king's desire for simple sense pleasures but the king's envy, vanity, or even spiritual sloth. Nevertheless, Mencius often treats the problems presented as if they resembled those found in cruder cases. Moreover, his more theoretical treatments neither examine subtle vices nor present them as major impediments to human flourishing.[52]

One crucial reason why Mencius's account takes the form it does is captured well by Legge's comment. He identifies as central to Mencius what he calls the radical defect of the orthodox moral school of China: the principle that "there only needs a knowledge of duty to insure its performance." We will discuss later whether accepting this principle constitutes a defect, especially when put in the context of Mencius's theory of action. More important here is that Legge, following many Protestants, could say Aquinas also accepts this principle and therefore has the same radical defect. Aquinas, in fact, usually does start from only a slightly modified version of the principle that to know the good is to do the good. His treatment, for instance, of the problem of weak will (akrasia), of acting against one's better judgment, generally follows Aristotle's account in which the principle is modified but defended.[53]

One can argue that we all at least must start from this principle if we are to make any sense out of human action. That is, only if we connect knowing and doing can we work from a context of intelligible agency. Mencius and Aquinas's use of the principle goes far beyond this, however, as we have seen. Both thinkers usually accept the premise that failures in action represent failures in knowledge. Vain people act as they do, for instance, because they misidentify the goods that should be pursued to receive worthwhile praise. Aquinas thinks that humans are more likely to misidentify goods than Mencius, especially in those areas where more subtle deformations operate. Although the difference is very important, as discussed, it ought not obscure the fact that both thinkers usually accept the principle.[54]

Nevertheless, and this is our second point, Aquinas differs from Mencius because he often is involved in analyses that challenge the principle that to know the good is to do the good. Aquinas constantly must deal with evidence from within his own tradition, including material found in sacred texts, that challenges the principle. One especially powerful example is St. Paul's statement in Romans that he cannot do the good he would do or avoid the bad he would avoid. Another is Augustine's depiction in the second book of the *Confessions* of an action, his theft of pears, that seems explainable to him only as an attempt to act against all possible goods. A third is the general phenomenon that spiritual apathy (*acedia*) describes, a state first identified by the desert fathers and a familiar feature of the monastic life. These examples, and a host of related ones, cannot be fitted easily (or perhaps ever) into the general principle that to know the good is to do the good.

Aquinas, for instance, employs the idea, which Aristotle built on the principle, that all character is of six types. The six are, at the extreme ends, the brute and the godlike, and in between them the virtuous and the vicious, and the continent or strong willed and the incontinent or weak willed. Aquinas, however, cannot fit crucial examples from his own tradition into any of the three categories in which they supposedly should fit. Augustine or St. Paul's actions and Cassian's treatment of *acedia* hardly seem to belong within the categories of the vicious or the incontinent, much less the brute. Example like these, as well as the ideas about human failure they spawn, lead Aquinas to produce treatments that ill fit the classical principle about knowing and doing the good.[55]

Aquinas, then, incorporates ideas or presents analyses that either conflict with the classical principle or (at the least) are in uneasy relationship to it. Deep tensions, perhaps even contradictions, thereby are introduced into parts of his analyses of human action. We will evaluate the seriousness of this problem differently, depending on how we understand the counter examples he examines; on how much we prize coherence; and on whether we think, in at least some areas, irreducible but productive tensions always are present and must be preserved. What is unquestionable, however, is that Aquinas's acceptance of the classical principle is constantly called in question by his own work.

Mencius, on the other hand, considers far fewer examples and ideas that test the principle that to know the good is to do the good. He rarely deals with the rich examples that we find in the text of Confucius's *Analects*, for instance. Moreover, he distinguishes between just two possibilities — refusal to act and inability to act — in cases where that simple a dichotomy seems much too facile. He does believe that ethical constancy depends on people possessing minimal material means of support. But he seems also to think that those minimal conditions just allow people to avoid the tragic choices that severe deprivation can produce.

Some features of Mencius's statements probably can be explained by his rhetorical strategies. He often attempts to persuade people that possibilities they have rejected are real, or at least are worth considering. Moreover, at times, he asserts that proper ethical leadership and social organization can produce what, to us, are astonishing changes. (Conversely, he also speaks, in places, as if cycles of decay can make human flourishing extremely difficult.) Both judgments, in at least their most dramatic form, rest on the results of his historical inquiries and secondary theories and show how practical theory can be affected by them.[56]

Mencius, on occasion, does display a striking sense for the difficulties inherent in acting well. An especially powerful illustration of this is his beautiful, poignant development of the image of Ox Mountain. A once luxuriant mountain that now is bald because humans defaced it, the mountain serves as a metaphor for how and why humans appear to be bad. Even that passage, however, ends with a ringing declaration about how people can become virtuous if only they will seek to become virtuous. Mencius continues to return, here and elsewhere, to the grand and uncompromising vision of why humans need not fail to flourish discussed earlier. Whatever vexing issues may surround our understanding of Mencius's ideas about people's ability to be virtuous, Mencius consistently proclaims that knowledge of the good is within the reach of humans and that such knowledge will always produce good action and character. Indeed, as Legge notes, he is able to say only that such people are not worth the trouble to talk with because they lack respect for themselves or confidence in themselves.[57]

Both thinkers, then, work from the premise that knowledge of the good produces good actions. Aquinas, however, is constantly, if not always coherently, dealing with cases and ideas that challenge the universal applicability of the idea. Mencius, in contrast, rarely treats such cases and ideas. Moreover, he usually holds much more firmly then Aquinas to the position that failures in action arise from failures in knowledge and even in effort.

The final distinction between Mencius and Aquinas's understanding of human failure emerges from each thinker's development of two ideas they both accept; that human capacities point in various directions and that full human flourishing involves a unified inclination to and delight in real goods. Mencius believes the possibility of becoming virtuous always is present. Although people are automatically drawn to objects that can mislead them, the sprouts of goodness are present in virtually all people and ways exists to contact and cultivate them. Aquinas also believes sprouts that incline people toward the good, as well as self-evident ideas about the good, always are present. But for him the dispositions we acquire, some before we can make real choices, make easy and agreeable only specific kinds of action. The human will does not swing back to indifference with every tick of the clock; past operations determine present orientations. A kind of passivity born of previous habituation largely determines human inclination.

This situation leaves us, Aquinas thinks, with a deep problem about how we can change ourselves. We are caught in a circle. We employ our dispositions as we will or please, but our willing and pleasing are product of our dispositions. Moreover, we need desperately to change ourselves because the circle we are caught in contains evil or at least imperfect inclinations. That is, Aquinas believes evidence from his own life and other peoples lives, as well as evidence from sacred texts, shows that our basic dispositional responses, our connatural loves, often are errant. Human beings either are turned toward vicious rather than virtuous states or, at the least, are turned toward some vicious as well as some virtuous states. Given this, Aquinas asserts that only a separate power, a power that transcends humanity, can fundamentally reorient people and thereby rescue them from the circle in which they are caught. To use traditional Christian language, he claims the avoidance of sin is impossible if human beings alone are the only possible agents of change, and therefore God's grace must save us.[58]

Mencius's position is radically different in so far as he thinks the existence of both the sprouts and the ability to cultivate them means people always are capable of becoming good, of achieving sagehood in his language. He, however, does describe empowering forces that extend beyond the normal; for example, forms of virtuous leadership (*te*) and psychophysical energy (*ch'i*) can help transform people, and the heavenly origin of the four sprouts gives them special potency. Moreover, Mencius's sense of the difficulties involved in changing people moves closer to Aquinas's when we remember his model of human nature is developmental. Unlike later Neo-Confucians, he thinks people must develop their excellences over time; they cannot discover them in a different, higher being or mind. (If that higher mind acted to aid such discoveries, this Neo-Confucian view would resemble Aquinas's solution more clearly than does Mencius's.) Finally, Mencius and Aquinas's ideas about the difficulties involved in changing people (if not their ideas about the solution) grow still closer if Mencius believes that people's upbringing in an appropriate society is crucial. He never consistently develops this idea and its implications, however, although doing so would allow him to explain why many people do bad things most of the time.

When Mencius speaks in his most voluntaristic fashion and claims we can reorient ourselves just by refocusing our attention, he differs fundamentally from Aquinas. When Mencius speaks in a less voluntaristic vein, however, he moves closer to Aquinas's position that only a separate power can rescue individuals from the destructive circle they inhabit. But even when Mencius speaks this way he usually asserts that human forces (if ones that draw on other powers) can affect the needed changes. Aquinas, in contrast, believes all human efforts are too corrupt to produce all the changes needed. That is, although he thinks statecraft and leadership can accomplish extremely important things, he does not believe they can ever solve the deep problems presented by people's errant inclinations.[59]

We will examine aspects of these topics, such as the issue of Mencius's voluntarism, in the following sections. Here, however, we can review the broad outlines of how Aquinas and Mencius treat the human propensity to fail. Despite the apparently stark differences between Mencius's idea that human nature is good and Aquinas's idea that it is sinful, and the massive difference between their secondary theories and historical inquiries, we do see resemblances. Both emphasize a developmental model of human nature in which inclinations to the good remain. Moreover, both share the notion that people at their best should and can delight in the world's omnipresent goods and that human deformations impede the ability to do that. Distinctions do appear when we compare Aquinas's focus on those deformations that engage higher human faculties and Mencius's normal focus on deformations that arise from lower capacities. Moreover, a clear difference, if a difference within a similarity, appears on the subject of whether to know the good is to do the good. Both accept some version of this principle, but Aquinas, much more than Mencius, continually deals with ideas and phenomena that call it into question. Finally, a distinction appears when we examine the way in which humans alone are capable of changing themselves, even if Mencius's account of how people can change themselves is more complicated than it initially may appear to be. Let us turn now to examine, with constructive intent, a topic on which the resemblances between the two are far more pronounced. That topic is the picture of the self that underlies their theories of virtue, especially the character and relationship of reasons, emotions, and dispositions.

VIII. The Picture of the Self Underlying This Type of Virtue Theory: Practical Reason, Emotions, and Dispositions

In the next two sections, we will complete our analysis of Mencius and Aquinas's theory of virtue by examining in a modern vocabulary and with constructive intent three interrelated conceptions that underlie their theories of virtue: the notions of emotions, practical reason, and disposition. Although each thinker develops these ideas and their relationship in a distinctive way, the basic conceptions of each are remarkably similar. We see here, then, the fundamental elements in that practical theory about the self on which a virtue theory like Mencius and Aquinas's relies.

Both think practical reason works from judgments made both in situations and on general goals. Both also think humans must utilize practical reason to activate dispositions and to influence, directly or indirectly, the form and power of emotions. This picture of the self differs from many prevalent modern pictures, and examining it helps us to understand and compare Mencius and Aquinas's ideas on virtue in general and courage in particular. Moreover, this picture, I think, makes as much sense as do the opposing modern views, even if it is bewitched by some serious problems, such as how we can hold people responsible for many of their dispositions. I normally will speak "for" not "of" their position, then, when discussing controversial questions about the character and relationship of dispositions, emotions, and practical reason. That is, I will be directly engaged in the constructive part of the comparative philosophy of religious flourishings.[60]

Mencius and Aquinas both hold to what can be called a *cognitive* or *interpretative* view of at least most emotions. This view appears in Mencius's notion of extension: he presumes a close link between cognitive judgments and emotional reactions. But it also appears in Aquinas's notion that the emotions resemble beings who have wills and therefore are subject to a political control. Most emotions, then, should be seen as more or less intelligent ways of conceiving a situation dominated by or involving a strong feeling. Emotions do involve physiological changes; for example, an increased pulse rate or the flow of additional adrenalin. They also involve desire conceived of mainly as the source of an inclination to act. Fear, for example, is the desire to escape from what is believed to be dangerous, or to avoid contact with it, or to confront it only by special effort. But the cognitive element is crucial; beliefs determine the appearance and form of most emotions. Only when I believe something is dangerous (whether that something be a tiger, or an open space, or an authoritative woman) do I feel fear.

The relationship of many emotions to their objects, then, involves a perceived import of the object, a significance seen in it. This import explains why the object matters and thus provides the cognitive basis for the feeling. We see the role of imports most clearly in cases where people say that they have mistakenly felt an emotion. I realize there was no need for fear, for example, if the person rounding the corner is elderly and feeble and not the tough young mugger I thought I saw. I recognize my shame was mistaken when I see that the laughter that erupted nearby was directed at someone else's joke and not at my own odd behavior.

With a few emotions, such as most kinds of physical fear, we can give an objective, reductive account of the import involved. But with others, like shame, that kind of account is impossible. Large, hostile people or animals underlie the import that produces physical fear, and we can provide an objective account of why that is so. But reactions of shame usually arise from personal qualities or actions, and their meanings depend on cultural norms and personal ideals. That is, they have no reality apart from the cognition or interpretation that produces them. A shrill voice, an effeminate manner, or an aggressive demeanor can generate shame in one culture and self-respect in another.

Most of the emotions that inform people's deepest understanding of their humanity resemble shame not physical fear in that interpretation is crucial. Dignity, admiration, contempt, remorse, and self-reproach, for example, all depend on interpretation. Indeed, even some kinds of physical fear depend on similar judgments. The experienced soldier and the raw recruit's reactions to the dangers that appear in battle differ considerably. The interpretative elements in emotions are crucial, then, because people are inclined to give and respond to their own understandings or descriptions of situations.[61]

An interpretative view of the emotions underlies several critical features of Aquinas and Mencius's theories of the self, such as their notion of how reason forms dispositions. I will discuss these later, but let me briefly note here how this perspective enables us to make analyses or highlight issues that enrich our understanding of virtue. We can utilize such a perspective to differentiate related emotions and thus the virtues that deal with them. For example, we can distinguish the fear arising from physical danger and the fear arising from shame, and therefore distinguish the kinds of courage that deal with them. (Distinctions like this, in fact, will underlie Mencius and Aquinas's account of courage.) Moreover, this perspective allows us, as students of past thinkers, to understand that people's insight into their emotional life can deepen and sharpen over time. We possess, for example, a far richer vocabulary to identify subtly different emotional states than did Aquinas and Mencius. No equivalents appear in their writings to distinctions we make among emotional reactions, say, that are reserved, diffident, shy, abashed, rebuffed, mawkish, callow, and embarrassed. It is important that we understand these differences exist and that we see their implications.[62]

Some of the implications become clear when we recognize that using this perspective allows us to highlight and understand an important process in the life of both individuals and cultures. People need always to check to determine if their emotional responses (those at least that depend on a subject's interpretation) are as mature as they should be; that is, whether their responses reflect or distort a full and sensitive view of the world. What I physically fear, in at least the simplest sense, has changed little since I obtained basic information, such as that knives or fire can cause pain. But what makes me feel shame changes considerably as I age: for instance, I move from a worry about how I appear to friends to a concern about whether I am furthering their welfare. A similar process often occurs as a culture changes. What is seen (or argued about) as shameful or degrading will change, even though the idea of what is to be feared physically remains relatively constant. Most emotions will have a history, then, and changes in that history will deeply affect people's understanding of the virtues that deal with such emotions. Indeed, such changes underlie both those transformations in the understanding of virtue that Mencius and Aquinas attempt, and those expansions of the meaning of single virtues they undertake.

The feature of rationality that produces interpretations that form emotions, then, constitutes one crucial feature of Mencius and Aquinas's picture of ethical rationality. It fits into a more general understanding of ethical reasoning that we now must examine. As discussed, we find a resemblance but not a correspondence between Aquinas's practical wisdom (*prudentia*) and Mencius's intelligent awareness (*chih*), mainly because each relates to other abilities in their respective pictures of the mind that are dissimilar. Nevertheless, the accounts of both Mencius and Aquinas belong within a general category that can be labeled *practical reason*, and the exercise of true virtue relies on its presence.

Practical reason involves three processes: situational appreciation; reasoning about means to ends; and a continuing consideration of the value of the ends sought. Reasoning about means to ends often is the major or sole topic of contemporary discussions about practical wisdom. The other two features of practical wisdom, however, will be the focus of this discussion. (I disregard the unjustified link of rationality to gender that is clear in Aquinas and implied in Mencius.)

Practical wisdom appears in any adequate specification, any appropriate description of what is to be heeded, realized, or safeguarded in a situation. Practical reason, then, relies on ways to focus and attend to a situation's most salient characteristics. In some situations the relevant factors are strikingly clear. When, in Mencius's example, I see a baby about to fall down a well, recognizing what features are salient is easy. In other situations, however, a more delicate kind of awareness is needed. For instance, I recognize, when others do not, that my aged mother will be sorely distressed by my attending a party given by a close friend, and therefore I stay with her rather than go to the party. I then also must decide how best to inform the friend, a means-end question that itself involves a perception of salient characteristics. Moreover, I may consider, if fleetingly, the worth of a life that values a parent's feelings more than immediate, pleasurable experiences and the maintenance of some features of friendship.

Practical reason's detection and interpretation of the relevant features of a situation characterizes virtuous activity. It also produces a problem with which practical reason must deal: the magnetic quality a virtue possesses and the tendency to expansionism and excess it generates. Part of the dynamic of virtuous dispositions is to seek situations in which they can be exercised. Although this often leads to beneficial actions, it also can create problems. My benevolence, for example, may lead me to see a helpless, wronged person whose plight moves me, and whom I must help. I never consider actions, that to my mind, would chastise her or cause me heartlessly to abandon her, even though what might best serve her is not benevolent succoring but chastisement or inaction. Courage is especially prone to such excesses, as discussed. A courageous person's tendency to see difficulties which must be overcome easily may expand into areas where a better response is to find an imaginative compromise. In a situation where different interpretations are possible, then, a person who possesses a particular virtue can use the virtue's cognitive aspect to focus salient features in a way that is inappropriate and makes almost inevitable the exercise of that virtuous disposition.

Virtues are magnetizing in that they attract situations in which they can be exercised. The possessor of the virtues either gravitates toward situations that will elicit them or, more important, promotes or even creates situations in which the virtues can be given full play. This means that virtues also tend to expansionism, they tend to exceed their appropriate areas and move into realms where they do not fit. That is, a person who either lacks the virtue or combines it correctly with other virtues will not think the situation is one in which the virtue should operate. To the person who possesses the virtue, however, the situation demands its exercise.

These expansionistic and magnetic tendencies in virtues can be controlled only by the application of sensitive, flexible, and powerful rational judgments. Such judgments must be sensitive to the correct description of a situation. Yet they also must be flexible enough to choose among a variety of possible descriptions and thus strategies. Finally, they must be powerful enough to control the magnetic quality that virtues possess. Perfected practical reason, then, provides those cognitive aspects of virtue that pick out a situation's salient characteristics, utilize a person's conception of the best way of life, form emotional reactions, and check the magnetic propensity that virtues possess.[63]

To see practical reason's role in ethical life in this fashion is to resist any attempt at systematic codification or generalized prescription. Excluding those rules that manifest injunctions, this means, as Martha Nussbaum says, that ethical

> rules and universal principles are [to be seen as] guidelines or rules of thumb: summaries of particular decisions, useful for purposes of economy and aids in identifying the salient features of the particular case. . . . Principles [and rules] are perspicuous descriptive summaries of good judgments . . . [and] are normative only insofar as they transmit

in economical form the normative force of the good concrete decisions of the wise person.[64]

Rules and principles are especially important in situations in which we
lack the time to scrutinize a situation carefully. They also provide us with
needed stability when we realize that emotion or bias could adversely
affect our judgment. They, then, can be significant aids to practical reason, but only if their characteristics, and thus limitations, are understood.

Characterizing practical reason in this way also leads to affirming that
particular perceptions are guided by a person's picture of the best way of life.
That picture may be difficult to specify, as is the way in which it informs action,
but it is crucial. The general position on practical reason (to quote an accurate if
recondite formulation) reflects a "context-conditioned evaluative objectivism":

> a conceptual framework which we can apply to particular cases, which
> articulates the reciprocal relations of an agent's concerns and his per-
> ception of how things objectively are in the world; and a schema of
> description *which relates the complex ideal the agent tries in the process of
> living to make real to the form that the world impresses, both by way of
> opportunity, and by way of limitations, upon that ideal.*[65]

In this picture of practical reason, we define ourselves not by our first-
order desires but by our second-order volitions. We define ourselves by
those values that produce desires we want to constitute our wills, to be
our regnant dispositions, to cause us consistently to act. I ordinarily may
be moved, for example, by prideful impulses that make me react angrily to
perceived slights. But I also can define myself as someone who does not
want to be that kind of person and then undertake to reform myself so
that my values rather than my present desires control my life.

These kinds of judgments lead me to make strong not weak evaluations, to use Charles Taylor's terminology. Weak evaluations arise when I
decide among a number of contingent desires all of which I would like to
fulfill if I could. The need for choice arises because of incompatibilities
among the desires themselves or problems in the circumstances surrounding their fulfillment. Strong evaluations, however, arise from a decision about what kind of person I want to be. I think of my desires in the
contrastive terminology of good and bad or worthy and unworthy. They
are data I evaluate rather than forces to which I respond.[66]

My decision to diet is a weak evaluation if it arises from a simple
weighing of my desire to eat against my desire to be seen as sleekly attrac-
tive, or my desire to lessen my chances of dying from a heart attack, or my
desire to avoid the purchase of a new wardrobe. If, however, my decision

arises from a judgment that I should cease being a person who is dominated by certain sensual impulses, if it arises from a decision about dignity and degradation as these features are evident in self-control and its lack, it is a strong evaluation. With weak evaluations I start from my given desires, setting aside alternatives on the basis of contingent incompatibilities. (If, for instance, a pill existed that allowed me both to gorge myself and to remain svelte, I would eat differently than I do.) Moreover, such judgments usually will have a quantitative form: "I can fulfill more of my desires or the most weighty and demanding of my desires by doing this rather than that." With strong evaluations, however, the decisions are set in contrastive terms and qualitative language is used. I am not simply weighing desires but using ideas of the base and the noble: "I do this because it is more noble than that." To use earlier terminology, my judgments involve expressive as well as acquisitive motives.

Such differences lead people to call the strong evaluator "deep" and the weak evaluator "shallow." This ascription of depth rests on the idea that a full conception of human life involves people in seeing themselves as specific sorts of human beings. A defender of weak evaluations may respond that her position is sensible and pragmatic rather than shallow. She may also call a strong evaluator "self-aggrandizing," "dogmatic," and "impractically romantic" rather than deep. Such a response, however, involves the weak evaluator in a contradiction. She now defends the use of weak evaluations by arguing their use produces a qualitatively better way of life. That shift signals a change in how she conceives of desire decisions, and actions; she has become a kind of strong evaluator. Such a shift in her argument makes clear, I think, that we face here two fundamentally different pictures of what human life ought to be.

People, then, must have an ideal of what they wish to be that they use to guide, reanimate, and change their desires and actions. To be a full human being is to move toward an unrealized human state that is perceived as a good, that can be realized, and that one is obligated to seek. Mencius and Aquinas's emphasis on the role of practical reason in the identification of proper ways of life and the actualization of natural inclinations shows that they believe human excellence arises from strong not weak evaluations. Moreover, they employ their own versions of the distinction between these two kinds of evaluations to differentiate virtues from their semblances.

The ability of practical reason to make strong evaluations shows that it has the power to *command*, *weigh*, and *form* emotions. The formation of emotions and the creation of dispositions it helps produce is our main concern. But we also need to look briefly at how reason interacts with emotions in the command and weighing models. Each reflects how an imperfectly virtuous person deals with an emotion, like fear, that interferes with the direction of reason. That emotion can "sweep away" reason's judgments or it can change the way reason calculates. With the *command* model, fear either overpowers or is overpowered by reason's judgment. If a large, hostile person makes nasty remarks about my crippled friend and his wheelchair, I want him to stop but I also fear confronting him. If my fear triumphs I avoid the confrontation, but if my rational judgment triumphs I overcome the fear by commanding myself. I bootstrap myself into doing something I fear to do.

The *weighing* model reflects a more subtle conflict between fear and rational judgment. Deliberating people can give more weight to certain elements in a decision than they (or normal people) usually would because those elements engender fear. I see in retrospect, for instance, the real basis of my supposedly reasonable decision not to aid a friend who was being undermined by a powerful person's malicious rumors. It rested on an overestimation of the possible harm that might occur to me. Cool reflection shows that my deliberations were corrupted by an excessive fear about the consequences for me that might result from my actions. I now recognize that my responsibility to the friend should have outweighed the possible harm to me. Armed with such a recognition, I proceed with more care the next time I face a similar situation. That is, I am particularly attentive to ways in which my weighing of alternatives might be affected by my fear. (The modern concern that such failures in weighing largely may be inaccessible to cool reflection because they arise from self-deception or unconscious obsessions raises questions that this model may not be able to deal with adequately.)[67]

Aquinas and Mencius think practical reason can do more than simply command or weigh emotions. They agree that these two options best describe many of the situations in which all but the most perfectly virtuous people will find themselves. But they think reason can also *form* emotions and thus creates new dispositions. Indeed, the proper formation of emotions and dispositions is the goal of self-cultivation. Reaching that goal produces effortless action, the mark of truly virtuous activity. Let us, then, turn to this subject, the last one in our examination of the picture of the self underlying this type of virtue theory.

IX. The Picture of the Self Underlying This Type of Virtue Theory: The Formation of Emotions and the Character of Dispositions

The formation of emotion occurs in two ways. Reason alters the emotion *indirectly* when it leads a person to undertake a process of self-cultivation that aims, over a long period of time, to change by training certain emotional reactions. It also *directly* alters emotions either almost immediately or over a fairly short period of time. Such formation can occur because emotions are seen not as irrational entities but as forces whose form is determined by interpretative processes. They are aspects of those strong evaluations that work from a picture of the most excellent human life.

In the *indirect* formation of emotions by reason, there are three ascending stages. These stages define the process of *self-cultivation* that is so crucial to both Mencius and Aquinas's practical theory of virtue. (In Aquinas's secondary theory, as we discussed, God ultimately is responsible, of course, for people's ability to cultivate themselves.) At the initial stage, judgment and emotion conflict severely and only flawed triumphs and frequent backsliding are possible. My reason, at best, can command my emotions or be particularly sensitive to how they may interfere with my judgment. The execution of any virtuous act will be difficult, and its form often will be marred. Either my willpower cracks and I take the third glass of wine, or my resistance needs such constant shoring up that my agitation makes me bad company for both myself and others.

At the second stage, my acts will have the form of a virtuous act but will not proceed from a virtuous character. Errant emotions still are evident and powerful, even though they are under control. I usually still want to drink the wine, but little question exists that I will resist; I need to thwart strong contrary impulses only from time to time.

At the third stage, the act proceeds from a fully formed character and no conflict occurs between emotion and judgment; even conscious self-control is unnecessary. No thought of drinking the third glass of wine is present. I cannot even identify a desire within me to do so, and I easily, almost thoughtlessly, refuse it. In Mencius's language my extension proceeds effortlessly and is informed fully by attention and intelligent awareness. In Aquinas's formulation, practical wisdom's deliberations are easy, effortlessly lead to decision, and result in a harmonious, political control of the emotions.[68]

This picture of ascending stages in the formation of emotions best fits inclinational virtues; they aim at the third state and their perfection is defined by it. However, it also can fit the perfected form of some activities of a preservative virtue such as moderation. The activity of moderating well the drinking of wine will more easily attain such a perfected form, for most people, than the activity of moderating sexual desires. A preservative virtue like courage, in contrast, can never (under any normal conditions) reach the final stage. It always involves conflicts among goods and a recognition that the conflict exists.

Indeed, the truly courageous person's state resembles the state of someone who is acquiring an inclinational virtue or a preservative virtue such a moderation. While I train myself not to drink the third glass of wine, I still find appealing the good represented by the taste of it and the results of drinking it. I carry out moderate acts but I am not yet moderate, and my inner perturbation shows that. With courage, however, the goods that I may lose through my actions continue to appeal. In fact, for example, the recognition that I may lose my job by standing up for my slandered friend constitutes part of the act's courage. A significant difference remains between a person who has a courageous character and a person who does a courageous act but lacks the character to be a courageous person. But the ideal of spontaneous ease that defines inclinational virtues and some preservative virtues cannot exist for courage. The conflict and reflexivity that arise from adversity never can be completely overcome, except in those versions of courage where transhuman powers intervene. The final stage attained in the indirect formation of emotions by reason, then, never can be attained by a virtue like courage.

Reason, however, also *directly* alters emotions either almost immediately or over a fairly long period of time. Understanding exactly how this often mysterious process occurs is difficult. Nevertheless, direct alteration of the emotions by reason does occur. Rational evaluation can destroy an emotion that operated at some previous point in a person's life. At one time, I may have reacted with intense emotional perturbation, for example, whenever anyone, even a dull-minded or odious person, failed to show respect for me. I also may have had such strong emotional reactions to the idea of being poor that I would never consider a job, however worthwhile, that would leave me in poverty. Those emotional reactions can simply cease to exist as my reflections on what I think is valuable clarify and inform more completely my general perspective. After I have come to understand that poverty is not a mark of disgrace or a state that destroys the ability to live well, I no longer have the same emotional reaction to my possible poverty. After I have grown to realize that only good people's judgments on me tell me anything of importance about myself, I no longer react with emotion to the judgments of dull or bad people.

In addition to destroying certain emotions, rational reflection also may diminish emotions' power and even modify their form. For example, the reactions I have when rejected by a loved one may be profoundly modified by reflection. These refections may affect not only my explicit fear of rejection but also my pride in self or guilt about failure. If, for instance, I have come to believe that the changes that inevitably occur in life make all personal relationships unstable, show them all to be extremely frail, then a rejection of me may fail to surprise or even perturb me. Even less obviously relevant products of reflection also may change emotional reactions: for example, if I obtain either a new sense of how problematic I am as a partner or a deeper appreciation of the difficulties involved in understanding another human being.[69]

The exact character of the reflections that generate these changes often is difficult to articulate or even trace. The reflective process usually is not explicit, and it often relies on necessarily vague pictures of the world's character and a human being's ideal way of life. Few moments appear when a person consciously makes a decision between two opposing, general viewpoints by weighing up the evidence for each and deciding what human attitudes and attributes are most valuable. Indeed, we often can be surprised to discover that a new viewpoint is now dominant and has formed our emotional responses. The intricate, slow movements that govern these changes, then, are unclear. Nevertheless, such changes do occur, and they manifest practical reason's direct formation of emotion. (Mencius's depiction, for example, of how extension operates in an imperfectly virtuous person, where resemblances must be laboriously pursued and maneuvered into place, shows one kind of direct formation.)[70]

Despite the difficulties in specifying the components in the process, the changes that occur with both direct and indirect formation are rational. The people involved or astute outside observers can give an account of why the change occurred and how the new beliefs replaced the old beliefs. They can respond to questions about why the new position is justified or at least paint a picture that makes it understandable. Indeed, much of the virtue theory in Mencius and Aquinas serves the purpose of presenting the outlines of just such a rational justification.

A fairly simple example of this kind of change and how it affects our emotional life is evident when we think about the difference between our first love, or first few loves, and all subsequent loves. The particularly sweet pleasures of first love, the especially intense invigoration of self it brings, arise in part because we have no real sense that it will (or perhaps even could) end or go rancid. We live within a naive, truncated picture of the world and lack the context provided by reflection on experience. Such reflection forces us to see the more vexing sides of even the finest relationships and peoples: the possibilities for betrayal, for the cooling of inflamed passions, for the reanimating by others of passions thought to be dead, and for changes over time, caused by various events, that none could foresee.

The rational realization of such things literally changes the valence, the form, and the import of the relevant emotions. We become *incapable* of feeling a certain sort of love because of what our reason tells us. The message delivered does not simply generate caution in us when some emotion arises. (Reflection *also* can do that, as when it calls in question the strong attraction we feel toward a particular kind of neurotic person.) Rather reflection presents us with a different view of the world and human ideals, and that literally changes the form of the emotional reaction. We need not act on the new reactions, of course. Considered judgment can show us that although our new emotions are truer than our old ones, commitments made partially on the basis of old emotions still should be honored.

These shifts in rational judgment can involve clarification or crystallization of inchoate ideas and responses. They also can involve fundamental changes in what one thinks, although most of these major changes are probably just the result of long processes containing discrete crystallizations. The shifts can involve only particular events — I come to understand what a feminist critique of the tenure process means. But they also can involve more general viewpoints — I come to understand the way in which my picture of intellectual excellence involves specific cultural attitudes. These changes affect my emotional reactions at both the particular and general levels: both how I feel when faced with a feminist protest about a tenure case and how I feel about my general intellectual activity. These rational changes, with their formation of emotional reactions, dispose a person to behave in a new way. They generate a virtue, a disposition to act in ways that constitute human excellence, if the rationality is sound. They generate a vice, a disposition to act in ways that manifest human failure, if the rationality is unsound.

The concept of disposition thus provides us with another way to formulate the role of practical reason and the interaction of it with the emotions. Moreover, when we discuss both its focal and secondary meanings, we can identify more precisely those features that distinguish virtues from their semblances. The conception of disposition, therefore, is of the utmost importance in itself and as it helps us to understand and compare Mencius and Aquinas's theories of virtue. But the concept also is complicated, and we need to begin by discussing its intricacies.

The concept of disposition, to many people, connotes behavioristic ideas that seem to reduce humans to the level of animals. But the behavioristic use of the concept restricts it to invariant connections between a stimulus and a response, to those "if-then" situations where if A happens then B also will happen. This usage reflects the logic of all inanimate dispositions and some animate ones. That is, an occurrence generates a stimulus that produces an action. For example, "glass has a disposition to be brittle" means that if glass is struck then it will break; "my dog has a disposition to mark his territory" means that if he smells something foreign he will urinate on it.

Proponents of the virtue theory we are examining recognize that such invariant reactions exist, but they distinguish between them and fully human dispositions. In Aquinas's language, the focal meaning is found in human dispositions, the secondary meaning in invariant reactions. Mencius makes a similar point when he distinguishes between what is automatically drawn to its objects and what is not, and then argues the latter constitutes the fully human.[71]

Distinctively human dispositions rely on natural and acquired capabilities, but they also involve choice. They involve a tendency toward actions, but they do not always manifest themselves in characteristic ways when specific circumstances occur. Another person's pain does not produce my benevolence. Rather it provides the impetus for my appraisal of the situation and for my possible activation of a benevolent disposition. A disposition in this theory, then, is not a "substantial something"; I cannot give one to someone else or possess two of a particular kind. Therefore, it ought not be hypostatized: the relationship of a disposition and its exercise is a matter of logic. A disposition is defined by its exercise, it does not account for its exercise.

The notion of dispositions is best seen as a middle term in a conceptual framework that contains two other terms: capacities or potentialities and actions or actualities. A potentiality signifies what something can do or be; an actuality signifies what something is or is doing. A disposition signifies less than an actuality in the sense that no act is occurring. But it signifies more than just a potentiality, what something could do or be. The presence of appropriate circumstances and sound judgment make it very likely that a specific kind of action will occur. With a disposition a real inclination toward an action exists. Dispositions, then, are real additions to the self that fundamentally change what a person is likely to do.

If I am a normal human being, for example, I have a capacity to be generous; it is within my power. I have the disposition to be generous, however, only when I have a generous character and yet am not at the moment being generous and therefore actualizing it. More than a simple capacity is present because even if I am not now utilizing the disposition I can actualize it when an appropriate situation arises. Indeed, I will be very likely to be generous if specific circumstances arise, such as that some person manifests a need I can meet. But the action will not inevitably arise. For a variety of good reasons I may decide not to behave generously: if, for instance, the need is expressed by someone who, in my judgment, has tendencies to become overly dependent on the generosity of others.

Virtuous human dispositions consist in a person being disposed toward both appropriate actions and astute judgments. They do not resemble, then, the simple responses of either instincts or some skills; they are unlike anyone's reaction to a hot object or a gifted pianist's reaction to an especially difficult passage. Those two classes of actions are both more easily describable and more clearly predictable than the actions of virtuous dispositions because complex rational judgments do not function as centrally.

Virtuous dispositions usually will rule out some kinds of behavior. They do not ensure that specific kinds of action will occur, however. Two courageous actions — those of a teacher facing censure by misguided par-

ents and those of a soldier facing danger in battle — may share few if any
outward features. Moreover, even if the agents and circumstances are
quite similar — for example, two teachers facing censure by similar communities — the actions may be quite different and yet still be instances of
courage. Furthermore, the apparently successful completion of courageous actions may be semblances of the virtue. The soldier and the teacher's perseverance through danger may be due to arrogance, naiveté, or
anger rather than to true courage.

In thinking about dispositions, then, we can distinguish two senses of an
ability or power, and only the second occurs in virtuous action. The first kind
of power is identified by its behavioral expressions: the behavior of arriving
on time identifies the punctual person. But the second kind of power is less
directly related to behavior. That is, two people can be said to possess a power
when they behave in similar ways, and that behavior manifests the same
power. But two people also can be said to possess the same power when each
of them is in the same state, and that state explains their behavior.

We have no way to identify the courageous person's behavior that
resembles "arriving on time" as the identifying mark of the punctual person's behavior. Neither the power of standing firm nor the power of fleeing
identifies courageous behavior; either may express brave or cowardly
actions. We can describe the virtuous actions, then, only as those actions
that would be carried out by a courageous person, by someone who was in a
courageous state and had the requisite aims. Our account of courageousness
depends on our account of the courageous person: courageous actions will
be those actions produced by a courageous person. In Mencius or Aquinas's
language, the only criterion for a virtuous act is that a sage or good person
would do that particular act in that specific situation.[72]

Put schematically, I think four kinds of action belong within the category of disposition when that category is defined most generally. The four
fit on a spectrum where general distinctions are clear; only one, for
instance, is the term's focal meaning. But boundary lines can be sinuous. At
one end are *invariant reactions*. They inevitably produce actions when an
appropriate stimulus or occurrence happens. Dispositions in this sense
appear in both the inanimate and animate world; sugar can be said to have a
disposition to dissolve and my knee to have a disposition to move when
struck correctly. At the other end are *intelligent dispositions*, dispositions in
the fully human sense, the term's focal meaning. They involve both rationality and inclinations, arise from complex training not rote conditioning,
and produce activities that fit into no easily identifiable class of actions. In
the middle are *habits* and their close neighbors *propensities*, dispositions that
characterize only animate beings. They normally are acquired by conditioning, and in human beings both require little attention and move within
rather than against the grain of people or a person's inclinations.

Invariant reactions are relatively unimportant; they can be under-stood easily and clearly differ from the other three. But the character of and relationship among the other three is both complicated and significant. An intelligent disposition will make an action easier, such as behaving generously, than if one did not have the disposition. But it dif-fers from a habit, such as smoking, where not smoking is harder than if one lacked the habit. I can choose more easily to be generous when I have generosity as an intelligent disposition than when I do not. But the choice is not automatic, except perhaps for the most perfected people. Being generous is still harder than not being generous because generosity goes against the grain, corrects a human tendency to the contrary. With a habit, however, the action is almost automatic. At the least, it goes with rather than against the grain; it is easier to smoke than not to smoke.

"Propensities" manifest deeply ingrained human qualities. Although they closely resemble many habits, they are closer to intelligent dispositions than to some habits, such as smoking. Propensities, then, display not just a tendency toward action but a latent actuality that can easily appear. For example, if I have a propensity to be vain and encounter a large group of interesting people, I will push myself forward, wonder about the impression I am making, and feel uneasy if I am not the center of attention. (In this sense, propensities resemble more closely intellectual dispositions, such as the ability to speak German, than they do the will's intelligent dispositions.) Propensities lack the simple, almost automatic, responsiveness that charac-terizes habits. But they also fail to exhibit the fullness of choice and thus variation that characterizes intelligent dispositions. Moreover, they do not correct normal human inclinations, they do not go against the grain. The normal human inclination to vanity arises from a different kind of capacity than the possible human inclination to generosity. Generosity must correct other normal inclinations, but vanity need not.

The distinctions among these four kinds of action help us to under-stand Mencius and Aquinas's accounts of virtue. Both reject the idea that invariant reactions characterize virtuous activity, and both agree that the presence of intelligent dispositions defines fully virtuous activity. Mencius, for example, claims most sense reactions are invariant and dis-tinguishes them from virtuous actions on those grounds. Similarly, Aquinas argues virtuous activity depends on how reason controls the invariant features present in even good natural inclinations.

Furthermore, they both believe that people need to understand the differences between intelligent dispositions and habits to grasp the distinc-tion between virtues and their semblances. A common failure, they think, is to mistake habitual reactions for virtuous actions. That leads people to underestimate the crucial role played by practical reason and its formation of the emotions. People then become liable to all those ethical difficulties that, as discussed, arise when semblances of virtue are confused with true virtue.

The idea of propensities, in turn, helps us to understand Mencius and Aquinas's ideas of perfectly virtuous activity. Although the capacity for good never can become a habit, since rationality must operate, it can become a defining propensity. To reach such a state, however, the transforming presence of transhuman powers is needed; only they can permanently and completely overcome the contrary movements that normal virtues must constantly correct. That is, in this kind of perfected activity people no longer correct contrary inclinations. They instead move from those higher inclinations that arise, for Mencius, from their true nature and powers such as Heaven or *ch'i*, and that arise, for Aquinas, from the still intact features of their nature and grace's healing action.

Finally, these notions also help us to understand the relationship of virtuous and nonvirtuous behavior. Neither thinker holds that the habits or even propensities manifested in evil behavior can fully define humans. (This is true at least for those humans who fit securely within the category of the human.) Selfishness, for example, runs against part of what defines humans; it must correct tendencies to generosity or benevolence. For both, then, the sprouts of virtue remain, even if, as discussed, Mencius usually sees them as much more powerful than does Aquinas.

Examining the conception of disposition helps us, then, both to understand a crucial idea in virtue theory and to compare Aquinas and Mencius. It also allows us to specify some very general characteristics of each thinker's theory of virtue, and ideas about why humans fail to be virtuous, and with that specification we will end this chapter. Theories of virtue of the kind we have been examining fit on a spectrum defined by three points. Proponents of theories that fit at one end believe that humans should be guided by their natural inclinations. We called this the *Stoic position* and argued it fits a discovery model of human nature. Proponents of theories that fit at the other end believe that humans can and should choose among their various natural inclinations. We will call this the *voluntarism position*. It fits into a version of the development model of human nature that is less biological than the one discussed because changes, or developments, can occur very rapidly. Proponents of theories that fit in the middle of the continuum believe humans should be guided by rational judgments that interact with emotions to form intelligent dispositions.

Both Mencius and Aquinas's theories fit in the middle of the spectrum. Each thinker, however, tends toward one of the poles, as we saw in examining their views on human failures to be virtuous. A tendency to voluntarism is present in Mencius that is largely absent in Aquinas. In some of his presentations of extension, for example, people are painted as having an almost unhindered ability to choose among their cognitive and emotional reactions and to replace inappropriate ones with appropriate ones. Aquinas, on the other hand, tends toward the Stoic position. Claims about the significance of the new dispositions that God produces through infused virtues or even the role of God's invigoration of the natural inclinations given in Creation display this tendency.

Both thinkers, however, finally fit closer to the middle of the spectrum than to either end of it. This is especially true when we concentrate on their practical rather than their secondary theories. Each recognizes the partial truth in the pole that differs from the one to which they are drawn. Mencius thinks that one must identify and live with those inclinations that arise from a higher source and truly define one. Aquinas thinks that reason must choose among inclinations and form even those that tend in correct directions. Finally, then, each thinker's theory of virtue fits into a middle position, a position where reason must interact with natural inclinations to form those emotions and guide those dispositions that generate virtuous activity. We can examine more closely exactly how they work out the problems inherent in holding to this mediating position by analyzing their understanding of courage, and to that subject we may now turn.

Chapter 4

Mencius and Aquinas's
Conceptions of Courage

I. Introduction: The Distinguishing Marks of the Virtue of Courage

Our examination of Mencius and Aquinas's ideas on courage focuses on how and why they both distinguish real courage from its semblances and expand the meaning of courage into a religious realm. Before beginning that examination, however, we need to discuss how courage differs from other virtues. Analyzing those differences will help us understand Mencius and Aquinas's accounts, but it also allows us to probe the characteristics of courage as a particular kind of human excellence. Our initial enterprise, then, is a constructive one. Moreover, I will pursue it at a sufficiently theoretical level so that we need not for the moment deal with questions about courage's social location. Ideas about courage reflect and reinforce ideas about, for example, class and gender distinctions, as discussed. But here I will focus on a theoretical account of what is involved in using the concept of courage, especially what differentiates its use from the use of other concepts that refer to human excellence.[1]

Courage is an intelligent disposition that allows people to respect but control the effects perceptions of danger produce. Courage, then, consists in having a character that lets neither fear nor confidence unduly change behavior. Courageous people carefully consider what is dangerous. But they believe their own safety, or even ordinary happiness, has only a measure of importance and may at times count for little. Courageous people also consider carefully the grounds for their confidence. They recognize that confidence can rest on illegitimate grounds and produce actions that damage both the agent and other people.

Nuanced rational judgments about what is pertinent and valuable will, then, establish the boundaries among the foolhardy, the cowardly, and the courageous. Those judgments, in turn, will depend on three factors. The first is what people think is fearful. The second is what they believe is worth pursuing despite the fearful consequences. The third is what they assume to be legitimate grounds for confidence. The content of each of these three usually will differ substantially from culture to culture and often can differ from individual to individual. Consider, for example, the different answers to each of these three that would be given by a samurai, an ascetic Jain, and a contemporary investment banker.

Nevertheless, we can give an abstract account of courage's structure that helps us identify and understand the concept itself and the similarities and differences among various expressions of courage. In courageous actions a person overcomes the fear caused by some perceived difficulty in order to reach a desired end. That is, in a courageous action a person acts on the justified belief that doing something is dangerous and yet worth the risk. The person also recognizes that he or she could fail to act without suffering some inordinate punishment. Finally, the person understands that most people would think the danger sufficiently formidable to find acting difficult.[2]

Courageous actions manifest an *external goal*, an *internal goal*, and a "countergoal," an *objectionable result*. The external goal consists of the hoped-for state of affairs that animates the action; for example, the restoration of the reputation of a friend unfairly attacked by powerful people. The internal goal consists in the agent's belief that both the actions aimed toward the goal and the goal itself are good or noble. Both acquisitive and expressive motives operate here; the restoring of a deserved reputation is simply something worth doing. Finally, the objectionable result, the difficulty, consists of the unfortunate state of affairs that also will or may result from the laudatory action. If helping my friend results in my losing the beneficent regard of powerful people, that loss is an objectionable result; it represents a legitimate object of fear.[3]

Courageous acts, then, necessarily involve *conflicts* in which a person must sacrifice desirable goods. The most obvious conflict, and usually the most crucial one, is between the loss of one good and the acquisition of another. That is, it is between the objectionable result and both the internal and external goals. The conflict between my loss of powerful people's beneficent regard and the noble act of helping my friend illustrates this kind of conflict.

The internal and external goals also can conflict, however, and in a fashion that leads a person to cease pursuing the internal goal. In these conflicts, the agent does not consider alternative actions, but considers the reasons to act and chooses a reason that produces a semblance of courage. I do not really consider betraying my friend by remaining silent, for example, or by joining the attacks on her. My motive, however, is not that I think acting to help her is noble, but that I fear other people's censure (now or at a later time) if I betray her. I just balance different and commensurable fears in deciding what to do. My question has ceased to be how important is my safety, given the act's nobility. It has instead become which action will yield more safety.

Truly courageous action, then, always involves a focus on the internal goal; without it only a semblance of courage appears. This means a second order of motivations, a *reflexivity* or executive control, always must be present. This fact differentiates courage from most other kinds of virtue. The fully virtuous person who displays inclinational virtues (as discussed) has only a first-order motivation: to be truly benevolent is simply to see suffering and to respond to it. Indeed, to possess a second-order motivation, a desire to manifest the virtue, is to show a reflexivity that debilitates the virtuous activity. If I see a suffering person, want to think of myself as a benevolent person, and then act to accomplish that goal, the action's value is diminished considerably.

With a preservative virtue like courage, however, reflexivity constitutes part of the virtue's perfection. I am not misdirecting my attention when I seek to manifest the virtue because I value it and consider carefully what must be surrendered for me to obtain it. If I confront a thug attacking someone, my understanding that I may be hurt if I intervene is part of the courage I display. Indeed, to lack that understanding is to be insensitive to an important feature of the situation and the action. Courageous people must recognize both that they will pay a price and that courageous acts, which they consider valuable, always involve paying such a price. Reflexivity and executive control are essential parts of courage, but they vitiate or even destroy inclinational virtues.

Moreover, the facts that courageous action involves the loss of legitimate goods leads to another, if related, characteristic that differentiates it from many virtuous actions. *Contrary inclinations* will be a constitutive feature of courageous actions. People who are just, for example, appear to lose something only from the perspective of the unjust; the just themselves put no value on what is lost. The money or prestige a lie would bring provides a just person with no reason to act and its absence no reason for regret. With courage, however, valuable goods are lost, and that loss provides an agent with reason to act differently and to regret the loss that occurs. In this sense, as noted earlier, the corrective character of inclinational and preservative virtues differs considerably. The former correct a general human tendency, but the latter correct a present psychological state. With inclinational virtues the agent says "I will do this" and knows that he or she foregoes no real goods. With courage the agent says "I will do this even if I must forego or lose that" and acts despite the loss involved.[4]

The presence in courage of different goals and thus of loss, conflict, and reflexivity produces still another difference from other virtues. Courage displays in *exaggerated fashion* three characteristics all virtues share. They are difficulties in identifying easily which acts are virtuous; difficulties in specifying how pleasure connects to virtuous activity; and difficulties in unraveling how virtues are best cultivated. The first difficulty, then, is that virtuous activity fails to fit into easily identifiable categories. All virtuous actions have this characteristic, but with most virtues we have legitimate general expectations about typical actions and exceptions will be few. Refusing to drink oneself into a stupor, almost without fail, can be labeled an instance of moderation. With courage, however, we have no rules that allow us to specify whether an act is courageous or not. Fleeing, attacking, or standing firm may or may not be instances of courage. Judgments about those actions always will depend on our evaluation of the situation and the agent. Courage differs in degree not kind from other virtues here, but the difference is important, and it arises because courage deals with significant dangers and weighs real but conflicting goods. Therefore it must rely on delicate rational judgments and complex formations of emotions.

The connection between virtuous activity and pleasure is a second way that courage displays in exaggerated fashion a feature of all virtues. With most manifestations of most virtues the connection to pleasure is firm, but with courage the connection is strained. Although, for instance, benevolent actions may produce some kinds of pain, such actions usually are pleasant for benevolent people. They easily do what they wish to do and forego nothing that they want to possess. Courageous people, however, must surrender something they wish to possess, and that surrender produces either pain or some dissatisfaction. Courageous people do find a kind of pleasure in what they do. But they usually (to use Anthony Kenny's terminology) find pleasure only in the accomplishment that terminates a "performance" and not in the "activity" itself. I may take pleasure in an inherently unpleasant courageous activity; for example, if I save my family from a burning house. But the pleasure arises not from the activity of rushing through the flames but from a performance that manifests nobility and, I hope, accomplishes the desired end of rescuing my family.[5]

The third distinction covers differences between cultivating courage and cultivating other virtues. As discussed, normal courage cannot reach through cultivation that state where actions exhibit neither conflict nor reflexivity. Courage, then, differs from inclinational virtues and some preservative virtues. But the very ways in which courage is cultivated also show two other features in exaggerated fashion: the need for indirect cultivation and the significance of acquiring skills.

The cultivation of courage must necessarily be far more *indirect* than the cultivation of other virtues. The situations that call forth many forms of courage are too rare to allow people to practice meeting them. I often will face the opportunity to indulge my taste for food or wine, but thankfully I rarely face the opportunity to test myself against a person aiming to injure innocents physically. Furthermore, courage's exercise often depends on people's ability to act on general beliefs about what is valuable when they are under stress. When this fact and the infrequency of opportunities to practice courage are combined, it is clear that courage's cultivation must involve a variety of indirect exercises. People will need to strengthen their ability to surrender desirable goods, for example. They also will need to reflect regularly on the significance of self-sacrifice for important goals.

The cultivation of courage, moreover, unlike the cultivation of most inclinational virtues involves acquiring *skills*, abilities that aim to produce a product. Skills and virtues differ in three significant ways, and distinguishing them is important. (Benjamin Franklin's ideas on virtue look so odd, for example, just because he fails to distinguish them.) The agent's internal state is crucial with virtues but not with skills. Artists' pictures not their character concern us. Furthermore, the reliable production of specifiable results is crucial with skills but not with virtues; the potter's consistently beautiful vases manifest her excellence. Finally, the skillful can display their abilities by deliberately acting unskillfully but the virtuous cannot display their virtues by deliberately acting unvirtuously. We know the pianists' quality by her ability to distort the sonata.

Despite these differences between virtues and skills, the cultivation of courage usually involves developing skills. Courageous people, for example, must acquire the skills that enable them to deal easily with situations that would frighten people who lack those skills. They also must be able to distinguish between real and false dangers and have the abilities that allow them, as far as possible, to encounter real dangers skillfully. We may think people (such as sufferers from phobias) are courageous when they confront the fears that arise from their lack of proper understanding or ability. But we also think such people should develop the understanding and ability that would enable them not to feel fear in such situations.[6]

The cultivation of courage involves skills, then, and often may have to be indirect. These characteristics, as well as the link with pleasure and the relationship to identifiable categories of action, show how courage manifests in exaggerated form features that all virtues share. All these exaggerations arise from courage's distinctive structure, those marks that differentiate ordinary courage from most other virtues: the presence of external goals, internal goals, and objectionable results; and therefore the existence in courage of conflict, loss, and reflexivity.

Let us now turn to our main subject, Mencius and Aquinas's understanding of true courage, its semblances, and it religious forms. My analysis will concentrate on the details of their respective accounts or arguments, because in this chapter I undertake the most specific and textured of the inquiries. Comparisons of the two figures, then, will emerge only from within my detailed examinations of each. Most of the comparisons, moreover, will appear only in the treatment of Mencius because we need to go through Aquinas's detailed account before we can compare it to specific features of Mencius's account. Finally, the constructive aspects of my enterprise, except for what was contained in the preceding analysis, will appear only in my examination and evaluation of the specific arguments or perspectives each thinker presents. However, in the final chapter, I will focus again on more general comparisons between the two and also discuss the constitutive features present in both the products and the processes of such comparisons.

II. Aquinas's Analysis of Ordinary Courage, Especially the Roles in It of Fear and Confidence

Aquinas's major treatment of courage appears in a simple, apparently unified treatise. I think it contains three separate if related analyses, however. The first shapes the concept of ordinary courage. Especially important is his analysis of the differing roles of fear and confidence in courage, and his examination of how semblances of courage differ from true courage. In the second, Aquinas expands the concept of courage by examining those virtues that share courage's essential character but differ from it in important ways. Most important here are the arguments he makes in defending two seemingly implausible claims: that every courageous act involves a willingness to die and that endurance is courage's defining mark. In the third, Aquinas develops the religious meaning of courage that appears in his expansion of the concept. Especially important are two exalted states. One is found in the operations of the supernatural virtue of patience, the other is found in that rare kind of perfected courage, produced by the Gift of Courage, where no contending appetites appear. Aquinas's treatment of courage, then, can be said to move from an examination of ordinary courage's formation of those appetites that can impede normal virtuous activity to a religious state where the ability to endure as one should is the defining mark.

Put in terms of the formation of emotions, the full range of courageous activity involves dealing with three possible hindrances to the following of appropriate judgments in both the ordinary and religious sphere: the emotions of fear, confidence, and sadness or sorrow (*tristitia*). Failure in forming any of them produces semblances of courage. Forming the first two underlies normal courage and forming the third, religious courage; moving beyond the need to form any of them is the rare state produced by the Gift of Courage.

I will examine separately each of his three analyses in what follows, beginning with the first, as they can be said to build on each other. My treatment of his shaping of the conception of ordinary courage can be brief. It resembles closely the analysis just discussed, although an often very different vocabulary is employed. Moreover, Aquinas's more distinctive and interesting discussion of ordinary courage appears when he examines the role of fear and confidence in courage and analyzes the semblances of courage.

Aquinas thinks courage protects the activities of practical wisdom against those difficulties the contending appetites produce. Courage deals with "the revulsion of the will from the end suggested by reason, because of some opposing difficulty"; it concerns the removing of "the hindrance which holds back the will from following reason." The evaluation of courageous acts, then, will rest on whether an agent has good reasons to pursue some goals and reject others. In this sense, courage exemplifies Aquinas's general principle that because "virtue is concerned with the good rather than the difficult . . . [the] stature of a virtue should . . . be measured by the criterion of goodness rather than difficulty." No matter how heroic is the overcoming of a difficulty, appraisal's ultimate criterion remains the goods preserved. As he says, the "praise accorded to courage derives in a sense from justice," and justice here refers to what is "concerned to impose the order of reason in all human affairs."[7]

Aquinas, then, clearly emphasizes the significance of the objectionable result and especially the external goal. But he also thinks that courageous people act for an internal goal, the nobility of the courageous act. In his rather odd formulation of the expressive motive for virtuous action, he says people are motivated by the goal of impressing their own likeness onto something, by a desire to express what they think they are. The recognition that courage is a good quality and one they possess provides people with a motive to express that quality in action. They want to imprint, however successfully, their own picture of the good on an indifferent or even hostile landscape.

For Aquinas, then, courage is an executive virtue that recognizes a possible objectionable result but aims at both an internal and external goal. This conception of courage also leads Aquinas to argue that courage

illustrates in exaggerated form the three common characteristics of virtues
we noted earlier. It fails to fit into easily identifiable categories of action;
at times it will not connect directly to pleasure; and it involves indirect
forms of cultivation, some of which include the acquisition of skills.[8]

Critical to Aquinas's distinctive understanding of courage is his analysis of the roles of fear and confidence in it. These two emotions underlie
courage's normal and expanded forms, and each has a distinctive semblance. In analyzing the roles of fear and confidence in courage, Aquinas
employs the Aristotelian idea of the mean. That is, he approaches virtues
as states of emotional balance that have characteristic forms we can
describe in terms of a mean, or right amount, and the poles of excess and
deficiency. For example, the person who feels great anger at a trivial slight
has an excessive emotional and cognitive reaction, and the person who
feels only mild annoyance at the battering of a child a deficient one.

Most contemporary scholars agree that the idea of the mean works
better with some virtues than with others, although some doubt it helps
us to analyze any virtues, a judgment with which I disagree. In any event,
a problem clearly does arise when Aristotle uses the idea of the mean to
analyze courage. We will note that problem briefly, as it illuminates
Aquinas who follows this aspect of Aristotle's account, and then will examine Aquinas' own account more closely.[9]

Aristotle claims courage is a mean with regard to fear and
confidence. Modern scholars generally (if not universally) agree, however,
that his analysis of courage covers not one tightly unified virtue but two
different if closely related aspects. This occurs because courage concerns
not one but two emotions: one is fear (*phobos*) and the other is confidence
or "cheer" (*thairos* or *thaieos*). Fear and confidence are different enough
emotions that they are not even opposite poles on a single homogenous
scale. Fear is a desire to flee from danger. Confidence, however, is not an
appetite for risk or a love of danger. Rather, it is an expectation that safety
is close at hand. Moreover, when we analyze each emotion in terms of the
mean different pictures emerge. Confidence's mean state is discretion or
caution; its deficiency is timidity; and its excess is rashness, a tendency to
be overly bold or daring. Fear's mean state is bravery; its deficiency is cowardliness; and its excess is insensitivity to fear or fearlessness. (Complete
insensitivity to fear may be rare, or perhaps even nonexistent, but an insensitivity to the fears that a normal, sensitive person feels is common.)

The differences between the two can be illustrated by looking at
their respective deficient states. Timidity or insufficient daring, the
deficient state of confidence, arises from specific temperamental propensities. It does not result from an overt fear of clearly perceived risks as does
cowardliness. Timid people refuse to take risks, but they lack a clearly

defined sense of what the risks are. They possess only a vague, general belief that many risks exist in a world that is too dangerous for their tastes. Their fear, then, rarely takes the specific form of actual felt reactions, of inclinations with physiological consequences, and that state differs considerably from the coward's deficient state. Indeed, timid people can be brave. But to be brave they must overcome their normal temperament, their usual likes and dislikes. Cowardly people, however, just refuse to take a specific risk because of their fear.

Aquinas does not specifically pinpoint the issue modern scholars have noted in Aristotle's analysis, and at times his examination of the issue is confused, or at least confusing. But his account, I think, can be plausibly (and revealingly) reconstructed to show that he thinks *normal* courage concerns not one but two emotions. For him, as for Aristotle, it therefore is one virtue with two closely related aspects. Moreover, courage in its expanded and most significant *religious form* involves, as noted, still another emotion, sadness or sorrow (*tristitia*). This form of courage, which has no analogue in Aristotle, relates in special ways to both fear and confidence, and we will examine it at length later. Aquinas, then, thinks that courage concerns three emotions: fear, confidence, and sorrow. Let us begin by analyzing the treatment of fear and confidence.

Aquinas thinks normal courage's essential characteristic is to overcome those hindrances that impede people's ability to follow their rational judgment. Two possible hindrances, fear and confidence, are most important, and they differ substantially. Each represents a different state of character, produces different semblances, and therefore, relates in distinct ways to practical wisdom. Aquinas claims courage chiefly concerns fear but that it also deals with daring, the excess of confidence.

> [R]etreat from a difficult situation is characteristic of fear, for fear connotes withdrawal before a formidable evil. . . . Accordingly courage is chiefly concerned with fears of difficulties likely to cause the will to retreat from following the lead of reason. But courage ought not only to endure unflinchingly . . . it ought to make a calculated attack. . . . Such action . . . belong[s] to daring. Therefore courage is concerned with fear and acts of daring, restraining the first and measuring the second.[10]

When people deal with fear (*timor*), the excess is fearlessness, the deficiency cowardliness, and the mean is bravery. When they deal with confidence, daring is the excess, timidity is the deficiency, and discretion is the mean.

Timidity and cowardliness, the two deficient states, can be understood relatively easily. Each represents a straightforward response that fits the descriptions given in examining Aristotle's analysis. The one responds to obviously fearful objects, the other to a world that contains too much danger. Understanding the excess states of fearlessness and especially of daring is, however, more difficult. Both appear, from Aquinas's perspective, to violate the natural reactions appetites have to specific objects they confront. That is, they seem to pursue the disagreeable and to love the fearful. An explanation of these reactions, then, can rely only on understanding how they relate to a previously existing set of emotions and judgments.

In the case of *fearlessness* (*intimiditas* or *inpaviditas*), Aquinas thinks three origins can exist. One is pride, an overestimation of one's abilities. Another is lack of reason, a failure to see clearly the goods that may be lost. A third is insufficient love, a general inability to love properly the various goods in the world. The fearlessness that rests either on a prideful overestimation of one's abilities or on a failure to appreciate those goods that may be lost, for Aquinas, is easily understandable. But the fearlessness that rests on an insufficient love of worldly goods remains mysterious to him because he thinks people have an inbred love of their own life and those things that contribute to it. (Living after Freud, with his explication of masochism, we may not share Aquinas's difficulty.)[11]

An explanation of *daring* (*audacia*) also must turn to previously existing states. This emotion arises, Aquinas thinks, when people face difficulties with the confidence that they can overcome them, with a security about success that rests in part on their natural spiritedness. Daring people, then, do not pursue the frightening or disagreeable because they find pleasure in it — that would be "darage," an appetite for risk. (General Skobeleff, discussed earlier, seems to personify darage.) Rather they pursue them because they believe they can overcome them and therefore attain some good, if perhaps only the good of triumph. Daring people do pursue the frightening or disagreeable, but the good of success is the object of their hope, and victory is thought to be assured.

The excessiveness, the unreasonableness, of the daring rests on the fact that daring people, unlike courageous people, falter when they encounter difficulties that are greater than they anticipated them to be. This faltering shows that the hope that dispels their fear rests on false judgments and arises from imperfectly informed spiritedness. Daring people lack the courageous person's persistence. They fail to possess the persistence that arises from calm deliberation, adherence to a real good, and the full formation of the emotions.[12]

For Aquinas, then, normal courage is one virtue that deals with two separate emotions. With fear, bravery is the mean, fearlessness the excess, and cowardliness the deficiency. With confidence, discretion is the mean, daring the excess, and timidity the deficiency. The two differ in various ways. Most important to us, however, are the different roles practical wisdom plays in each mean state and in the cultivation that produces it. When fear is the central emotion, reason's role is relatively straightforward. Those basic processes we described at length in our examination of the direct and indirect formation of emotions will constitute its operation. (The indirect formation of fear, nevertheless, could involve a delicate cultivation process if people had to analyze their failure to love goods that should be loved in order to overcome their fearlessness.)

When confidence is the subject, however, reason's role in both the direct and indirect formation of the emotions is more complicated. With daring, there must be a detailed and difficult examination of whether the grounds for any feeling of confidence are reliable. Moreover, such an examination often will face the added problem of considering the role of high spiritedness, the temperamental propensity to react with more confidence than is reasonable. A similarly difficult situation appears when practical wisdom must modify timidity. Explicit fear plays little role in timidity. Modifying it, therefore, involves people in the subtle, taxing examination of what in their temperament and general perspective leads them to see the world, or some part of it, in an overly cautious fashion. Both discretion and timidity demand, then, nuanced examinations of subjects that are hard to probe. People must analyze basic attitudes, ways of viewing the world, and procedures for interpreting information and making judgments.

Both aspects of courage share the essential feature of overcoming hindrances that impede people's ability to follow reason's judgments. But the character of the hindrances differs, as do the ways to remove them. Giving a proper weight to discrete objects of fear and forming one's fearful reactions in appropriate ways is relatively straightforward. But with confidence (and a few aspects of fearlessness) people have to probe deeply into their temperaments and general views of the world. They constantly must turn over and evaluate the judgments that underlie the confidence they feel.

People's ability to evaluate the confidence they feel is especially important when courage's religious manifestations are the subject. If they use normal standards, the confidence they feel often clearly is excessive. They, then, must decide whether their confidence manifests the theological virtue of hope, the direct prompting of the Holy Spirit, or a presumption that rests on idolatry or some other deformation. This issue is important, and we will discuss it at length when we examine how Aquinas expands courage into the specifically religious realm. Here we can note just that understanding the differences between courage's two aspects provides the needed background for that examination. Let us now examine more closely another subject that illuminates Aquinas's understanding of normal courage: his treatment of five semblances of ordinary courage.

III. Aquinas's Differentiation of True Courage from Semblances of Courage

Aquinas's best single treatment of this subject occurs when he examines those five kinds of people that Aristotle claimed represented lesser manifestations of courage. The treatment is condensed, even by Aquinas's standards, but it remains a good point from which to start.

> On occasions when persons not possessing virtue perform what is outwardly an act of virtue, they do so from a motivating cause other than virtue. This is why Aristotle proposes five types of persons who are called brave because they appear to be so, who in a way act bravely but without the virtue of courage (*quinque modos eorum qui similtudinarie dicuntur forte, quasi exercentes actum fortitudinis praeter virtutem*). This happens in three ways. First are those who rush into a difficult situation as though it were not difficult, and in them three types of action can be distinguished; sometimes they act through ignorance, not realizing the immensity of the danger; sometimes through optimism about overcoming danger, for example when somebody has previous experience of often escaping dangers; and sometimes through knowledge and skill (*scientiem et artem*), as is the case with soldiers, who do not think of the serious dangers of war because of their skill in arms and their training, reckoning that they can be shielded from them by their skill. . . . Secondly, a man performs an act of bravery without virtue under the impulse of feeling (*impulsum passionis*) — whether depression (*tristitiae*), which he wishes to throw off, or anger (*irae*). Thirdly, he does it because he chooses not what is right but rather some worldly advantage such as honor, pleasure or gain; or to avoid some disadvantage like obloquy, pain or loss.[13]

Aquinas's treatment follows Aristotle's in usually referring to people in warfare. The more general import of his ideas, however, can be seen if we employ other features of his account of virtue to develop the portraits which he presents here.

Each portrait of a semblance can be labeled as follows, the label referring to the quality on which the semblance rests. People suffering from *simple ignorance* fail to recognize the danger they face. People characterized by *tempered optimism* fail to see all the features of the danger they face because they fail to evaluate well both the situation faced and their own history. When *acquired skill* forms people's actions, it leads them to misread their capability to deal with the dangers they face. *Spirited* people, in contrast, are moved to action because of powerful emotions imperfectly formed by reason. Finally, people acting from *perceived advantage* simply calculate between or among commensurable goals and choose the courses of action that will most surely preserve their safety or other closely related goods.

Examining these five semblances enables us to probe critical features of Aquinas's understanding of normal courage; moreover the five will be useful in the later analysis of his ideas about patience. They are important enough, then, to treat one by one. In doing so, I will sometimes speak of individual acts for stylistic reasons, but in all cases the critical reference is to character, to the kind of person who would act in that way. That is, I will speak of "a choice made to gain an advantage," for instance, but I could say instead "a disposition to make choices to gain an advantage."

The last semblance, *perceived advantage*, illustrates in strikingly clear fashion one crucial feature of the distinction between courage and its semblances. Action here rests on a choice made to gain an advantage or to avoid a disadvantage. Truly courageous people choose to endure the fearful for the sake of a good, but people displaying this semblance merely calculate what they most fear to lose. (Calling it "political courage" in another context, Aquinas declares these people act from "fear of loss of status, or of punishment."[14]) People who manifest this semblance, then, choose between commensurable goals that fit on a single scale; the fear of losing the good of other's respect, for example, and the fear of losing the good of physical well-being. Truly courageous people, in contrast, choose between incommensurable goods; for instance, they choose between physical safety and undertaking a heinous act.

Courageous people focus on the act's internal goal and make strong evaluations. They both use the contrastive language of the noble and base and make judgments about what kind of life a human should lead. Acting for the sake of the admirable action, they aim to express their conception of what the best life demands. In contrast, people who let perceived advantage guide them make weak evaluations. Such people would like to realize all their desires and see these desires as contingently not basically incompatible. They would avoid both the community's judgment and the action's dangers, if possible.

The semblance of perceived advantage illustrates well a fundamental distinction between virtuous action and its semblances. The remaining semblances display other facets of the difference. The first three semblances — simple ignorance, tempered optimism, and acquired skill — can be grouped together. They all manifest (in even clearer fashion than perceived advantage) failures in practical wisdom's ability to deliberate and decide. The remaining semblance, spiritedness, manifests both those failures and an inability to form emotional responses correctly.

The clearest and least interesting of these semblances rests on *simple ignorance*; the absence of a full understanding of the dangers (rather than goods) involved in a situation characterize this semblance. Such ignorance, Aquinas says, often arises from lack of experience, from having seen too little to know that dangers are present or will occur. A paradigmatic example would be a naive young woman who defied a vengeful individual and later was genuinely surprised to discover the person's vengeance has turned against her. The next two semblances involve more complicated forms of ignorance. In each of them a significant aspect of the situation faced is misunderstood because of some fault in the agent's ability to evaluate danger. Each semblance concerns, then, the grounds of justified belief and the role of such belief and the confidence it produces in the evaluation of courage.

Tempered optimism illustrates this particularly well. The optimism of these people is tempered, it arises from experience not from simple ignorance. That is, their confidence rests on their past and limited experience of triumphing over or escaping from danger. Nevertheless, their judgments, and thus their confidence, is faulty. Either the evidence that underlies the confidence is too limited to form a reliable base for judgment or the people who evaluate the evidence do so in an inadequate way. Such people, for example, will act bravely because they are accustomed to winning in the past, accustomed to overcoming obstacles. They rely on habitual responses or propensities, then, not on astute perceptions and intelligently activated dispositions.

Many observers think people of this sort exemplify courage because they appear to be solid and balanced when adversity appears. Those observers fail to recognize that tempered optimists act from temperamental characteristics that may serve them well in simple situations but that can cause problems in complex situations. Tempered optimists are predisposed to be unreflective and sanguine, even phlegmatic. They therefore rarely either seek out challenging information or reflect on the information they possess in ways that might change their behavior and attitudes.[15]

Acquired skill, the next semblance, also rests on confidence, but the confidence it produces arises from an evaluation of native capacities an learned expertise. Training leads these people to develop their capacities both to evaluate possible dangers and respond well to them. The result is that they usually do not fear what many others fear. Developing such skill, as discussed, is an important part of cultivating courage. But if possessing such skill leads people to feel no fear, their actions cannot be called courageous. We can judge whether such people are truly courageous only when we see how they face situations where their skill does not prevent them from feeling fear. The semblance of courage that rests on acquired skill is evident, then, only when three conditions are satisfied. A person must face some situations fearlessly that would involve fear in the unskilled; the person would fail in situations where such fear was felt; and the person has undertaken no self-conscious acquisition of skill to overcome some kinds of fear.

The last and most complicated semblance is the one that rests on *spiritedness*. This semblance relies on powerful feelings (such as anger, depression, or pain) that either directly impel people to act or cause strong reactions that indirectly move people to act. The spirited, thus, confront dangers mainly by means of powerful emotions inadequately informed by reason. Anger (*ira*) exemplifies a spirited emotion. As a strong feeling, it can produce vigorous, confident action against a person or situation that has harmed or could harm one. Actions generated from anger, however, differ from courageous actions. (In fact, as discussed, one of anger's permutations, for Aquinas, counts as a capital sin.) Simply angry actions arise only from a passion, but courageous actions arise from a passion formed by reasonable judgments that aim at appropriate goals.

Indeed, the relationship between practical wisdom and anger illustrates well how rational judgments and emotions need to inform each other in the case of courage. Anger depends on its cognitive component even more clearly than many other emotions just because it aims to apply good to evil; that is, to respond correctly and passionately to violations of justice. Unlike hatred or even simple desire, the rational component in anger not only identifies the emotion's object but also evaluates the degree to which the injury received is unjust. The cognitive judgement, in turn, must be informed by a strong feeling. I ought not just coolly judge that some horrible act has occurred, for instance; I must also be angry. Anger, then, must rely on correct cognitive judgments, but it also must involve a desire to inflict punishment for a suffering received.

The passionate side of anger often is especially important when courageous action is needed. The passion can generate the added impetus that allows a person to overcome fear or some other difficulty. The passion, however, always must be formed by practical wisdom because a passion like anger easily can slip into powerful and irrational forms. Anger, therefore, will be a potentially dangerous and always ambivalent part of courageous action. Even more than with most emotions, practical wisdom must exercise a political control of a spirited element like anger. It must both form and respect the emotion if truly courageous action is to occur.[16]

Some aspect of practical wisdom's ability to deliberate, decide, and then inform action is absent in each of these five semblances. Truly courageous actions rest on practical wisdom's astute judgments about situations, personal capacities, and justifiable goals, as well as on its ability to make those judgments inform emotional responses. Certain features of practical wisdom, however, do operate with each of the semblances. Actions that rest on perceived advantage involve judgments, but they produce only weak evaluations. Similarly, the semblances of courage that rest on tempered optimism and acquired skills rely on a rational evaluation of a person's capacities and past experience. But they lack the complicated and nuanced view of the good that practical wisdom provides. Finally, simple ignorance lacks almost all of what rationality provides and spiritedness, in at least its lowest forms, manifests an imperfect formation of the emotions. Semblances of courage, then, appear when practical wisdom is either virtually absent or present only in one of its deficient forms.

One other possible deficiency in practical wisdom (and an especially important one when courage is the subject) is highlighted only imperfectly in this account of courage's five semblances. This deficiency appears when a person lacks a comprehensive enough view of the kind of life that generates full human flourishing. It produces a person who pursues limited ends and focuses on ultimately insignificant fears. In considering this deficiency, a version of which we see in Mencius's accounts of semblances, two ideas discussed earlier are important. One is the idea that the self-sacrifice evident in some kinds of courageous actions is only an extreme instance of the virtuous person's normal attitude to virtuous action. The second is the idea that a virtue can be genuine by one standard and a semblance by another. These ideas and the analysis of this semblance inform Aquinas's understanding of courage's more clearly religious dimensions, and therefore we need to examine, if briefly, this deficiency in practical wisdom.

Aquinas thinks any pursuit of a life plan that fails to understand correctly God's plans and actions is inadequate. The deficiency arises from the failure to identify what really ought to be feared. What Aquinas calls a *solicitude about temporal concerns* appears, then, when people fail to grasp how Christ's teachings, especially those about providence, enable people to overcome their normal fears about meeting fundamental needs. Aquinas says, people should not be possessed by

> needless fears, as when a man is afraid of doing what he ought to do lest he should fall into want of the necessities of life. Our Lord rules out such fear on three grounds. To begin with, God has given us greater blessings, namely a body and soul, beyond what human solicitude could provide. Next, he provides without human help for animals and plants proportionately to their natures. Finally, in consideration of divine Providence, of which unbelievers are ignorant, and so are preoccupied with the pursuit of earthly goods. He [Christ] concludes, therefore, that our first care should be for spiritual goods, while yet hoping that temporal goods will be forthcoming provided we do what we ought.[17]

Aquinas paints here neither a simply supportive world nor an easily reached supernatural reward. The difficulties in being saved or knowing one is saved remain, and great need and suffering obviously can arise in such a world; animals, plants, and people, for instance, can die from drought. Aquinas does say, however, that people ought to excise needless fears and constantly think about two present goods that provide reasons for gratitude and assurity. One is the possession of body and soul. The other is the presence, without human help, of aid that is proportionate to the natures of animals and plants.

Aquinas firmly believes a prudential concern for future states always should inform people's practical judgments. He says people ought to plan "according to human custom," and he even declares the teaching "take no thought for the morrow" concerns only the dangers that arise in preoccupying oneself with possible future ills. Nevertheless, spiritual goods should be truly virtuous people's first concern, and hope in providence should modify their fears about the loss of temporal goods. Aquinas never claims, then, that Christ teaches that temporal goods will appear if spiritual goods are sought. He does claim, however, that spiritual goods should be people's major concern, and they should hope (not presume) that temporal goods will appear. The person possessing true practical wisdom and courage, for Aquinas, does not assume that normal needs will be met. Such a person just understands which goods must be sought and which fears overcome if human flourishing is to occur, whatever may be the apparent cost to the virtuous. The higher perspective of "a view to the final good for the whole of life" allows people to understand the crucial issue of what really ought to be feared. The major fear courage ultimately should deal with is the fear of not possessing fully the spiritual goods virtuous people pursue and manifest, as Christ's teachings on providence both underline and illuminate.[18]

For Aquinas courage protects practical wisdom's judgments against the difficulties the contending appetites present. The character of that protection is clarified when we examine his understanding of the failures present both in the five semblances of courage drawn from Aristotle's account and in that semblance represented by a "solicitude about temporal concerns." Moreover, we also saw how that protection takes different forms depending on whether fear or confidence is the emotion dealt with; indeed, that courage is one virtue with two closely related aspects. The foregoing examination completes our investigation of how Aquinas shapes the concept of normal courage. We can now turn to his expansion of the conception of courage and his argument for two critical claims involved in it: that all courageous actions involve a willingness to die and that endurance is central to courage.

IV. Aquinas's Expansion of Courage and the Place of Endurance and the Willingness to Die

Aquinas's expansion of the conception of courage by means of the idea of parts of a virtue contains those general problems and possibilities we discussed in examining his list of virtues. Most important here, however, is a specific line of argument, or thread, in his analysis that I want to reconstruct and examine closely. The thread is woven into a rich and diverse tapestry; the line of argument draws on many other ideas and arguments. Briefly put, however, Aquinas links courage specifically with a willingness to die, then argues that endurance not attack is courage's most characteristic act, and finally presents patience as the religious consummation of courage. Before beginning the analysis, however, let us review succinctly the outlines of Aquinas's expansion of courage.

Aquinas links four major virtues to courage: perseverance, patience, magnificence ("great making"), and magnanimity ("great souledness"). Each is a component part, an element needed for the virtue's full functioning (*pars integralis*), if the action concerns death, courage's distinguishing mark. But it is an allied virtue if the action concerns difficulties less pressing than death (*pars potentialis*). Allied virtues share the virtue's general attributes and even may surpass it in some ways, but they fail to express fully its paradigmatic character.

Patience and perseverance refer to those qualities people need if they are to endure in the pursuit of a good over a long period of time. Each is concerned with a separate difficulty. Perseverance, with its opposed vices of obstinacy and softness (a too easy yielding to pleasure), concerns the need to adhere to the good sought. Patience concerns the need to overcome the sorrow brought by the inevitable loss of some goods. Magnificence, in contrast, concerns the planning and performance of great deeds that display spirited resolution and constancy and therefore manifests a person's grandeur. Expensive, public projects are its main subject, but, by extension, it includes any substantial "making," even of the self, and its deformations, pettiness and wasteful vulgarity, relate to both. Magnanimity concerns those grand actions that rest in a justified trust in the self. It leads a person both to be free from insignificant anxieties and to aspire to and undertake great and honorable projects. (Aquinas's lengthy discussion of magnanimity — unsurprising given the subject's historical importance — covers many important topics, especially in his analysis of its deformations: pusillanimity [small souledness], presumption, vainglory, and ambition.)[19]

Underlying Aquinas' expansion is the distinction he makes between a broader and narrower meaning in courage:

> The term "courage" can be taken in two senses; first, . . .[as] steadfastness of mind, and in this case it is a general virtue or rather a condition of each and every virtue. . . . Secondly, courage can be taken as meaning firmness of mind in enduring or repulsing whatever make steadfastness outstandingly difficult; that is, particularly serious dangers.[20]

Steadfastness undergirds the continuity in response that defines all virtues. As a condition of the love that constitutes all virtues, it also informs hope about obtaining what is loved and distress about losing it. But the steadfastness that distinguishes courage from other virtues concerns only pronounced dangers, especially the death that may occur when a good is pursued.

Aquinas, following Aristotle, claims that warfare exemplifies a situation where people's pursuit of goods may produce death. But he widens considerably the meaning of warfare when he includes under it cases where, for example, "a judge or even a private individual refuses to be moved from a just decision by . . . any peril whatsoever. . . . [Or] when a man does not shrink from attendance on a sick friend for fear of deadly infection, or when he does not shrink from a journey on some matter of duty because of fear of shipwreck or bandits."[21] Aquinas expands the conception of warfare to encompass non-military situations where people face possible death. Moreover, he extends the range of meanings included in the idea of facing death. A pursuit of the good must be involved; "passive courage," meeting an inevitable fate, counts only if it involves adherence to a good. But death need not be as likely as it is in battle. It is enough to face a situation or pursue a goal that possibly might lead to death.

Aquinas, then, claims that courage as firmness or steadfastness underlies all virtues, but that courage's specific nature appears only when people pursue goods that lead them to face the danger presented by death. That claim serves many purposes. It allows him, for instance, to present a clearer conceptual analysis, to solve various technical problems about how to relate parts of the virtue, and to demonstrate how Aristotle's analysis helps to solve contemporary philosophical and theological problems. Aquinas's focus on the centrality of death in the idea of courage, however, also contains a deeper and more controversial claim.

He believes, I think, that every real fear we encounter prefigures our fear about death just as every confidence we feel rests on our confidence about meeting death. Actually facing death as a result of the pursuit of a good provides the paradigm for a host of more normal occasions in which people encounter dangers to help others or even to understand themselves. On such occasions, people risk their immediate well-being, accept insecurity, and abandon their usual self-centered hold on life. In all such situations, people must overcome their powerful desire for survival. That overcoming is extremely difficult to achieve, Aquinas thinks, because the desire has both natural roots in the inclination to self-preservation and spiritual roots in the necessary human affirmation of the goodness of being.

Every courageous act, then, has as its deepest root a readiness to die.

The truthfulness of such a claim is hardly obvious, and we need to examine Aquinas's reasons for asserting it. Aquinas's claim rests on two ideas. The first is that

> he who stands firm against greater evils naturally stands firm also against the lesser, though the converse is not true. [The second is that] a virtue by its nature always presses to its utmost objective. Now the most dread of all bodily ills is death, which removes all bodily goods. . . . Therefore the virtue of courage is concerned with the fears associated with dangers of death.[22]

The second, less significant, idea is defensible insofar as it means people can define a virtue best when they see its fullest expression. It is problematic insofar as it means that virtues inevitably tend to their fullest expression.

The first idea, that people who resist great evils also will resist lesser evils, is much more important and much less evidently defensible. Obvious counterexamples come to mind. We all know of people, for instance, who have acted heroically when confronted with the dangers that battle or deadly assault present and yet have reacted in a cowardly fashion when faced with racist or sexist behavior. Such examples seem to show that people's ability to stir themselves to heroic sacrifice is only contingently related to their ability to behave courageously in less dramatic situations. Courageous behavior may be manifested most clearly when people face the obvious threat of death. But that fact does not seem to imply the conclusion that what is manifested in those situations necessarily will appear in less dangerous situations.

An explication, and also defense, of Aquinas's claim can take two forms. The first relies on his notions that virtues manifest intelligent dispositions, and that an intelligent disposition expressed in a difficult situation always also will be expressed in less difficult situations. That is, the relationship between the two expressions is necessary not contingent; it arises from the very logic present in dispositional concepts. Counterexamples that purportedly show how heroic courage and normal courage are unrelated merely reveal that an observer has made a mistake about why a person behaved heroically. The dramatic act was a semblance of courage, and the observer failed to realize that. If a person faces death willingly in a war that aims to preserve the best American values and then mistreats blacks because they are blacks, we should realize that the intentions that animated the first action were not what we initially thought they were.

The second defense of Aquinas's claim rests on his idea that people's general perspective, their horizon, fundamentally informs their particular attitudes and actions. Aquinas assumes that people's perceptions of and reactions to specific events are controlled by the framework or horizon within which they place those events. A change in horizon therefore will generate many other changes. A horizon, for example, may lead a person to picture humans as hardy beings who control their own destiny, or at least to picture them in a way that does not highlight their frailty. Such an horizon will affect how the person sees and reacts to all that occurs in his or her life. If a recognition of death's role and the fragility it implies changes the horizon, most specific activities and perceptions also will change. The new horizon then will affect the ability to stand firm both in dramatic situations and ordinary ones. Indeed, the effect of the new framework often will be especially pronounced when lower stakes are involved — and therefore little conscious reflection occurs — than when more is at stake.[23]

Aquinas claims that people will resist lesser evil if they resist greater evil, and therefore that all courageous acts are rooted in a readiness to die. The claim rests, as said, on his ideas about the roles played by both horizons and dispositions. Moreover, his insistence on courage's relationship to death underlies his assertion that the chief activity of courage is not to attack but to endure. Endurance involves being both passively affected by outside events and actively clinging to a good. Aquinas, then, is arguing that, in many important ways, courage is more concerned with forming fear than with forming confidence.

The notion that courage is centrally concerned with *endurance* is extremely important, and an examination of it takes us into the heart of Aquinas's expanded sense of courage. Aquinas employs two kinds of arguments to explicate and defend the idea that endurance is courage's chief activity. One presents philosophical reasons and often echoes Aristotle's analysis. The other, more crucial one presents a variety of theological claims about the Christian's place in the world. The philosophical arguments hardly clinch Aquinas's case. His analysis rests on the idea that daring or even fearless people fail to persevere when some kinds of dangers become clear. But his claims about daring fail to cover all cases, and much of what his claims do cover fails even to qualify as courageous action. Moreover, he does not adequately account for two facts. The first is that, when failure is possible, unjustified confidence is at least as difficult to control as fear; and the second is that the mechanism for controlling both of them is a judgment of reason that effectively forms emotions and actions.[24]

Aquinas's philosophical arguments, however, do point toward a more interesting and justifiable position. Most important, they underscore his contention that acts of courage finally can be evaluated only in terms of an agents intentions, dispositions, and emotional states. The exact character of these components normally becomes clear (either to the agent or an out-sider) only if they can be studied in a variety of different manifestations extending over a long period of time. Short-term actions, then, rarely pro-vide the tests and information needed for astute evaluations. This contention reflects Aquinas's focus on the evaluation of character not acts. Moreover, the contention leads to the more theologically informed analysis of courage that underlies his emphasis on the importance of endurance in courage.

With the introduction of theological considerations, changes occur in both the concepts Aquinas uses and the form of analysis he employs. His agenda no longer is set mainly by Aristotle. The crucial concepts he uses now come from Stoic and especially Christian sources; perseverance and patience replace fear and daring as key ideas, for example. Most important, the focus of Aquinas's analysis shifts away from the components of a particular act of courage and the character it manifests. He now focuses on the general point of view, the specific way of existing in the world, that real courage represents. The analysis, then, moves from a consideration of the actions of people who encounter specific dangers to a consideration of a variety of human actions and attitudes, and a set of long-term undertakings, that fall under the umbrel-la of courage. Especially important to Aquinas is an analysis of the correct way for a Christian to encounter all those myriad difficulties that constitute a life lived on earth and in sin but directed to God and the beatific vision. Ideas drawn from his secondary theory, such as those about the character of grace, become more prominent. Most important to us, however, is his examination of a closely related group of concepts (allied virtues of courage) that are pre-sented to him by the discourse of his times and those traditions to which he is responsive. Most notable are *patience, perseverance,* and *forbearance.*

All three concern the kind of courage that long-term undertakings demand. Aquinas makes fine — at times overly fine — distinctions among the different ways people can endure over time. He also addresses, how-ever, the more general question of how Christians should operate in a world beset with difficulties and dangers. The endurance manifested in patience is most important to us, but we also need to treat briefly the two other virtues. They reflect Aquinas's normal distinction between the posi-tive and negative elements in an attitude, and they highlight an important distinction in endurance.

Forbearance (*longanimatas*), the negative element, refers to what occurs when people endure difficulty and pain over a length of time. Perseverance (*perseverantia*), the positive element, refers to what occurs when people's enduring is characterized by a continuing concentration on the good sought. Such a distinction may seem to be virtually meaningless, to be yet another example of how Aquinas labors to bring together the divergent discourses of (forbearance) differs significantly from moving through a task largely because of an attachment to the goal sought (perseverance). The buoyancy and probable productivity of the persevering often contrasts sharply with the long-suffering demeanor and probable inefficiency of the forbearing. Moreover, we never are inclined to wonder why the persevering continues, but with the forbearing we often may wonder.

Nevertheless, both perseverance and forbearance usually are necessary, and either alone may reveal a deformed character and result in a project's failure. The persevering, for example, may be overcome by difficulties that they had failed properly to attend to; they can unexpectedly stop, declaring themselves completely, if suddenly, overwhelmed by the problems involved. The forbearing usually will persist, but they can be so constantly downcast that their persistence manifests only a habitual action or a virtually unrecoverable second order motive. The distinction between perseverance and forbearance therefore enables us to give a more finely grained analysis of endurance over time than we otherwise could give. It also highlights (although Aquinas rarely emphasizes this) that perseverance's adherence to a good is closer to the best state than is forbearance's emphasis on difficulties. Here as elsewhere the good rather than the difficult provides the final criterion of value.[25]

The distinction between the two may be relatively insignificant when all that is involved is the completion of some ordinary task, such as finishing a manuscript. But when the subject is people's relationship to God, when it concerns the quality of their life as pilgrims who face difficulties — as people "on the way" (*status viatoris*) — the distinction can be of crucial importance. Christians, Aquinas thinks, must adhere to the goal sought and manifest both the joy and the equilibrium generated by the theological virtues. This, however, should not preclude real contact with the sadness that events in life produce.[26]

Indeed, this particular combination of sadness and joy in the religious realm is the subject matter of patience. With patience, then, we see the full theological content of the idea that endurance is courage's chief activity. That is, we see why the essence of religious courage appears clearly only when all that it is possible to achieve is a special kind of enduring. Patience forms the sadness or dejection that is the last of the three emotions with which courage deals. It represents the ultimate religious form that courage attains, unless a rare, direct prompting by God (a Gift of the Holy Spirit) allows a person to transcend the need to form any contending appetites. Let us, then, examine the final two manifestations of courage.

V. Aquinas on Courage's Specifically Religious Dimension, the Virtue of Patience, and the Highest Religious Dimension, the Gift of Courage

Aquinas claims that patience (*patientia*) depends on grace's direct action and therefore has only a supernatural form. He also portrays what appears to be a natural form of patience, however. This seeming confusion between what Aquinas says and what he does probably is best explained by assuming patience's focal meaning is religious and its secondary meaning is natural. In any event, examining the natural form helps us grasp the distinctive character of the religious form.

Patience as a natural virtue enables people to endure all those difficulties that arise from the sadness produced by the loss of desired goods. As Aquinas says, "a man is said to be patient . . . because of praiseworthy conduct in enduring immediate injuries in such a way as not to be unduly dejected by them." The injuries endured include those that arise from the suffering of others, as people generally desire that human beings should not be made unhappy without reason. Patience thus protects people from the dejection that comes either when they are unable to obtain what they themselves desire or when they see other people's legitimate desires thwarted in an undeserved way. Patience is the "virtue which preserves the good of reason (*bonum rationis*) against dejection (*tristitiam*), to ensure that reason does not yield to it."[27]

Although dejection is its main concern, patience also indirectly affects the fear and confidence with which normal courage deals. It helps to form those specific fears that arise from clearly perceived risks. More important, it can transform timidity, that overarching attitude to risk, arising from temperament and a general view of the world, which constitutes confidence's deficiency. Patience's indirect effect on both of these emotions arises, however, from how it relates to dejection. Dejection (*tristitia*) is one of the six categories into which the affective appetites are divided. As pleasure's (*delectatio*) contrary, it refers to what occurs when a person cannot reach and enjoy a loved object, and it normally is translated as dejection, sadness, or sorrow.

Dejection exemplifies the cognitive or interpretative character of emotions. Unjust injury and thwarted aspiration are, of course, constant features of life. Responses to them, however, and thus dejection's exact character, always depend on a person (or a culture's) overall perspective or horizon. That is, the responses will rest on what goals are valued, what expectations considered legitimate, and what failures thought inevitable. Specific problems always threaten people's happiness or undermine it, but people's belief's determine which of them produces dejection. The effect of people' beliefs on the dejection they feel leads Aquinas to differentiate kinds of dejection. He focuses on dejection as a religious phenomenon, as a reaction that arises from a set of distinctively Christian beliefs.[28]

A true understanding of created things, for Aquinas, includes an insuperable sadness, and dejection must reflect it. Patience will form that dejection so that it does not debilitate a person, but its formation will be political, will respect the integrity of the emotion. Sadness that rests on Christian beliefs neither can nor should be lifted by natural means; it reflects a correct view of the world and is useful. Indeed, Aquinas thinks that this judgment about the place of sadness in a fully flourishing life shows a crucial difference between Stoic and Christian ideas. He believes, for example, that Christ's suffering on the cross exemplifies the role of sorrow in defining a true religious vision. Moreover, the Beatitude "blessed are those that mourn for they shall be comforted," he thinks, contains a similar meaning. As he puts it, in discussing the motives behind the Beatitude: "Knowledge, through which one knows the deficiencies in himself and in worldly things, is the chief motive for mourning, according to what is written, *He who increases knowledge, increases sorrow* [Ecclesiasticus 1:18]." True understanding of the world and the self, then, necessarily involves sadness. Such understanding also makes clear that real goodness often can manifest itself only in powerlessness and thus endurance. Aquinas argues, for instance, that the Beatitude declaring that those who hunger and thirst after justice will be filled, a Beatitude associated with the Gift of Courage, refers only to a supernatural fulfillment. The world, he thinks, rarely satisfies those who pursue natural justice. Enduring evil and grasping firmly the good that enables them to persevere often will be all that can characterize such a pursuit. Christians who honestly face themselves and the world, for Aquinas, must be dejected. They must be saddened by their own frailty, by the suffering present in the world, and by their inability to change either fundamentally.[29]

The deep dejection this somber picture produces is what patience must both honor and control in its formation of the emotion. The emotion's integrity, the cognitive judgment it manifests, must be respected and even, at times, followed. But people can be unduly affected by such sadness and patience must stop that from happening. Patience must prevent people from falling into depression, despair, or even spiritual apathy (*acedia*), states that lead them to fail to pursue the goods they can and must. As Aquinas says, "Patience is to ensure that we do not abandon virtue's good through dejection of this kind."[30] Patience, then, allows people to be properly saddened by their own and the world's state and yet also to remain unimpeded in their pursuit of and adherence to valuable goals.

The two sides evident in patience — dejection and the overcoming of it — represent in microcosm the two-sided attitude Christians always should display. They should be "in but not of the world," they should be involved with normal life and its sorrows and also attentive to a higher, finer reality. The endurance manifest in patience differs sharply from the joyless, self-immolating attitude that, for some people in Aquinas's time, characterized Christian endurance. Patience endures, but it is not dominated by sadness or grief. As Aquinas writes, in commenting on the phrase (in Luke 21:19) "in patience you shall possess your souls," "Possession connotes peaceful rule. So a man is said to possess his soul by patience in so far as he utterly uproots the feelings, aroused by hardships, which trouble the soul."[31]

Patience, then, contains joy, manifests peaceful rule, and yet faces the sadness present in life. This fundamental, and complex, Christian attitude is manifested so clearly in patience that Aquinas thinks grace must empower it and charity be present in it. As he says:

> The soul hates pain and sorrow in themselves, and so would never choose to suffer them for their own sake but only for some end. Therefore it is necessary that the good for whose sake someone is willing to suffer evils should be more desired and loved than that good whose absence inflicts grief which we patiently bear. But that someone should prefer the good which is grace before all natural goods whose loss can give rise to grief, involves charity, which loves God above all things. From this it is evident that patience as a virtue is an effect of charity.[32]

In normal life, people are patient about many matters. Almost all will be patient about painful things, such as medicine or fever, that enable them to regain bodily health. Most will be patient about those passing moments of acute dejection that arise either from personal failure or the recognition of another's pain. But the dejection Aquinas focuses on arises only when people are constantly sensitive both to their own failures and to the general suffering evident in the world.

Most important, this true dejection arises only if people measure themselves and the world against two things. One is the standard provided by the transcendent sacrality of God and the other is God's presence, through charity, in their own lives. The recognition of both that standard and that presence, and the distance of normal life from each of them, is characteristic of the deep dejection patience forms. Recognizing them however, also produces the joy (*gaudium*) that is an effect of charity and can be combined with sadness. This joy that makes us delight (*gaudet*) in the divine good as shared by us . . . can be impeded by something contrary to it, [so that] our joy can be mingled with sadness (*tristitiae*), in the sense that we grieve over what opposes this participation (*participationi*) in the divine good in ourselves, or in our neighbors, whom we love as ourselves.[33]

Neither a simple recognition of evil nor a simple suffering of evil for the sake of a future good is what truly patient people face. Both the dejection they face and the future good they pursue, sense intimations of, and even participate in are far greater than what a normal person encounters. Patience occurs only when people combine two different, even apparently paradoxical, attitudes. They must judge the sadness of earthly life by means of the standard evident in God's goodness, expectations, and just judgment. Yet they also must adhere to two goods: the future good of possible union with God and the present good evident in God's manifestations in the world and participation in people's lives. Both sides of the attitude are crucial. A person's sadness must persist in extremely intense form. However, it must not overwhelm a pursuit of the good, an accurate recognition of its manifest forms, and a correct belief about the world's ultimate character. This attitude is distinctive enough that it can arise, Aquinas thinks, only from the theological virtues. Charity's friendship with God is most crucial, but the attitude manifest in patience also rests on faith and displays the mean between presumption and despair that appears in hope.

Patience's character can be illuminated, as was ordinary courage's character, by examining its semblances. Aquinas never undertakes such an examination, but I will develop one by applying to patience his analysis of normal courage's five semblances: simple ignorance, tempered optimism, acquired skill, perceived advantage, and spiritedness. The three semblances of courage that arise from the faulty workings of practical wisdom resemble three semblances of patience, but the theological virtues, especially faith, usually play the role in the religious realm that practical wisdom plays in the natural realm. The semblance constituted by ignorance arises when people fail to possess either the trust that the theological virtues produce or the dejection that an understanding of the world's injustice ought to produce. That is, it arises when people fail to maintain the distinctive, two-sided attitude that characterizes patience. Similarly, the semblance of tempered optimism appears when people either rest too confidently on their past experiences of overcoming dejection or manifest a phlegmatic or unreflective disposition at inappropriate times. Their optimism, then, reflects a flawed hope that is close to dullness or presumption. It displays an untempered attitude that expresses itself in the naive belief that all will turn out for the best.

A major source for such an attitude can be people's untutored reliance on acquired religious practices that resemble skills. Unlike skills, these practices cannot always produce results, and the agent's interior state is important. Nevertheless, reorienting the self when suffering occurs by means of prayer, sacraments, and holy texts involves using practices that resemble skills. That is, as with acquired skills in normal courage, these religious skills play an important role in nurturing true patience. However, they can hinder a person from perceiving accurately and then reacting correctly.

These three semblances of patience all rest on faulty forms of understanding. Each fails to reflect the two-sided attitude that arises from a true understanding both of human finitude and sin and of divine goodness and power. An especially debased form of deficient religious understanding appears when people act from perceived advantage to gain an advantage or avoid a disadvantage. In such cases, the belief that overcomes dejection arises just from a balancing of fears. A person pursues God's goodness simply because the fear of eternal damnation outweighs other fears. In Aquinas's language, such people act from servile fear not filial fear. They follow a rule or pursue commendation because they fear punishment. They do not act from love of the person who promulgates the rule; they do not desire to please the person by pursuing the way of life the person represents. Servile fear, Aquinas thinks, has a legitimate role in the preliminary stages of the religious life. Indeed, its role resembles the one perceived advantage plays in the acquisition of true courage. The need for servile fear, however, is greater because God's character is understood less easily than the character of most objects of courageous action. Nevertheless, servile fear ultimately must be replaced by filial fear for true virtue to exist. People must respond just to God's goodness not to the advantage that God can produce for them.

The last semblance of courage, spiritedness, may appear to have few religious analogues. A natural buoyancy of spirit, however, can help people overcome or moderate dejection. But this buoyancy easily can distort the theological virtue of hope and the supernatural virtue of patience, as each of them relies on a clear perception of what legitimately generate sadness. Moreover, other emotional reactions that could fit within the category of spiritedness can warp the supernatural virtues. Natural reverence, wonder, or love, for example, are all laudatory, but they can distort the two-sided attitude patience manifests. Their proper role resembles anger's proper role when it aids courage's exercise but is formed by practical wisdom. In all these cases, "natural" emotional reactions are valuable in themselves and may be extremely helpful. But they need to be formed by a correct spiritual perspective or only a semblance of virtue appears.

The supernatural virtue of patience, then, can be said, to have five semblances that resemble ordinary courage's semblances. Examining them illuminates the distinctive kind of enduring the virtue manifests and reveals the deformed kinds of enduring to which it is liable. The endurance that patience represents manifests the highest religious form courage normally attains. An extraordinary, direct prompting of God, however, can produce a state that exceeds the state present in patience, that found in the Gift of Courage. Aquinas says little about this Gift, but what he does say is extremely important in itself and for our comparison with Mencius.

The Gifts, as noted earlier, are dispositions that make people more responsive to the Holy Spirit's promptings or more obedient to them. Actions manifesting the disposition that is the Gift of Courage, then, will depend directly on the actions of the Holy Spirit. In such actions, the Gift of Courage produces a state where a person, say a martyr, is "protected against the dread of dangers" in a very distinctive manner. Aquinas describes it in the following fashion:

> The Holy Spirit moves the human mind further [than the steadfast-ness of normal courage], in order that one may reach the end of any work begun and avoid threatening dangers of any kind. This tran-scends human nature, for sometimes it does not lie within human power to attain the end of one's work, or to escape evils or dangers, since these sometimes press in upon us to the point of death. But the Holy Spirit achieves this in us when he leads us to eternal life, which is the end of all good works and the escape from all dangers. And he pours into our mind a certain confidence (*fiduciam*) that this will be, refusing to admit the opposing fear.

The Holy Spirit generates confidence about an eternal reward, not about earthly success, and that confidence literally excludes the fear that a person normally would feel. The difference the Gift makes is truly monumental. As Aquinas says: "Courage as a virtue make the mind competent to endure any dangers. But it has not the resources to make us confident (*fiduciam*) of escaping each and every danger; this is the role of that courage which is the Gift of the Holy Spirit."[34] People do not simply endure dangers they know may destroy most or all of what they value. Instead, they are assured that they are protected against all dangers. Their confidence, it seems, includes more than just an assurance about what will happen in the future. They also feel assurance about the meaning of those signs that ensure them the Holy Spirit moves them and that they are participating in the relationship of friendship with God that characterizes charity.

Indeed, the presence of charity and its accompanying Gift, the Gift of Wisdom, means that people are fundamentally changed. I already have discussed how charity changes people, but we need here to examine the operations of the Gift of Wisdom that accompanies it, as those operations help to explain the confidence evident in the Gift of Courage. The Gift of Wisdom contains both theoretical and practical dimensions. The confidence felt, then, has both cognitive and affective aspects, but it rests largely on love. Knowledge, for Aquinas, operates by taking the object known into the knower, and thus is subject to the limitations of the knower. Love, however, can move subjects beyond themselves and into a relationship with an object different from them and, in this case, transcending them.

This position, critical to understanding how the Gift of Wisdom operates, leads Aquinas to make claims that some might think surprising to find in him. He says, for example, that "a man can make his way to God more swiftly and surely when he is drawn passively through love (*amor*) by God himself, than through the activity of his own reason." This claim rests, in turn, on the general notion that it "can therefore happen that a thing is loved better than it is known (*cognoscatur*), for it can be loved perfectly without being known perfectly." Moreover, even the very operation of the animating love will only be grasped imperfectly. Movements of love, unlike movements of knowledge, lack their own proper vocabulary. Imprecision in terminology and a lack of full conceptual understanding, therefore, must accompany investigations into love's activities and effects. The role of love in the confidence that characterizes the Gift of Courage means that its confidence never can be put in clear propositional form. It can neither be defended adequately nor even understood fully. Nevertheless, those features of love and the necessary obscurity they produce, Aquinas thinks, do not diminish either the power or the significance of the confidence felt.[35]

The confidence present in the Gift of Courage, in turn, produces a state where the contending emotions' character changes fundamentally. Aquinas boldly describes the new state when he declares:

> Now virtue restrains man from following the irascible [contending] emotions in not allowing him to go beyond the rule of reason; but the Gifts restrain him from them in a more excellent way, viz. so as to leave him completely tranquil, in accordance with the will of God (*donum autem excellentiori modo, ut scilicet homo, secundum voluntatem divinam, totaliter ab eis tranquillus reddatur*).[36]

Aquinas speaks here about a state of being in which the Holy Spirit's actions generate a confidence that excludes fear and leaves a person completely tranquil. The direct action of deity produces a state where a preservative virtue becomes an inclinational virtue. Adverse movements no longer need to be resisted; only animating inclinations are present. Neither present psychological states nor actual tendencies must be corrected by the preservative virtue. The only correction that occurs, then, is of a general human tendency.

In this state, courage ceases to exhibit any of its distinctive marks. The defining structure of external goals, internal goals, and objectionable results disappears. Courage, therefore, will no longer be characterized by evident conflicts among goals, the necessary presence of contrary inclinations, and the need for executive control, a second order of motivations. The division and reflexivity that normally defines actions involving the contending emotions are replaced by the harmonious action that characterizes inclinational virtues. Indeed, if we use this form of courage as a standard, all lesser forms of courage are only semblances of courage.

The perfection described here, furthermore, displays affective and cognitive qualities that differ in fundamental ways from the qualities that normally characterize human life. In this state, people's practical wisdom operates in a most extraordinary fashion. Perfected people deliberate and decide by means of a special participation in and grasp of God and His will. Moreover, they possess a new ability to form themselves, and it provides a very distinctive kind of motivation. Total assurance apparently replaces the normal doubt that informs any action of practical reason and almost all aspects of faith. Similarly, complete tranquility replaces all forms of perturbation, apparently even those that dejection produces. The Gift of Courage, then, manifests a state that passes beyond not only normal courage but even the integral religious manifestations of courage that patience displays.

Aquinas's analysis of courage, I think, moves from normal courage to the religious courage found in patience to that distinctive form the Gift of Courage presents. He treats normal courage as the virtue that protects practical wisdom's activities against the difficulties the contending appetites produce. He goes on to treat patience's formation of sorrow, however, and ends with an examination of that apparently rare kind of perfected courage where no contending appetites appear. Courage, then, forms three possible hindrances to following tempered judgments, with failures in any of these formations producing semblances of courage: the emotions of fear, confidence, and sorrow. The formation of fear and confidence characterize normal courage, and the formation of sorrow characterizes patience. The expansion of the concept of courage into the religious realm found in patience is completed by the transcendence of all kinds of formation evident in the Gift of Courage. Striking similarities, as well as noteworthy differences, are present in Mencius's treatment of courage and to that subject we may now turn.

VI. Mencius's General Conception of Courage and the Importance of Proper Self-Respect

Mencius's presentation of courage differs remarkably from Aquinas's. He provides little analysis that even vaguely resembles Aquinas's analysis of the structure of a courageous act, the various parts of courage, or the different emotions with which courage is concerned. He never makes and argues at length for complicated claims such as that endurance is courage's defining mark or that every act of courage involves a willingness to die. Indeed, if intellectual sophistication equals a version of what Aquinas does then Mencius's treatment of courage is woefully unsophisticated. Different kinds of intellectual sophistication surely exist, however, and in comparative studies we must be especially wary of giving undue privilege to any single approach. (This counsel may be especially apt in this case because we have evidence that Mencius could do more rigorous analysis when he chose.) We see in Mencius, I think, a powerful and sophisticated examination of courage.

Moreover, the topics Mencius covers usually fit many of those that appear in Aquinas's analyses of courage. Mencius, for example, focuses on the role of the more comprehensive goals that courageous people pursue, examines the place of different kinds of confidence, and analyzes semblances of courage. Furthermore, he treats, in a most distinctive fashion, questions about the cultivation of courage and the place of reason and the emotions in its exercise. Finally, closer examination also can enable us to see connections between topics in the two thinkers that we initially may have thought were unrelated. (The opportunity to see connections that we might otherwise miss, as discussed earlier, is one of the benefits of comparative studies.) One example we will discuss at length is the relationship between Mencius's ideas on the "unmoved mind" (*pu tung hsin*), "fate" (*ming*), and Heaven (*T'ien*) and Aquinas's understanding of patience and the Gift of Courage.

The way in which Mencius examines these topics differs considerably, often radically, from the way in which Aquinas does. But the very differences in the style of presentation and extent of analysis present important and fascinating problems to us as comparativists. The methodological implications of such differences will be treated in the final chapter when we discuss how best to choose focal and secondary terms and establish systematic relationships among apparently discrete virtues. Now, however, I will examine Mencius's analysis of courage, concentrating, as was the case with Aquinas, on the details of his account. (The interpretative process, of course, will differ from the one used with Aquinas because Mencius's aims and modes of presentation often differ.) However, I will utilize the analysis of Aquinas already done to compare briefly the two thinkers' ideas, especially when the subject is courage's expanded religious forms. General comparisons between the two, nevertheless, will appear only in the final chapter; and the constructive feature of this enterprise will be displayed only in my evaluation of specific ideas or arguments.

Courage is a very important virtue for Mencius. But he does not include it among the four basic virtues, to which he returns constantly, that he says define human nature: righteousness, benevolence, propriety, and intelligent awareness. Moreover, none of those virtues resemble courage or fulfill the exact functions it does. Mencius's view of the role of courage is especially striking because it contrasts with the views found in a significant strand of the early Confucian tradition. In that strand, courage is considered to be a central virtue. In the *Analects* of Confucius, for example, courage (*yung*) twice is specifically linked with two virtues that Mencius does think are central: benevolence (*jen*) and intelligent awareness (*chih*). Moreover, the *Doctrine of the Mean* (*Chung Yung*), a very influential work often thought to be part of the Mencian stream of Confucianism, quotes Confucius as saying: "Wisdom, benevolence and courage, these three are virtues universally acknowledged [or binding] in the Empire." This highlighting of courage does combine with a recognition that its value always depends on the goals served. When Confucius is asked, for instance, if the gentleman considers courage a supreme quality he replies: "For the gentleman it is morality (*yi*) that is supreme. Possessed of courage but devoid of morality, a gentleman will make trouble while a small man will be brigand."[37] Nevertheless, the emphasis on courage's importance persists.

The exclusion of courage from Mencius's list of four central virtues probably occurs for three related reasons. First, he focuses on those four virtues to show that inclinations toward ethical action are natural. Courage, however, is not an inclinational virtue, and few could doubt humans naturally display at least some form of courage. Second, Mencius tends to see all virtues as arising from impulse or affective emotions, a tendency reinforced by his reliance on a developmental model of human nature. This leads him to think inclinational virtues, like benevolence, are the paradigmatic virtues. Moreover, it also leads him to picture perfected virtuous action as spontaneous, free of real conflict, and simply pleasurable. Ordinary courage, however, is a preservative virtue; moreover, reflexivity, some form of conflict, and a complicated relationship to pleasure define it.

Third, Mencius worries (perhaps even more than Confucius) about the horrible consequences that can accompany a misunderstanding of courage's role in the virtuous life. He lived in an age when military ideals and adventures wreaked real havoc and often corrupted visions of human excellence. Sensible people in his time (like some in our time) questioned whether courage, as it is usually understood, fit only with a harsh age and a questionable idea of true heroism. Mencius's response to this problem was to expand the meaning of courage and to distinguish true courage from its semblances. Like Aquinas, then, he reinterpreted true courage, focusing on how it differs from its semblances, and expanded it into a religious realm. Features of his reinterpretation (as we will see) resemble closely aspects of Aquinas's understanding of, for example, the meaning of confidence, the control of fear, the place of a willingness to die, and the role of endurance. Mencius, however, even less than Aquinas, was wedded to the centrality of the military ideal of courage. Aquinas drew on a tradition, evident even in Aristotle's own reinterpretation of heroic courage, that still focused on the military meaning of courage. That tradition's ideas remained important to Aquinas, despite his massive transformation of it, in a way that no similar tradition was important to Mencius. This means that Mencius, in some instances, can carry forward aspects of Aquinas's deeper intent more easily, and perhaps more completely, than Aquinas.[38]

Even though Mencius does not portray courage as one of his four central virtues, he clearly does think courage is a crucial component in the good life. At one level, he focuses on the importance of courage as steadfastness, to use Aquinas's term for courage's broader meaning. Courage defined this way is what fuels self-cultivation and enables a person to overcome the myriad difficulties that confront anyone who pursues virtuousness. In fact, Mencius eloquently claims that all virtue's highest forms arise only through the courageous overcoming of those adversities caused either by one's self or by outside events. As he says:

> Heaven, when it is about to place a great burden on a man, always first tests his resolution, exhausts his frame and makes him suffer starvation and hardship, frustrates his efforts so as to shake him from his mental lassitude, toughen his nature and make good his deficiencies. . . . Only then do we learn the lesson that we survive in adversity and perish in ease and comfort.[39]

Overcoming adversity courageously, then, underlies any high human realization.

Indeed, one distinguishing mark of a sage is "strength." Although Mencius never precisely distinguishes between the kinds of ways in which people can endure over time, this strength resembles, in Aquinas's terms, perseverance not forbearance. That is, the sage has the ability to persevere through difficulties and to maintain a grip on what should animate a human being. As he says, in a passage that discusses various kinds of excellences:

> To begin in an orderly fashion is the concern of the wise while to end in an orderly fashion is the concern of a sage. Intelligent awareness is like

skill, shall I say, while sageness is like strength. It is like shooting from beyond a hundred paces. It is due to your strength that the arrow reaches the target, but it is not due to your strength that it hits the mark.[40]

Mencius thinks any pursuit of ideals involves a person in conflicts that demand the exercise of courage. Furthermore, as we will see, he often focuses on situations where correct action involves considerable sacrifice, perhaps even the sacrifice of one's life.

Underlying all such conflicts and possible sacrifices, and thus Mencius's understanding of courage, is the issue of what characterizes genuine honor, what constitutes true self-respect. Mencius shifts the focus of discussions about courage from overcoming physical fear to overcoming impediments to true self-respect. He thereby moves the discussion from a context where the relevant emotion often is objectively understandable to one where the emotion's context, and thus force, depends upon the interpretation given it by people and their culture. This change in context also enables Mencius to claim that most people fail to understand the real foundations of self-respect. The actualization of the qualities that Heaven gives constitutes, he thinks, the basis of true self-respect; and only a few people really recognize and value those qualities.

Mencius's project, then, resembles the one in which Aquinas is involved. Aristotle changes the standard of true honor from what conventionally respectable, often military, people honor to what good people honor. Aquinas, in turn, changes the standard to what God honors (and finally will judge), arguing that good people's judgments reflect but sometimes distort the ultimate standard. Mencius lacks the kind of secondary theory that informs, and makes clear, Aquinas's change, but he does contrast, for instance, the honors bestowed by humans and the honors bestowed by Heaven. Moreover, their practical theories about these changes contain some remarkable resemblances. Aquinas's treatment of confidence, for example, involves analyzing many of the same issues that appear when Mencius treats proper self-respect. Similarly, Aquinas's examination of magnanimity, a part of courage, often turns on answering questions about the appropriate grounds for honor. Let us, then, examine Mencius's account of what in Thomistic terms would be called several of the key *parts of courage* or elements that underlie it.[41]

We should not read modern ideas about the importance of self-respect into Mencius's culture. People in that culture valued the ideal of individual integrity less than most moderns and evaluated people in terms of their performance of given social roles more than most moderns. But any culture contains, if only implicitly, complicated pictures of what people should be, should do, and should allow to have done to them both as

they inhabit roles and as they move among roles and therefore are captured by no single role. These pictures underlie notions of self-respect,
notions of what one ought honor both in one's self and in others. In fact,
the distribution of sanctions (such as punishment, prestige, wealth, and
power) that rest on those notions is a concern of most thinkers in any culture. That concern becomes especially pronounced if, in the culture,
divergent pictures of human flourishing conflict with each other, with
accepted ideas about injunctions, or with new pictures that innovative
thinkers present. Mencius faced a situation of this sort. Various positions
on the basis of true self-respect were in conflict. Each had different ideas
on the goals courageous action should pursue and therefore each contained different judgments on courage's character.

Five of these positions can be extrapolated from Mencius's writings
and be said to constitute, for him, the semblances of true courage. Several
of them will be examined at length later, but, sketched briefly, the five are
as follows. People in one group accepted a military ideal that valued
beyond life itself the ability to stand up bravely against real or imagined
insults to one's self or one's community. In another group, people thought
self-respect arises from the praise and positions given by those in power
and believed everyone should valiantly pursue them. Still another group
was constituted by conventional, often priggish moralists who clung to an
untextured view of social forms; they would protect heroically rules and
institutions that should be changed. These three kinds of people, the last
two of whom are variants of Mencius's "village honest person," were
prone to endanger themselves or others in order to achieve dubious goals.

The last two positions are more philosophically sophisticated.
Proponents of one, evident in strands of Mohism, argue the kind of rational
deliberation that produces rules constitutes real human excellence and thus
underlies true self-respect. Courage's role is to protect such deliberations and
help people follow those rules that reason produces. Proponents of the other
position (surely evident in strands of early Taoism and probably part of
Yangism) argue for a kind of "refined cowardliness" in which people aim only
to protect themselves. These thinkers argue that almost nothing is so valuable
that people ought to die or even imperil themselves for it. Courage is the ability to resist the calls to sacrifice that many ethical, religious, or social leaders
make, unless such resistance in itself threatens to bring destruction.[42]

All five of these semblances are versions, albeit in a substantially different context, of that general semblance of courage Aquinas thinks arises
when people lack a comprehensive enough view of human flourishing.
What Aquinas calls a solicitude about temporal concerns, with its lack of a
more general perspective on life's ultimate goals, informs all of Mencius's
semblances. None of Aquinas's five other semblances, however, easily map

onto Mencius's five semblances. Nevertheless, it is worth noting briefly how Mencius and Aquinas's semblances relate to each other.

The semblances in Aquinas that rests on spiritedness has perhaps the closest analogue; that is, to those whom Mencius says embrace the military ideal. The semblance resting on perceived advantage resembles especially that semblance where people pursue the praise of the powerful. It also resembles, if less clearly, the semblance where people defend the conventional. In each case, if particularly in the first, people balances what they mistakenly think are commensurable goods. Finally, the semblance of acquired skill bears a faint resemblance to that found in refined cowardliness, and still fainter is the relationship between tempered optimism and the semblance, in Mencius, of those who rely too much on the protection of the kind of deliberation that produces rules. That is, skills allow people to escape danger and tempered optimism arises from a belief in the efficacy of one's practices. Whatever may be the resemblances, however, the distinctions are equally striking, especially with all except the first two of the five. On this subject Mencius's aims and modes of analysis contrast sharply with Aquinas's, except when the topic is how a person's general view of human flourishing should inform specific judgments.

Mencius criticizes these five pictures by questioning their ideas about self-respect or honor. He believes the embryonic virtues given by Heaven constitutes the distinctively human, the basis for true respect. Everyone possess something that far exceeds what any mere human could give to them, but most fail to realize it because they fail to attend as they should. As Mencius says: "All men share the same desire to be exalted. But as a matter of fact, every man has in him that which is exalted. The fact simply never dawned on him [fu ssu; i.e., he has not attended to it]. What man exalts is not truly exalted." Mencius's claim rests on distinguishing sharply between what comes from Heaven and what comes from man, and he employs that distinction to reinterpret the basis of respect. Using people who pursue political honor (our second kind of semblance) as his example, he puts it this way:

> There are honors bestowed by Heaven, and there are honors bestowed by man. Benevolence, dutifulness, conscientiousness, truthfulness to one's words, unflagging delight in what is good — these are the honors bestowed by Heaven. The position of a Ducal Minister, a Minister, or a Counsellor is an honor bestowed by man . . . . Men of today bend their efforts towards acquiring honors bestowed by Heaven in order to win honors bestowed by man, and once the latter is won they discard the former. Such men are deluded to the extreme, and in the end are sure only to perish.[43]

Most people, Mencius thinks, both use their desire for self-respect and develop their Heaven-given capacities only in the service of conventional social ideals. He, however, wants to harness the energy manifest in that desire and those capacities and turn it in directions that lead people to respect themselves in the right ways.

The task, he thinks, is to convince people that a true regard for the self arises from a respect for and cultivation of those natural capacities that arise from Heaven. Actualizing those capacities will involve courage, but the courage needed differs from what most people think courage is. Mencius, then, aims to reorient people's ideas about what is valuable and therefore also to reinterpret common views of courage, by showing that courage is a virtue that enables people to reach full human excellence. His understanding of exactly how courage helps people manifest the true development of their Heaven-given capacities is our next topic, and to it we turn.

VII. Mencius's Understanding of Perfected Courage: The Specific Features of His Analysis

My discussion of Mencius's account of perfected courage begins with an examination of specific texts, ideas, and even controversies that contain his account or illuminate it. I then turn, in the following section, to a more theoretical account of Mencius's understanding of the character and operations of perfected courage, relating it briefly to what Aquinas called the *Gift of Courage*. I end, in the last section, by examining how Mencius expands the idea of courage and makes it underlie the appropriate religious attitude toward legitimate sources of frustration and sadness. This expansion resembles that found in Aquinas's treatment of *patience*, and I will also discuss that resemblance. Let us begin, however, by examining several key issues and ideas that inform Mencius's understanding of courage.

Mencius's account of perfected courage arises from his rethinking of those common ideas on courage, semblances of courage to him, that most in his day affirmed. Those who saw the warrior as the paradigm of courage, as discussed, were even less important to Mencius than to Aquinas. Nevertheless, he remains indebted to the ideas he reinterpreted, including those found in the ideal of the warrior. (That debt may help to explain, incidentally, the lack of a notion of supererogation in Mencius.) Specific qualities characterize both the soldier and the sage, qualities like endurance, resolution, loyalty, vigor, skill, and quick adaptation to changing circumstances. Moreover, a military ideal and Mencius's spiritual ideals contain other less obvious connections. People who represent both ideals operate in a world that displays heroic dimensions; they often will find pallid the normal concern for petty matters and prudential accommodations to the unpleasant or unethical. Dramatic confrontations rather than sensible adjustments mark both worlds, as does the notion that people are caught up in battles in which everything of value can be gained or lost. The significance of the goals sought and the difficulties encountered are similar. Both these features distinguish their worlds from the ordinary one of compromise, adjustment, and caution.

Despite these connections one crucial difference distinguishes perfected courage and other lesser forms of courage. Perfected courage alone relies on consulting, developing, and following all the virtues that define human nature. Mencius alludes to this difference when he distinguishes between small and large valor in a discussion with King Hsüan. (The discussion also shows Mencius's understanding of how courage's expansionistic character leads to disastrous results when it informs political judgments about the need for war.) The king, who enjoys noting his own weakness, declares that Mencius's words are grand but that he is fond of valor. Mencius then responds: "I beg you not to be fond of small valor. To look fierce, putting your hand on your sword and say, 'How dare he oppose me!' is to show the valor of a common fellow which is of use only against a single adversary. You should make it something great." Great valor, for Mencius, is exemplified by King Wen and King Wu, two sage kings; they "brought peace to the people of the Empire in one outburst of rage." That is, through vigorous internal and external action they produced a proper social order. They overcame attackers, administered appropriate justice and education, and even ensured that "bullies" — improper exemplars of courage — did not thrive.[44]

A similar distinction is examined in a much more complicated way in a lengthy passage composed largely of logia and aphorisms. The relevant parts of the passage are elliptical, even cryptic, but various ideas of critical importance to Mencius's account of courage appear in it, and other passages can be used to shed light on these ideas. The passage opens with Mencius being asked if his failure to change a king's actions has "moved his mind"; that is, caused him anguish. Mencius replies, "It does not; I have not moved my mind [pu tung hsin; it has not been agitated] since I was forty." This leads the interlocutor, who praises Mencius's achievement, to ask, "Is there a way not to move the mind?"[45] The wide-ranging discussion this question sparks uses courage as its primary example. Threats to the desired equanimity are present especially in situations that demand courage. Moreover, many may have equated the possession of an unmoved mind with the kind of courage shown by people involved in military affairs. Mencius aims to show that the actions of most such people represent only semblances of courage. They misunderstand the real basis of self-respect. Therefore what they feel confident about and what they fear, and thus their courage, is flawed.

One such figure noted in the passage, Pei-kung Yu, returns any insults no matter by whom they are given; another, Meng Shih-she, concerns himself neither with victory nor defeat but only with the absence of fear. Both, in different ways, manifest inadequately the defining qualities of virtue. Intelligent awareness does not guide them; their responses are governed instead by rules, by obedience to others, or even by invariant reactions. Moreover, righteousness and benevolence play almost no role in their action, and the yielding that produces propriety seems to be rejected totally. Neither manifests the exemplary kind of courage Confucius described to a disciple.

> I once learned of great acts of courage from the Master [Confucius]: If upon turning inward I should find that I am not "ethically correct" (*so*), then although my enemy is but a coarsely clad servant would I not be made to gasp in fright by him? But if upon turning inward I find that I am ethically correct then although I face a myriad of men I will march forward.[46]

We, unfortunately, are unsure of exactly what *so* ("ethically correct") means. It probably refers, however, to the poise and confidence that arises from contact with those virtuous inclinations that come from Heaven and define human nature. What is clear, nevertheless, is that the ethical state described in the passage connects a person with *ch'i*, and the connection is extremely important.

I will not translate *ch'i* in what follows. *Psychophysical energy* probably is the best single equivalent, but the search for any equivalent or set of equivalents exemplifies the difficulties in establishing commensurability between truly different systems of thought. (The term, as I will discuss, also illustrates well the way in which secondary theory can inform practical theory.) *Ch'i*, a basic term in early Chinese cosmology, refers to a pervasive and continuous stuff-energy that in grosser and finer forms makes up the whole universe, animate and inanimate. Mencius's presentation of *ch'i* draws on a physicalist discourse in which *ch'i* is pictured as a circulating fluid. But he also thinks *ch'i* has potentially numinous qualities; it can be a spiritual energy when it operates in perfected human beings. Although the notion clearly fits within an organic framework in which nothing fundamentally transcends anything else, *ch'i*'s numinous qualities enable humans to transcend their ordinary modes of being and action.[47]

Especially important is what Mencius calls the *flood-like ch'i* (*hao jan chih ch'i*), which he says he excels at nurturing. This

> is the *ch'i* which is largest and strongest. Nourish it with forthrightness and do it no harm and it will fill the space between Heaven and Earth.

> It is the *ch'i* which is a counterpart to righteousness (*yi*) and which adheres to the way; without these it would shrivel up. It is what is

produced by joining with righteousness; it is not what righteousness
captures through surprise attack.
If one's actions do not satisfy the mind it will shrivel up.[48]

Mencius can be said to "moralize" the idea of *ch'i* in that he declares the
presence of its grandest form, the flood-like *ch'i*, depends on correct ethical
action. Unless *ch'i* is joined to righteousness it will shrivel. Mencius may be
criticizing here some proponents of the position I labeled refined cowardliness; that is, people who hope to attain fulfillment by fleeing engagement in
the world and cultivating *ch'i* through meditation. He, however, surely is
opposing a position represented by Kao Tzu when he asserts that people
must contact righteousness in the correct way. They must tap the natural
inclination to righteousness, Mencius says, and not just the inclination to
follow rules that will produce supposedly righteous acts.

Kao Tzu is a figure of substantial enough accomplishments to have
also attained an unmoved mind. According to Mencius, he thought that
righteousness was stimulated by a recognition of objective facts about
people's relationships. Moreover, Kao Tzu believed it manifests itself in
an adherence to correct rules or doctrines (*yen*). The mind or heart (*hsin*),
for him, lacks natural inclinations that when developed lead to righteousness. But the mind does have the ability to identify the objective aspects
of a situation, to give a thin but true description of it, and to make actions
conform to specific doctrines or rules. The distinction between Mencius
and Kao Tzu corresponds to the distinction between an approach that
emphasizes rules or duty and one that emphasizes virtues. (In their language, the question is whether, for example, righteousness is "external" or
"internal.") This fundamental difference underlies Mencius's rejection of
Kao Tzu's idea that "if you do not get it from doctrine (*yen*) do not seek it
in the mind (*hsin*)." That is, Mencius thinks the mind has natural inclinations to righteousness that Kao Tzu overlooks because he refuses to turn
to the mind and focuses instead on rules.

Especially important to us in considering this disagreement are
Mencius's ideas about how *ch'i* relates to and aids activity, especially courageous activity. He agrees with Kao Tzu's assertion that one ought not seek in
ch'i what the mind cannot also give or help produce. But Mencius thinks that
will (*chih*), the direction of the mind, is "the lead of *ch'i*." If will is unsupport-
ed *ch'i* will be desiccated, will fail to empower action as fully as it can.
Moreover, Mencius claims that the flood-like *ch'i* is fully activated only if a
person acts through a natural inclination to righteousness. Kao Tzu's righteousness, which is produced only through following a rule, cannot connect
properly with *ch'i*. As Mencius puts it, *ch'i* "is not what righteousness captures through surprise attack."

Interpreting Mencius's ideas on this subject brings us into the technical arcania surrounding the conception of *ch'i*, and we understand only imperfectly the different theories about *ch'i* operating at the time. Nevertheless, many crucial features of Mencius's position are clear, even if the technical ramifications remain murky. Mencius asserts that *ch'i* necessarily adheres to the will (*chih*) and the righteousness it can manifest. Predisposed to follow such natural inclinations, *ch'i* shrivels up if linked only to rules.

Actions arising from virtuousness, then, will have different characteristics than actions arising from the application of rules. Most notably, virtuous actions release more energy, produce more efficacious results, and generate a fuller sense of tranquility and assurance than dutiful actions. Spontaneity, joy, and equanimity accompany virtuous actions and even help validate and reinforce them. The idea of *ch'i* provides for Mencius an explanation, at the level of secondary theory, of why these characteristics appear. That is, the flood-like *ch'i* produces powerful effects, such as assurance about one's goals, added energy to reach them, and even joyful reactions while acting. As I will discuss, an explanation at the level of practical theory also can produce an account of why these characteristics appear, an account that enables us more productively to compare Mencius and Aquinas's ideas.[49]

More important here, however, is Mencius's idea that these manifestations of *ch'i* are especially necessary when courageous action is demanded. The fear produced by the loss of real goods can either prevent people undertaking a courageous act or impede the performance of it. *Chi*'s manifestation, however, can help ensure that the tumultuous forces released by legitimate fears will be overcome. Moreover, these manifestations help to ensure the agent that ethical inclinations are present. They help to maintain a person's legitimate confidence by validating the correctness of the courageous act's goals. Mencius's explication of perfected courage ties together a variety of notions: for example, the poise and confidence manifest in ethical correctness (*so*), the numinous power that *ch'i* can display, and the relationship to the true sources of one's Heaven-given nature apparent in real righteousness. Most critical here, however, is the way in which the presence of the fullest *ch'i*, with the power and satisfaction it brings, depends on correct ethical responses.

A striking picture of what occurs when a perfected person faces situations that call for courageous action appears in a passage where Mencius contrasts the desire to live with the desire to be righteous.

> Life I desire, righteousness too I desire; if I cannot get to have both,
> rather than life I choose righteousness. On the one hand, though life

is what I want, there is something I want more than life. That is why I do not cling to life at all costs. On the other hand, though death is what I loathe, there is something I loathe more than death. That is why there are troubles I do not avoid. . . . Not only men of worth have a mind which thinks like this, all men have it; it is simply that the worthy are able to avoid relinquishing their hold on it. Here is a basketful of rice and a bowlful of soup. Getting them will mean life; not getting them will mean death. When these are given with abuse, . . . even a beggar will not accept them. Yet when it comes to [an income of] 10,000 bushels of grain, one accepts them without regard for propriety and right. . . . What I would not accept in the first instance I now-wrongly-accept merely for the sake of having beautiful houses, wives, and concubines, and the gratitude I would reap by generosity to needy friends.[50]

In this passage, Mencius employs that reasoning by resemblances discussed in examining his theory of virtue. He uses it here to explicate the claim righteousness has on people and the role courage has in helping people to meet that claim. Moving from situations where people easily would choose one item over another and display the courage needed to act on that choice, he attempts to show that human beings may just as naturally desire some things more than they desire life. Stark alternatives are formulated, but Mencius presents them in a way that aims to show that making the correct decision is far less difficult than might seem to be the case.

Mencius's rhetoric is dramatic, and he makes no attempt here to give us a nuanced picture of deliberation. Nevertheless, the passage illustrates the operation of perfected courage. When courage is needed, correct inclinations will triumph easily if people will utilize the thinking by resemblances that combines attention, extension, and intelligent awareness. Such thinking relies on contact with Heaven-given inclinations, unleashes the flood-like *ch'i*, and makes the easy apparently difficult or even impossible.

This portrait of perfected courage, as well as the one Mencius develops in relation to the unmoved mind, express an exalted ideal of perfection. It resembles, I think, the one found in Aquinas's depiction of the Gift of Courage, although the resemblance is surely one marked by both similarities in differences and differences in similarities. Let us now examine that state and, briefly, the relationship to Aquinas. In that examination, I will develop at a more abstract level than Mencius does the processes involved in the operation of perfected courage. That is, I will engage in the dangerous but illuminating task of constructing a practical theory about the state of perfected courage that is more explicit than the one we find in Mencius.

VIII. Mencius's Understanding of Perfected Courage: A Theoretical Account and Brief Examination of the Resemblance to the Gift of Courage

Mencius's depiction of perfect courage seems to describe a state in which the truly courageous person has no fear of the objectionable results, of the loss of real goods. Many contemporary Western thinkers would call this a portrait of fearlessness or overconfidence rather than of courage, a judgment that reveals much about Mencius, as well as about contemporary Western thinkers. I think it most productive, however, to assume that we see here a perfected state that resembles the state Aquinas describes as resulting from the Gift of Courage. Both manifest an exalted human realization that rests on religious grounds. Examining how this state operates, then, allows us to probe one feature of that religious consummation of courage Mencius thinks defines the highest possible virtuousness.

As discussed in the previous chapter, Mencius thinks emotions like shame and some kinds of fear have three components. The cognitive component consists in a judgment about an object's value, the desire component consists in an inclination to act, and a final component appears in various physiological changes. That is, a normal person will believe something is dangerous and thereby be inclined to flee from it, and those two components will generate physiological changes, such as an increased pulse rate.

In Mencius's understanding, however, the truly courageous person knows that something is dangerous, but neither inclines to flee from it nor manifests the normal physiological reactions. Such a person differs, then, both from the fearless person who lacks all three components and from a normal person who manifests all three. When this person sees an obviously deranged person about to attack a child, she knows the person is deranged not normal, that such people can be dangerous, and that this deranged person will hurt the child and probably anyone who interferes. The appropriate cognitive judgment occurs, but the components that normally accompany it are missing; she lacks the desire to flee and numerous physiological reactions. Indeed, those noncognitive reactions that do appear arise from another judgment and lead to virtuous actions. That is, she feels only a desire to aid the child and has the concomitant physiological changes. The animating desires in the two possible acts, to flee and to move forward, contrast sharply then, although some physiological reactions, such as the release of adrenaline, may be identical.

Put schematically, two distinct judgments exist in the perfected person's mind. One is that a deranged person is ready to attack and that such a person can harm both the agent and the child. The other is that the child is in danger and should be helped. The two reactions (desires and physiological changes) that normally arise from the first, fear-inducing judgment are disconnected from that first judgment. But the two reactions that normally arise from the second judgment remain, and a benevolent action that also manifests courage takes place. The virtues that constitute a human being's true nature fully operates, but the cognitive judgment about an object's dangerousness remains. Put in the language of extension, both intellectual and emotional extensions occur with the virtue. With fear, however, only an intellectual extension occurs. A person just places the object, the deranged person, in the proper category; it is a fearful object rather than a benign one.

Reaching this perfected state will involve that regimen of direct and indirect self-cultivation, the general structure described in the previous chapter. Mencius, for example, thinks that benevolence and righteousness can be obstructed by errant intellectual ideas, such as the "heresies" of Yang Chu and Mo Tzu.[51] Therefore, people must be sure that their ethical ideas are correct, well-understood, and firmly held. Moreover, they should practice extension and reasoning by resemblances. (More arcane meditational techniques also may need to be employed, although we have little evidence about such techniques.) Training like this allows people to disconnect the normal relationships between the three components in an emotion. It enables them to make judgments but neither feel the desires nor have the physiological reactions that usually accompany them.

Mencius, as discussed, believes that humans can alter themselves or be altered in fundamental ways. The training they receive or undertake is crucial, then, because errant training can cause disconnections that deform rather than produce human flourishing.[52] (Cultivating the unmoved mind may exemplify the potential problems: differences between Kao Tzu and Mencius's versions of that mind may rest on which disconnections they nurtured.) People, for instance, should retrain emotions, such as fear, that are likely to cause problems unless the components of the emotion are disconnected. But they ought to foster not retrain other connections because they are natural, arise from heaven, and lead to the unleashing of the flood-like *ch'i*. Learning how to extend correctly involves being able to strengthen the connection between, say, a benevolent judgment and the inclinations and physiological reactions that accompany it. Moreover, it also involves people training themselves to extend such connected reactions from places where they operate easily to places where they do not.

The results of such training are that the three components in a virtue's emotional reaction operate whereas only the cognitive element operates in a possible disabling emotion, like fear. The judgment about danger is disconnected from the inclinations and physiological reactions that normally accompany it, while all three components in the virtuous reaction sweep into operation. Unhesitating, ethical action occurs, but in the presence of an object perceived to be dangerous. This means in most circumstances the perfected person has neither a full awareness of courage's divergent goals nor feels conflict. The correct action is clear, and a fully connected reaction reinforces it and easily overcomes the almost impotent, unconnected reaction of fear.

In Mencius's view, then, perfected people do not just form emotions. They replace one emotion with another emotion, in the sense that the appropriate emotion sweeps over the inappropriate one. In some cases, the change virtually destroys the emotion that is replaced. When I change by extension my temporary lassitude toward a suffering friend into benevolence, my lassitude remains only as a thin cognitive judgment, only as a possible way of conceiving and reacting to the situation.

In other cases, and courage exemplifies such cases, some aspect of the replaced emotion must endure. The cognitive judgment about an object's dangerousness must remain hearty. I must understand that the deranged person I face is dangerous, and I must recognize the implications of that understanding. Nevertheless, the only passions that fully operate are ones that arise from my virtuous impulses. I know the person is dangerous, but I have none of the desires to act or physiological reactions that normally accompany such judgments. Only inclinational virtues, then, remain as motivating forces in the perfected person, even in situations where courage is demanded. Perfected courageousness thus reaches the last stage the cultivation of virtue can provide. The only conflict arises from the cognitive judgment that an object is fearful. The only reflexivity occurs when a person maneuvers the virtuous disposition into position, and that process will be preconscious and almost instantaneous.[53]

Many characteristics of the phenomena evident in Mencius's picture of perfected courage's operation resemble those found in Aquinas's description of how the Gift of Courage operates. Differences, however, also are present. The secondary theories of the two thinkers, of course, are radically different, and these theories, at places, affect the characteristics that are highlighted, as when Aquinas focuses on confidence about eternal reward. Furthermore, Mencius's greater voluntarism and his different ideas about why people fail to be virtuous does make such an analysis fit more easily into his position than into Aquinas's. Mencius also may think far more people, far more often, attain the perfected state.

Nevertheless, the similarities are striking. Both thinker's ideas on the emotions enable them to analyze coherently this kind of perfected courage. (It is even plausible to assume that a version of the disconnection among components of emotional reactions that is central to Mencius's account also operates in Aquinas's account, and helps us understand what takes place.)

Moreover, both describe a state in which the character of contending emotions changes so that only animating inclinations are present and most forms of conflict and executive control cease. In addition, they also both speak about a confidence that excludes many normal features of fear and generates an extraordinary kind of tranquility. Finally, both think this confidence arises, in part, from participation in a state that transcends the normal and rests on kinds of knowing that differ from many kinds of ordinary reasoning. That state, they argue, is contacted in part through ethical action, and it enables people to overcome the normal reactions fear invokes and therefore makes all virtuous action resemble the action of inclinational virtues.

Our understanding of each thinker's portrait of this state has striking lacunae. Aquinas says remarkably little about exactly how the Gift of Courage operates, and Mencius's treatment of the fully perfected state of the sage or the daimonic (*shen*), who surpasses even the sage, for example, often is extremely brief. Moreover, the differences between those aspects of their secondary theories that are relevant to this subject are pronounced enough to induce caution. Despite this, we must recognize that both thinkers believe humans are susceptible to transformations so total as to make people fundamentally different from what they normally are. Furthermore, some characteristics of that transformed state show remarkable resemblances, as do significant features of the practical theory that explains it.

Let us turn now to another aspect of Mencius's account of courage that also resembles Aquinas's; that is, shows similarities in differences and differences in similarities. The subject is Mencius's ideas about how a belief in fate and Heaven's purposes affects the way in which a person reacts to sadness. Differences in the secondary theory also are crucial here, but we see in Mencius's analysis, I think, an expansion of courage that compares in important and fascinating ways with Aquinas's ideas on patience.

IX. Mencius's Expansion of Courage: The Appropriate Attitude to Fate and Heaven and a Brief Examination of the Resemblance to Aquinas's Patience

Mencius, like Aquinas, aims to expand the conception of courage. He draws on but fundamentally transforms the idea that a warrior's conduct provides the paradigmatic examples of courageous action, as discussed. Indeed, he believes, I think, that a particular kind of religious attitude is an extremely important manifestation of courage. This attitude, which resembles that part of courage Aquinas called the *virtue of patience*, involves a combination of two apparently diverse states. On the one hand, contact with shortcomings in the self and with the injustices of the world and the sufferings in it legitimately produce sorrow. On the other hand, assurance about the character and power of the good generates confidence and equanimity.

Grasping the nature of the state Mencius commends, however, is considerably more difficult than grasping the nature of Aquinas's patience. Understanding it involves interpreting some of the more mysterious ideas and passages in Mencius. Moreover, those interpretations often rest on decisions about how best to understand Mencius's account of forces that transcend the human and those human excellences that allow people to participate in them. I discussed earlier several general questions that affect these interpretations, and I will return to them in the concluding chapter. Here, however, our focus is on Mencius's practical not secondary theory and on attitudes or virtues that Mencius may never label or even highlight but that are central to his understanding of full religious flourishing.[54]

Mencius's analysis begins with the simple notion that most desires produce contentment if satisfied and agitation if unsatisfied. A person may reduce agitation by limiting desires and Mencius recognizes that in some cases such a reduction is wise. However, he rejects an idea that probably was beginning to become prominent in his day: that people can attain a fully human equanimity simply by reducing or eliminating all desires. Two related sources of discontent (of dejection in Aquinas's terms) must remain, he thinks. One arises from the desire to see other people avoid suffering that is produced for no good reason. Mencius's organismic cosmology leads him to see many evils as a necessary part of the whole, as discussed.

Nevertheless, a desire to see people not suffer arises from the sprout of benevolence and links with the sprout of righteousness. The unjust suffering that remains in the world, then, should generate both sorrow and attempts to overcome the suffering. A second source of discontent arises from the fact that all but the most perfect people will continue to worry about their own self-cultivation. Normally virtuous people will continue to make strong evaluations, and thus to have second-order desires about what they ought to be. Equanimity for Mencius must coexist with the agitation produced by the suffering evident in the world and by the shortcomings evident in the self. Each combination of agitation and equanimity needs to be examined, and we can begin with the one that arises from the need to cultivate the self.

Mencius thinks equanimity, a peaceful assurance or confidence, informs the life of virtuous people. It arises, however, from their understanding that they are on the correct path not from their sense of having reached their destination. In his developmental model of human nature, the crucial factor (for all save a very few perfected people) is that the development is proceeding as it should, that the capacities that should be growing are growing. Mencius's notion of perfection, then, connects intimately with an image of process. (That connection helps explain the lack in him of those virtues of regret or remorse that appear in Aquinas.)

His depiction of Confucius's excellence illustrates this notion. Confucius's excellence, Mencius says, consists in the fact he "simply never tire[s] of learning nor [grows] weary of teaching."[55] Learning and teaching are activities — one directed to the self, one to others — that must be seen as ongoing endeavors. They can be moved through in better or worse fashions, but reaching a state of completion is impossible. Moreover, they are processes in which failures inevitably occur, but processes that produce satisfaction for a person and help to others if their integrity is maintained.

Mencius's acceptance of such a developmental picture of human excellence means he, like Aquinas, never doubts that a kind of perturbation must remain in virtuous people. Some perturbations (as I will discuss) arise from seeing other people's unwarranted suffering. Most important for now, however, is Mencius's understanding of the differences between those perturbations that arise from people pursuing goals, from their having second-order volitions, and those that arise from the effects of external events. As he says:

> While a gentleman has life-long cares, he has not a single morning's misfortunes. His worries are of this kind: Shun [a sage] was a man; I am also a man. . . . That is something worth worrying about. . . . On the other hand, the gentleman has nothing he would count as misfortune. He never does anything that is not benevolence; he does not act except in accordance with the rites. Even when unexpected vexations come his way, the gentleman refuses to be perturbed by them.

Perennial worries will exist: virtuous people want to maintain contact, as did the sages, with the true inclinations of their nature. But nothing that can be counted as a misfortune, a vexation, will affect virtuous people. Their cares are about how they connect with the Way, about their knowledge of and movement from their given nature and the social forms produced by the sages. As Mencius says:

> A gentleman steeps himself in the Way (tao) because he wishes to find it in himself (tzu te). When he finds it in himself, he will be at ease in it; when he is at ease in it, he can draw deeply upon it; when he can draw deeply upon it, he finds its source wherever he turns. That is why a gentleman wishes to find the Way in himself.[56]

One source of this ease is the delight that arises when people sense the actualization of virtues within themselves or see them flourish in others. Mencius says this recognition leads people to react with such joy that "the feet step in time with them, the hands dance them out." This ease also generates an equanimity that, in turn, produces steadfast purpose. The virtuous person will neither be moved to action nor perturbed by the fears and temptations that affect most people. (These ordinary temptations as discussed earlier, are crude rather than subtle deformations, however.) As Mencius says, a great man "cannot be led to excesses by wealth and honor, be deflected from his purpose by poverty and lowliness, nor be made to bend by power and force."[57] Equanimity, then, arises from a cognitive and emotional assurance. It, in turn, rests on a belief in and contact with those self-validating inclinations that Mencius thinks are produced by Heaven and make Heaven present on earth. But that equanimity coexists with an agitation that arises from the need to overcome shortcomings in the self and pursue the state of fully perfected virtue.

Another, if more elusive, kind of assurance and equanimity affects the second source of discontent, those perturbations generated by the suffering evident in the world. This state rests more on beliefs about, say, Heaven than on the evidence that, for Mencius, arises from contact with the virtues natural to humans. It also reflects Mencius's contention that people should make a sharp distinction between what they can affect and what they cannot affect. People always must pursue anything where, in his phrase, "seeking is of some use to getting," especially the development of those capacities that can become virtues. But they also must realize that many matters are beyond their control, notably the success of their actions, or even the consequences of them.

Mencius, then, focuses here on the vexing questions of what benefits virtuous actions bring and to whom. He probes the meaning, if you will, of his own comment that "there is neither good nor bad fortune which man does not bring upon himself."[58] Aspects of the older idea of virtue's effectiveness linger in Mencius, as discussed, and he sometimes speaks as if virtue always will bring evident benefits to both the virtuous and the society. But another, more sober view about virtue's benefits is more common in him. This view probably results from his own failure to change people and policies, and it surely manifests a more realistic picture of life. Virtuous action will not always bring to others the benefits desired, he recognizes, and therefore unjustified suffering will exist in the world. That suffering must affect virtuous people, but it should affect them in a way that destroys neither their assurance nor their equanimity.

Understanding how the achievement of such a state of mind is possible involves examining two of the more complex terms in Mencius: Heaven (*T'ien*) and fate (*ming*). Each clearly is a part of his secondary theory but each also affects deeply that part of his practical theory in which appropriate equanimity is a central concern. *Ming* is best rendered as "fate" or "destiny" but its root meaning is to command or decree. Mencius uses it to refer both to the quality of ethical appropriateness present in events and the quality that shows actions are not entirely within human control. It covers, then, two apparently distinct ideas. One is that which is ordered by forces beyond the human; the other is that which is manifested in the proper human domain, including even the special vocation of a particular person. The proper attitude to take to these two sides of fate, Mencius says, is to resist becoming double minded: "Not being made double minded [or doubtful, *erh*] by [prospects of] premature death or long life and cultivating oneself to await it (*hsiu shen yi ssu shih*) — this is the way to stand firm on ming (*li ming*)."[59] Thoughts about length of life should not introduce division into people. People should act solely on their virtuous inclinations and neither make plans nor specific decisions on the grounds that they will make possible a longer life. Fate as manifest in the ethically appropriate should guide them, but they also must cultivate themselves to await whatever fate, as what is beyond human control, brings them.

Heaven, like fate, refers both to the qualities underlying or found in appropriate human action and the quality of not being entirely within human control. The potential in humans for virtue arises from Heaven; it is their source, although humans must grasp and nurture the capacities they have. Moreover, human actions can manifest both Heaven's purposes and something of Heaven's power. But Heaven also is an overarching power that produces effects that surpass what humans can generate. This aspect of Heaven has qualities like human qualities, and it links with some human aspirations, even though it need not always serve them. Heaven, for example, can have desires, give responsibility, and be a source of political power; furthermore, people can fear Heaven, serve it, and recommend rulers to it.

Despite possessing such qualities, whenever Heaven's agency appears in areas that are not firmly in human control it links closely with fate. The combination *T'ien ming* does not occur in Mencius except when he quotes earlier texts. In many of these earlier texts, *T'ien ming*, the "Heavenly Mandate," refers to an important myth in which Heaven selects a good person and his family as rulers and helps them attain the kingdom. The two however, are linked in other contexts that refer to what humans do not cause. Mencius says, for instance, "What is done without being done is [due to] Heaven; what comes without being worked is [a matter of] fate (*ming*)."[60] In all these cases where Heaven is the mysterious presence behind what escapes human control, its purposes often are inscrutable, especially when it acts in history. It confers its mandate on lineages not individuals, for example, but a lineage cannot possibly be good in the sense that an individual is good. Moreover, it often appears indifferent to human suffering and even seems to violate its own apparent rules about how and when it will work.

Heaven's character and actions, at best, are unclearly presented when Mencius works at the level of secondary theory. But a more coherent and compelling picture appears in his practical theory. The proper response to the evident difficulties in grasping Heaven's purposes is to adopt a complex attitude that Mencius expresses well in what may appear to be a non sequitur. Leaving a state where he has largely failed in his mission, Mencius seems to be unhappy and is asked:

> "Master, you look somewhat unhappy. I heard from you the other day that a gentleman reproaches neither Heaven nor man."
>
> "This is one time; that was another time. Every five hundred years a true King should arise, and in the interval there should arise one from whom an age takes its name. From Chou to present, it is over seven hundred years. The five hundred mark is passed; the time seems ripe. It must be that Heaven does not as yet wish to bring peace to the Empire. If it did, who is there in the present time other than myself? Why should I be unhappy?"[61]

Heaven has not acted as Mencius expected it would, and we might think from his initial statement that he would be perplexed or upset. But Mencius is not discontent. He reassures himself that if Heaven wished to act, he would be its instrument. He doubts neither Heaven's purposes or will nor the fact that he is a chosen agent of Heaven. (Moreover, he continues to believe in the efficacy and value of the Confucian tradition, although it seems both weak and dated to many in his time.) Yet he also recognizes that the world's ills are severe, and that Heaven does not appear to be acting to ameliorate them.

Mencius affirms, then, that however perplexed and distressed events leave him a joy remains at participating in Heaven's activities, even though they are inscrutable. This attitude to Heaven resembles the proper attitude toward fate. People ought not be made doubtful by events outside their control. They, instead, should concern themselves with proper self-cultivation and action. The two attitudes differ, however, in one important way. With Heaven people should presume a legitimate purpose exists, but with fate they should not.

When faced with such attitudes, we may think Mencius's approach is woefully unsophisticated or even displays that kind of self-deception to which religious people are liable. In evaluating our response, however, we must recognize that Mencius does not operate with easily separable ideas of the transcendent and the immanent. Indeed, the whole question of what Heaven controls and what humans control, for him, has a given and acceptable lack of clarity. (A similar situation exists with fate, which refers both to human excellence and inhuman forces, but no presumption of intelligent purpose, as noted, works with fate's inhuman manifestations.) The causation of important human activities, Mencius thinks, often is inscrutable. Nevertheless, he continues to believe that what occurs is the achievement of the strenuous efforts of both Heaven and human beings. Most important here, the position he expresses, I think, reflects a profound spiritual attitude. That attitude resembles the one found in Aquinas's notion of patience. Their secondary theories differ greatly (although we need to be careful about presenting too simplistic a picture of what Aquinas thinks people can know about deity's causation of events) but the attitudes, and the practical theories they reflect, contain important resemblances.

Mencius exhibits a keen sense of what humans can neither control nor understand. But he also thinks people can know and control something of unsurpassed value: those sprouts of virtue Heaven implants and people must cultivate for both their own and other's good. Indeed, the value of those potentials for virtue is highlighted by the paradoxical linking, in the concepts of fate and especially of Heaven, of what is and is not in human control. The presence of potentials for virtue is as alien to much of what we normally consider human as is the presence of other events, such as earthquakes or floods, that also manifest Heaven or fate. The possibility of humans becoming virtuous should strike us, Mencius thinks, with the same awe and wonder as other events that manifest nonhuman activity. The potentials are numinous realities, fascinating and sacred mysteries. Mencius, then, employs a religiously charged vocabulary to describe the part of the self that people should most fear to lose, that aspect of their being the loss of which should legitimately generate a hatred of the self.[62]

Most important here, Mencius thinks that if people recognize these potentials as a gift, they will better understand the complex character of a human being's most crucial task. People must cultivate and manifest virtue, but they must undertake that task in light of the inscrutable processes of Heaven. To recognize a virtue's origin in fate and especially Heaven is to see how its character transcends the normal. To understand how powerful and mysterious are the effects of fate and Heaven on the world is to see how much of importance lies outside human control. Grasping these matters should lead people to realize that the consequences of their actions as well as much of what happens to them will be outside their control. But it should also make them realize they have religious reasons to continue both to act virtuously and to believe in Heaven's beneficent if mysterious purposes. This attitude underlies Mencius's comment, noted earlier, on his understanding of Heaven's purposes. It also appears in a sober but calm statement that echoes the notion of virtues as expressive: "All a gentleman (*chün tzu*) can do in starting an enterprise is to leave a tradition which can be carried on. Heaven alone can grant success. . . . You can only try your best to do good."[63]

Indeed, this perspective undergirds Mencius's general ideas about how people ought to focus their attention. He puts the point in formulaic fashion when he says:

Seek it and one will get it, let go of it and one will lose it; this is a case in which seeking is of use to getting and what is sought is in me. [But if] there is a proper way (tao) in seeking it, [and if] there is ming in getting it; this is a case in which seeking is of no use to getting, and what is sought is on the outside.[64]

People can seek out and control the understanding and development of their nature. Cultivating the self and behaving virtuously therefore is both possible and obligatory. But if events beyond a person's control arbitrate success, as they often do, pursuit will bring neither what people want nor even what they should have. People, then, must realize that outside forces will determine much of what happen and concentrate only on what they can control.

This attitude for Mencius, as for Aquinas, does not mean that one disregards normal, prudential considerations. As Mencius says: "Though nothing happens that is not due to destiny (mo fei ming yeh), one accepts willingly only what is one's proper destiny (shun shou ch'i cheng). That is why he who understands destiny (chih ming che) does not stand under a wall on the verge of collapse."[65] People's primary business is to cultivate the potentials for virtue that Heaven has given them. That process, however, should join with reasonable caution and an understanding that many events and consequences of actions must just be accepted, must be seen as decreed.

The attitude Mencius commends may appear to amount to little more than the one that arises from the common-sense view that people should do what they can and recognize that the success of their efforts often depends on factors beyond their control. More than that is involved, however. Mencius distinguishes in effect between a "known" and a "unknown" Heavenly Mandate, and the less-evident distinctions that resemble it when fate alone is concerned. He argues that people should focus on the known mandate human nature displays because it provides all the guidance that people need. They should not seek to penetrate the unknown mandate, for example, to attempt to understand why the unjust thrive. That activity focuses attention improperly and drains energy away from the crucial task of self-development.

To accept the unknown mandate, however, is not simply to assume that no choice exists but to accede to necessity. Virtuous people should believe that significant purpose informs the unknown mandate's actions, even if they cannot understand it. Mencius asks people, then, to adopt an attitude that differs from the ordinary one where they see either meaning or its lack in events. People should believe that many events display purpose, even if the purpose is unfathomable and probing for it misuses humanity's limited energy. This double-sided attitude produces the distinctive steadfastness and contentment that Mencius commends.

It also represents a particular type if religious thought in which several features of practical theory are especially important. That is, one must decide about a problem's tractability and importance to religious flourishing when considering what to analyze and how deeply to analyze it. Moreover (and more controversially), with some problems the solution of an intellectual problem may be less important than instructing people how to think about it so that appropriate attitudes and actions will arise.[66]

The attitude Mencius commends and the rationale for it, I think, resemble features of Aquinas's exposition of the virtue of patience. For both thinkers, courage attains its highest religious perfection when humans maintain simultaneously two distinct perspectives. On the one hand, they must perceive clearly the injustices present in the world and the failures present in themselves and feel sorrow about them. But, on the other hand, they must also maintain both their pursuit of the good and their belief in, hope for, and even participation in a higher good. Immense differences, of course, characterize the secondary theories that inform this resemblance in their practical theories about this attitude. As discussed, there are almost no evident correspondences between the transcendent realm Aquinas presents and the higher realm that operates in Mencius. Moreover, none of the structures that define Aquinas's open religion operate in Mencius's locative religion. Finally, and related to these differences, important distinctions characterize their understanding of people's propensity to fail to be virtuous.

Nevertheless, as the comparison of their lists of virtues showed, human excellences in Mencius enable people to touch realities that exceed anything that normally could or should be believed in, hoped for, or loved. (Indeed the identification of such excellences illustrates how a comparative approach can help identify elements that otherwise might be missed.) Both thinkers believe humans can be empowered by sacred forces that not only make possible but also favor a specific human understanding of goals, principles, and actions. Such a participation is what allows people to be dejected by their own or the world's situation and yet also to continue to pursue and adhere to the most valuable goals.

We find in their expansion of courage, then, striking similarities within differences and differen ces within similarities, as we did in examining other features of their analysis of courage, such as their understanding of the operations of perfected courage. Let us, in the final chapter, examine two related topics. One is how real resemblances in their accounts of virtue relate to the evident dissimilarities between the two thinkers, a situation that can be unraveled by a further analysis of the different kinds of theories that operate in them. The other is the best way to do the comparative philosophy of religious flourishings, a theoretical discussion that uses examples drawn from the comparisons already made.

Chapter 5

Conclusion

My final chapter covers two related subjects. I review succinctly (in Sections I-III) the more striking, and possibly disturbing, results of this inquiry; in that review I also provide a more abstract explanation than previously given of how and why I proceeded as I did. I then, in the bulk of the chapter (Sections IV-VI), discuss the theoretical question of how we can best do the comparative philosophy of human flourishings. I argue for a general method, but draw my examples from the analyses in this book.

I begin, then, by reviewing those results of the comparisons that, I think, left us in a perplexing situation. We found either raw dissimilarities or thin resemblances between many of Aquinas and Mencius's ideas, and yet we saw real resemblances between their theories of virtue and accounts of some specific virtues. I explain this situation by examining the three different types of theories — primary, practical, and secondary — that operate in these, as well as most other, thinkers. If we distinguish among the character and products of these theories, we can understand why real resemblances appear in some areas and dissimilarities or thin resemblances in others.

I then turn to a more general discussion of how best to undertake the comparative philosophy of human flourishings. I argue that we can utilize features of Aquinas's approach, provided that we realize his aims and ours differ substantially and that we need to examine both his successes and his failures to understand the problems and the possibilities in his approach. I then examine carefully the most important feature, for us, of Aquinas's approach: those performances that arise from analyzing and utilizing analogical expressions, especially those in which we construct and relate focal and secondary terms. This pursuit of the similar in the different and the different in the similar rests on the operations of the analogical imagination. I end by examining those operations and arguing that we must use imaginative capacities to successfully do a fully comparative philosophy of human flourishings. Let us turn, then, to our first subject.

I. Dissimilarities and Thin Resemblances between Mencius and Aquinas

The general perspectives, abstract ideas, overall approaches, and cultural contexts evident in Mencius and Aquinas usually differ substantially.[1] Marked contrasts appear in the general perspectives within which they work. Mencius's Confucianism, for instance, is as striking an example of a locative religion as is Aquinas's Christianity of an open religion. Moreover, Aquinas's cosmology represents in paradigmatic form that kind of theism in which a deity creates and preserves the world but remains fundamentally distinct from it. Mencius's cosmology, in contrast, is organismic or even "familial": all elements are intimately interconnected; they are what they are only through their relationships with other elements and their place in the whole.

Evident contrasts also appear when we look at many of the more fundamental, abstract conceptions in each thinker. No equivalent to Mencius's notion of psychophysical energy that can be numinous (*ch'i*) exists in Aquinas, and Aquinas's idea of grace (*gratia*) appears to resemble no concept in Mencius. Indeed, these two notions seem to make sense only within each thinker's more general framework. Mencius's psychophysical energy requires an organismic framework as clearly as Aquinas's grace requires a theistic one.

Furthermore, the very way Mencius and Aquinas develop and analyze their general perspectives and abstract conceptions differ considerably. Mencius employs a technical vocabulary, makes distinctions, and prosecutes arguments. Such analytic procedures and tools, however, are peripheral parts of his approach. In contrast, they are at the heart of Aquinas's approach. Indeed, Mencius seems not to share Aquinas's belief in the significance of either the process of analysis or its results. The process of self-cultivation that, for Mencius, leads to proper understanding and growth is too delicate, too subtly balanced an enterprise to be well-served by emphasizing such analysis.

Finally, the ways of life, the cultural contexts, that each works within obviously differ greatly. Conventional social rules and roles are considerably more important to Mencius than to Aquinas, for example, and familial relationships are less significant for Aquinas than for Mencius. Even their respective notions of a thinker's social role often differ strikingly. Both do think they are articulating a true position and therefore must defend it against various false views. Mencius, however, usually battles fiercely against opposed views. Aquinas sees his task (except in a few cases) as harmonizing positions that, he thinks, are only apparently opposed or different. Moreover, Mencius spends considerable time and effort trying to persuade rulers. Aquinas at times deals with those in political power, but they are hardly the focus of action and thought for him that they are for Mencius.

Striking differences in Mencius and Aquinas's overall perspectives, abstract conceptions, general approaches, and cultural contexts, then, are evident. Resemblances, of course, also are present in some areas. Many of them, however, are *real but thin*; that is, the resemblances are rather insignificant. They appear in an area that is so narrowly circumscribed or at a level that is so abstract that they provide us neither textured nor extensive materials on which to work.

Mencius and Aquinas's treatment of the role of injunctions, for instance, shows clear similarities. Each thinks that humans are bound by unconditional negative obligations, such as that one ought not take innocent life without compelling reasons. They even would agree on some areas in which these obligations operate; for example, no ruler should allow people to starve to satisfy his own desire for better food or drink. Nevertheless, significant differences appear between them when we turn from these clear cases and ask how each would understand the meanings of key words; that is, how each would decide who is an "innocent," or even a "person," and what constitutes a compelling reason. Mencius and Aquinas's differing answers to such questions arise from divergences between their general frameworks and cultural contexts.

Even more important, both Mencius and Aquinas think that injunctions cover only a few kinds of cases. Neither thinks directives arising from injunctions apply to many areas of life that are extraordinarily important to full human flourishing. That is, they differentiate sharply between the realms of injunctions and virtues, and they believe that despite the importance of injunctions, the realm of virtues contains most of what is critical. Whatever resemblances between them may be present in the realm of injunctions, then, much that is crucial remains untouched.

The subject of human nature's abstract characteristics shows us another, different kind of real but still thin resemblance. Both thinkers agree humans have a given nature; both believe capacities that may or may not be actualized define it; and both think a higher power, in some fashion, is responsible for its character. When we examine their more textured accounts, however, substantial disagreements appear. For example, their ideas differ about how the higher power acted on that nature or now acts on it. Similarly, they differ on the question of how fragile are a human being's natural capacities and what exactly must occur if these capacities are to be actualized.

If we look at general frameworks, abstract conceptions, analytic approaches, and cultural contexts, we see substantial differences between

Mencius and Aquinas. Real and noteworthy resemblances also are present, but they often are only thin ones. We seem, then, to be left with a situation in which we possess either thin accounts of real similarities or thick accounts of dissimilarities. Indeed, some aspects of their accounts of virtue and virtues reflect this dichotomy.

A few similarities in Aquinas and Mencius's theories of virtue are real but thin; for example, their notion that capacities exist that can develop over time into actualities or virtues. This similarity is real, and it does differentiate them from proponents of a discovery model who believe people can uncover a transhuman actualization that will completely inform their characters. But the similarity also is thin. A more detailed examination shows noteworthy distinctions between their respective understandings of how sturdy are the capacities, what is involved in actualizing them, and how prone people are to fail.

Similarly, when we examine their respective thick accounts of actual virtues we sometimes see only differences. Aquinas presents many different kinds of virtues, but Mencius presents scarcely any. More important, few of Mencius and Aquinas's virtues seem clearly to correspond, and those that do often show dissimilarities when we examine them more closely and place them correctly within each thinker's structure. Mencius's benevolence (*jen*), for instance, seems to resemble Aquinas's benevolence (*benevolentia*), but the virtue is central to Mencius and peripheral to Aquinas. In fact, charity (*caritas*) often functions for Aquinas in the way that benevolence (*jen*) functions for Mencius, and charity differs substantially from benevolence.

Other, even more general differences also seem to be evident when we examine their textured treatments of virtues. The significance of religious virtues in Aquinas in contrast to their seeming insignificance in Mencius is a notable one. Another notable difference is the close tie of virtue to social roles in Mencius in contrast to the relative unimportance of that link in Aquinas. Moreover, both these features of their accounts affect not only their examination of almost every virtue but also their establishment and defense of the priorities among all virtues.

Given all this, little seems to remain of my brave claims about the productive relationships that would arise if we focused on virtue in the comparative philosophy of religious flourishings. We seem to be left with only the unhappy dilemma I described in the first chapter. On the one hand, examinations of the realm of injunctions produce real but rather unilluminating resemblances. On the other hand, examinations of ways of life produce textured accounts that usually are characterized by complex differences.

II. Real Resemblances in Mencius and Aquinas's Understanding of Virtue

I do think that in comparing Mencius and Aquinas's ideas about virtue and virtues we found more than just thin but real resemblances at the more theoretical level and textured but diverse dissimilarities at the level of more concrete descriptions. Indeed, I think we found a complicated set of interactions that show us how comparisons like this involve us in creating similarities within differences and differences within similarities. Let me begin with a review of some of the results of the lengthy discussions in earlier chapters, as it sets the needed background. I will again examine Mencius and Aquinas's more theoretical analysis of virtue and then turn to their accounts of concrete virtues.

Before undertaking this review, however, one general observation is in order. The examination, I think, shows the importance of working with the details of each thinker's accounts. A comparative philosophy of human flourishing that deals with sophisticated thinkers works best when we focus on specific subjects and textured presentations. General, comparative accounts of thinkers or traditions have their place, of course, and any comparative enterprise also must treat the general background. Nevertheless, adequate and illuminating comparisons normally will appear only if we include a careful examination of details.

The following example can illustrate my point well. Aquinas and Mencius seem to connect virtue and social role in very different ways. The link between the two is much closer for Mencius than for Aquinas, and that leads Mencius to make judgments with which Aquinas would disagree; for example, when Mencius validates the actions of a gamekeeper who risks death rather than respond to a ritually improper summons. Nevertheless, in their more detailed analyses both thinkers use the idea of semblances of virtue in ways that must make us hesitant about drawing any uncomplicated distinction between them. Mencius's ideas about the village honest man (*hsiang yüan*) display his understanding of the problems with any simple relationship between role and virtue. Similarly, Aquinas's account of some cases, such as that of a judge's responsibilities, shows that he believes virtue and role can be intimately linked. We may find, then, that apparently clear differences are much less clear than they seemed when we turn to each thinker's detailed, textured accounts; we therefore must focus on such accounts when we make comparisons. With that in mind, let us turn to the main subject.

When we examine Mencius and Aquinas's theories of virtue we saw some striking resemblances, especially in the conceptions of the self that underlie both theories. They develop similar positions on the character and interaction of practical reason, the emotions, and dispositions. Moreover, each thinker also focuses on the ideas of semblances and expansions of virtues, and they employ these ideas in ways that often produce similar results. Both, for instance, identify semblances of courage and expand courage into the religious realm, and they do so in ways that generate revealing resemblances. Real and textured resemblances, then, characterize significant parts of Mencius and Aquinas's theories of virtue, conceptions of the self, and ideas about semblances and expansions of virtue.[2]

Matters are somewhat more complicated when we attempt to establish productive relationships between the two thinkers at a more concrete level. Closer analyses may uncover important differences in cases in which similarities seemed clear, as with the virtue of benevolence. Similarly, a more subtle and imaginative account may uncover resemblances that were overlooked initially. Closer investigation showed us, for example, that despite the apparently obvious absence in Mencius of any virtues that correspond to either Aquinas's theological virtues or his supernatural virtue of patience, significant similarities are present. Indeed, highlighting those similarities cast a most interesting light on Mencius and also allowed us to see Aquinas in a new way.[3]

Detailed analyses can be carried out with any virtue, of course, but I have treated with the necessary care only the virtue of courage. ("Practical reason" also was examined extensively, but focusing on how it informs courage meant that significant aspects of it were discussed only briefly.) Mencius and Aquinas both agreed that courage was of crucial importance to human fulfillment, and their understanding of the virtue's abstract structure also showed striking similarities. Moreover, their accounts of the character and significance of courage's semblances resembled each other in broad outline and sometimes in specific detail. Finally, their treatment of the religious aspects of courage, a prominent part of their expansions of courage, displayed significant resemblances on the subjects of the character of fully perfected courage and of the role of appropriate endurance.[4]

In summary, then, we find real and textured resemblances between Mencius and Aquinas's understanding of both the conception of virtue and the virtue of courage. (Furthermore, as we will discuss more fully later, comparing them deepened our understanding of each thinker and led us toward some normative conclusions.) Their understanding of virtues shows similarities missing almost completely when we focus on their general perspectives, abstract ideas, overall approaches, or cultural contexts.

Especially striking is that resemblances evident in their accounts of virtues and virtue fail to appear in their accounts of many more abstract topics. This difference, I think, raises an important question about the status of each thinker's culturally given conceptual vocabulary, especially the most theoretical of the concepts they use. Similarities rarely are evident here. But resemblances appear when Mencius and Aquinas focus on more concrete issues, aim at a relatively "neutral" description of an agent's state, and operate with a less technical vocabulary than they have at their command.

This situation leads me to query whether each thinker's more theoretical ideas and conceptual apparatus always serve them well, at least when they deal with virtues. Both thinkers may point to phenomena, ideas, and values that can be better grasped and explained, at least by us, with notions that differ from the ones that they themselves present. This remains true even if we understand these matters far better by having worked through their explication of them and by having taken seriously their more abstract distinctions, especially those that relate most closely to their explications of virtue.

I will analyze this issue and examine its implications in several ways. I will argue, in the book's last sections, that utilizing a comparative method that relies on the analogical imagination helps us both to deal with it and, most important, to engage in a truly productive comparative philosophy of religious flourishings. Before undertaking this more general inquiry, however, I want to examine the problem more directly. I will do so by focusing on the relationship between ideas of a more theoretical or abstract character and those that seem more to reflect common sense. I already have briefly discussed this subject at several places where we needed to untangle the relationships among different kinds of theory to understand and compare our two thinkers. The topic is important enough, however, that we need to examine more closely both the general subject and how an understanding of it affects our comparison of Mencius and Aquinas.

III. Primary, Practical, and Secondary Theories in the Comparative Philosophy of Religious Flourishings

One influential and productive way to formulate the relationship of more abstract ideas and ideas that seem to reflect common sense appears in the work of the anthropologist Robin Horton. He distinguishes between the terms and structures of what he calls *primary* and *secondary theories* — Horton's own correction of his earlier distinction between "everyday discourse" and "theoretical discourse." Horton's analysis, and the controversy it has generated, usually focuses on the explanation of natural or material phenomena. The discussion, then, often centers on the character of scientific understanding or even, more narrowly, on the nature of medical understanding. Nevertheless, Horton's framework is helpful.[5]

Primary theories are marvelously efficient in helping people to explain, predict, and control most normal situations. These theories will not vary much from culture to culture, although some features of them will be more or less well developed in any particular culture. An agricultural culture whose people live in tropical lowlands and a herding culture whose people live in the mountains will share the ideas and practices that result from their primary theories about, say, the characteristics of heavy objects or the common changes in seasons. Their differing situations, however, also will lead people in the respective cultures to have more developed primary theories in some areas than in others; for example, about the long-term effects of excessive rain and heat on the growth of grain or about the way cloud formations signal sudden, severe shifts in weather.

Primary theories underlie people's ability to cope with the normal problems the world presents. The explanations they provide allow people to predict, plan, and thereby often control important aspects of life. Moreover, they usually appear to be obviously truthful to people within the culture and even to many outside it. These theories can then be said to have a universal character; that is, they often speak in one voice, they are similar in nature and content.

Secondary theories, in contrast, usually vary enormously from culture to culture. They can be said to have an equivocal character; that is, they speak in various voices, they are dissimilar in nature and content. Indeed, they usually appear to almost all people, even those within the culture, to be a mixture of the familiar and the strange. The origin and function of these theories helps to explain aspects of their character. People build secondary theories from primary theories to explain distinctive, peculiar, or distressing occurrences. They develop ideas about a realm of powers or class of beings, like benevolent spirits, that clearly differ from evident phenomena to explain or interpret those extraordinary, or even normal, matters that primary theories cannot deal with adequately. A mysterious outbreak of disease or a person's extraordinary capacity to cure, for example, could be phenomena that would lead people to produce secondary theories.

Human beings try to explain, predict, and control events in all areas of life. Distinguishing between primary and secondary theories helps us, as interpreters, to understand the different ways in which these enterprises operate. (This is especially important when the subject is "natural" occurrences; when human flourishing is the subject, as we will see, things becomes considerably more complicated.) The distinction between the two kinds of theories helps us sort out different aspects of Mencius and Aquinas's accounts. This, in turn, allows us to understand more clearly why we may find resemblances, analogical predications, in treatments of virtue and only thin resemblances or differences, equivocal predications, in other areas.

Certain of Mencius and Aquinas's important ideas are firmly anchored in secondary theory; for example, psychophysical energy (*ch'i*) or grace (*gratia*). These ideas rely on conceptions of a realm of power or beings that obviously differs from what is clearly evident, and they help to explain both normal and abnormal situations. Other of their ideas fit easily into primary theory; for example, their most rudimentary notions about simple human desires to nourish and sexually express one's self, or to avoid those life-threatening objects that induce fear.

These latter ideas, however, take on a more complicated conceptual form as soon as either thinker begins to examine them closely. When Aquinas discusses with care the subject of simple human desires, for example, he distinguishes between impulse and contending appetites; and when Mencius discusses it he distinguishes between attention (*ssu*) and invariant reactions. An even more pronounced change occurs when either thinker reflects on which objects of desire bring real satisfaction. Raw fear about life-threatening objects or powerful movements toward sexual expression no longer are seen as implacable, unrefinable parts of human character. That is, their understanding of the interaction of reason, emotions, and dispositions leads them to argue for a very different picture of what can and should motivate people than appears in their most simple primary theories. Both thinkers, then, produce theoretical accounts that differ from primary theories about basic human desires or fears, and yet they do so without expressing those accounts in terms, like *ch'i* or grace, that are most evidently parts of their secondary theories.

These kinds of theoretical accounts lead me to suggest that Mencius and Aquinas (and most other sophisticated thinkers about human flourishing) utilize not two but three kinds of theories. Indeed, when human flourishing is the subject, the most important level of theorizing often fits between what Horton calls *primary* and *secondary* theories. People who theorize on human flourishing work on the materials produced by primary theories — for example, simple human drives and fears — and they often can link their theorizing with those ideas full-fledged secondary theories produce, like *ch'i* and grace. That is, they aim at a more conceptually precise ordering of human experience than does primary theory; but they stay far closer to the particular, often murky, phenomena that make up much of human life than does secondary theory. Practitioners of this kind of theory will use concepts, even technical terms of art. But they aim to order the often confusing tumult of human experience to generate those forms of understanding that will better guide appreciation and action.

I label this third kind of theory *practical theory*, as the aim is to explain human activities to guide people's practices, and therefore lead them to a more complete flourishing. (This kind of theorizing resembles, in important ways, the approach to "action" [*praxis*] that Aristotle utilizes in his ethical works when he attempts to preserve but order appearances.[6]) A simple example illustrates important features of this kind of theorizing. An untutored eye watching a basketball game sees only ten bodies rushing about on a confined court and attempting to put a ball in a basket. Little more than chaos punctuated by whistles and cheers is observed. An eye tutored by ideas found in the practical theory that surrounds basketball, however, sees something different. Knowing what a pick-and-roll is, understanding what a double team is, recognizing the difference between a zone defense and a man-to-man defense, a different picture emerges of what is happening. The terms of art, and the theory of which they are a part, enable tutored observers to see form and pattern where before they saw only chaotic interaction. They also allow observers to understand who is playing well and who badly, and may even allow them — as coaches, players, or bettors — to be more successful than they would otherwise have been. Practical theory, then, generates a form of explanation, prediction, and control.

Basketball is a game, of course, and it possesses firm characteristics that life does not have. The analogy to the panoply of matters involved in human flourishing, then, is imperfect. Game-like phenomena, however, are significant parts of the virtuous life, as MacIntyre and others have argued, and they give us important information about how best to understand and live that life.[7] Nevertheless, and even more important, the example of a game can be misleading insofar as it concerns only the ordering of sense impressions, the data of observation.

Mencius and Aquinas's practical theory aims to order sense impressions. But the phenomena they work on as practical theorists also includes beliefs, interpretations, and the language of texts thought to be sacred. All these sources are critical for practical theory, and the need to use them illustrates how this kind of theory sits between primary and secondary theory. When they theorize about simple, observable data they come very close to primary theory. When they theorize about phenomena revealed in beliefs or sacred language they come close to secondary theory.

The connection to secondary theory is especially close, then, when ethical and religious phenomena are the subject, but differences between the two kinds of theorizing can be illustrated with the help of an example. Both thinkers examine closely the important, to them, phenomenon of empowerment, the state of being able to do easily and well what before could be done only haltingly or badly. This phenomenon is central to the discourses they use, appears in figures and texts they respond to, and also seems to have been a crucial part of their own experiences. Their secondary theory aims to capture it with notions such as, the link of righteousness (*yi*) and the flood-like *ch'i* in Mencius, and the differences between normal patience and the infused virtue of patience, or courage and the Gift of Courage, in Aquinas.

But they also examine the phenomenon in their practical theory, often either without the terms found in their secondary theory or in a way that allows us to distinguish their uses of those terms and the phenomenon they examine. These accounts enabled us to portray, for example, the operation of perfected courage or an attitude like patience in each thinker without constantly referring to the terms in their secondary theories. That is, we could examine those operations and attitudes without also focusing on their more theoretical treatments of conceptions like Heaven, fate, God, and infused virtues. This, in turn, enabled us to produce a comparison that would have been impossible had the terms of their secondary theory been central. Focusing on their practical theories, then, allowed us to compare them in ways we otherwise could not have.[8]

This approach also contains a danger, however: we can overlook not only the importance of their secondary theories but also the religious meaning that appears in these theories. The temptation to flatten their accounts, to exorcise from them those striking religious claims that often ill fit our normal presuppositions, is always present. The only real protection against this temptation, as with many other intellectual temptations, is easy to state and difficult to do. We need to remain constantly vigilant, always to be aware that succumbing to this temptation is possible. We must continue to highlight the importance of the phenomenon of empowerment, for example, even though we work with their practical not their secondary theories.

As I will investigate later, I think the best way we can give a concrete form to that vigilance is always to highlight the role of analogical predication in their practical theorizing. We need here to examine another issue, however: the question of whether either thinker usually is well-served when the subject is virtue by the ideas and terminology present in his secondary theory. All thinkers are liable to hypostatize or even reify ideas. They can make abstractions about mysterious realties into substantial entities that seem to be better understood than they possible can be. With the greatest thinkers this usually occurs only when they operate at less than their full power; their more clumsy followers (which too often unfortunately include us), however, can be veritable adepts at it. Aquinas and especially Mencius, at their best, are acutely aware of this problem. A kind of agnosticism, as discussed, informs their use of secondary theories. It rests on their acute sense of the mystery and complexity of the sacred, their beliefs that some ideas may create fictional and damaging realities, and their notions about the limitations of human understanding and the need to remain content with them and thus at peace with one's humanity.[9]

As interpreters of Mencius and Aquinas we must always remain aware of this strand in their thought and the truth contained in it. We always must take seriously their secondary theories and yet also realize how their practical theories may contain a more adequate, if also vaguer, picture than these theories, especially when virtues are the subject. Their secondary theories, at times, may hinder their more subtle analyses of human flourishing, just as they also may hinder the possible comparisons between them that we can make.

Practical theory is crucial, then, to Mencius and Aquinas's account of human flourishing. Fitting between simple primary theory and full-fledged secondary theory, it differs from but relates closely, sometimes very closely, to each. We often have concentrated on their practical theories, and this focus has allowed us to make comparisons that are analogical in character. It enables us to steer between the similarity or univocity we find in their primary theories and the differences or equivocity we often find in their secondary theory.

The concept of dispositions, a part of practical theories, provides us with an especially good illustration of how our comparative process operated. (The concept itself, of course, always is liable to being hypostatized and we must remember that dispositions are not substantial somethings; I cannot possess two of a particular kind nor give one to another person.) The practical theory of which the idea of dispositions is a part is considerably more prominent in Aquinas's account than it is in Mencius's account. Indeed, the idea is central to Aquinas's theory but seems hardly to appear in Mencius theory; it fits within a practical theory that Aquinas develops and Mencius implies but never develops. When we recognize this fact and see its implications, we can make comparisons that we otherwise might miss, see new features in each thinker, and pursue important constructive goals.

Nevertheless, the judgment that Mencius possesses but never develops this aspect of his practical theory does seem questionable. Judgments of this kind always will be controversial, and we must proceed with extreme care whenever we argue that aspects of a practical theory are developed by one thinker and only implicit in another. Such judgments, however, also can lead us to some of our most productive inquiries and formulations. For example, utilizing Aquinas's idea that dispositions have different forms enabled me to specify more clearly Mencius's position on semblances of virtue. Moreover, my desire to explain how a notion of dispositions could, and even should, operate in Mencius's practical theory led me to distinguish between development and discovery models of human nature. That distinction, in turn, helped me to formulate in clear fashion an important general point in Mencius: his denial that virtues simply can be discovered and his affirmation that they can and must be developed.

Finally, Mencius's nuanced account of aspects of the process of self-cultivation, as well as his profound, reasoned disquiet about some kinds of invariant responses, provided me with rich materials with which to test the adequacy of ideas in Aquinas's more developed practical theory. That testing also bore fruit in the constructive part of the enterprise. It led me, for example, to develop those distinctions among dispositional responses that provide, I think, a richer account of the idea. The results of the constructive enterprise, in turn, illuminated both strengths and weaknesses in Aquinas's practical theory, deepened the understanding of each figure, and enabled me to develop a more nuanced comparison between them.[10]

The example of dispositions, I think, shows that if we focus on Mencius and Aquinas's practical theories productive comparisons arise. With their secondary theories we may see only dissimilarities or real but thin resemblances. With their practical theories, however, we can probe real and illuminating relationships. This focus also helps us understand better each thinker and the traditions they represent, as well as to develop a more adequate constructive position on the character of virtue and virtues.

Recognizing the existence and importance of thinkers' practical theories, then, is of great importance to the comparative philosophy of human flourishings that focuses on different thinkers' ideas of virtue. Other elements also are critical to the successful execution of this enterprise, of course, and I now want to consider them. My approach up to now (despite a few prominent exceptions) has been to make actual comparisons and let illustrations of method or observations about it appear in that context. In the book's remaining sections, however, I will focus on general issues about method.

Models for doing comparative work are many. But I think we find ideas that point toward a productive model for the comparative philosophy of human flourishings in what initially may appear to be a very odd place: Aquinas's idea that virtues have parts and, most important, his ideas about analogical expressions. Roughly similar ideas and approaches are present in Neo-Confucianism and other traditions and may also even be present, in inchoate form, in Mencius. I will begin with Aquinas's ideas, however, because they are clearest to me, and we have already examined features of them.[11]

In beginning with Aquinas I am not claiming that any traditional approach to the problem of comparing virtues can provide us, as moderns, with a fully satisfactory method. I do think, nevertheless, that we find extremely useful ideas in Aquinas. Moreover, examining them both links us to an important tradition and shows us how we differ from it. In the next section, then, I examine the productiveness and limitations of Aquinas's model. In the final two sections, I move considerably beyond Aquinas's ideas and consider those general features that should inform our approach to the comparative philosophy of human flourishings.

IV. Problems and Possibilities in Aquinas's Model for Comparing Apparently Different Ideas of Virtue

Aquinas responds to and attempts to synthesize an astonishingly diverse group of thinkers; for example, classical Greek philosophers, neo-Platonic theologians, Roman ethicists, and biblical writers who in turn draw on various strands of Ancient Near Eastern religions. He aims to harmonize their different lists of virtues, perspectives on virtue, and understandings of particular virtues. The attempt rests on his presumption that (with at least most features of these different discourses) he can sympathetically appreciate them in their own terms and yet recast them in a way that produces a synthetic whole. This presumption differs considerably from a common modern presumption. Most sophisticated moderns think that apparently different discourses, grounded in evidently different cultures, cannot be harmonized unless someone simply imposes a categorical scheme drawn from one discourse.

Some contemporary thinkers, perhaps most notably Alasdair MacIntyre, have criticized this modern presumption. For them any healthy tradition contains diverse, often conflicting ideals and, most important, has powerful ways to adjudicate conflicts of all sorts. They argue that the tendency of modern thinkers to focus on unbridgeable kinds of diversity arises from a failure in understanding. They fail to grasp the force of the claim that a few vital traditions have within them resources and procedures that allow great thinkers to harmonize apparently divergent positions. Thinkers in such vital traditions, it is argued, can meet the challenges that diversity presents. They can incorporate different positions in a way that preserves the critical insights or formulations of those positions and also resolves internal problems in them and fills their lacunae.[12]

We must take seriously the notion that thinkers in vital traditions can call on powerful resources and procedures. Nevertheless, we still have good reason to be suspicious about attempts like that of Aquinas's. Few moderns share either Aquinas's ideas about the world's evidently rational structure or his exact theological beliefs. Both these features of his thought underlie his aspiration to harmonize apparently different discourses, and they help to generate his sanguineness about the success of his endeavor. Moreover, almost no sophisticated modern shares the ahistorical perspective and insensitivity to the social location of ideas that provides another critical motivational and intellectual support for Aquinas's attempt.

We do not, and should not, share some of the beliefs and presumptions that animate Aquinas. Nevertheless, we also must be careful not to oversimplify the ideas that support his enterprise. I discussed aspects of this issue earlier, but three points bear repeating. First, we must be wary of conflating two matters that Aquinas was usually careful to distinguish. One is the "fact" of a separate, rational ontological order; the other is the problems that plague any human being's full or clear knowledge of its character. Second, we must be careful not to overstate Aquinas's lack of historical and cultural understanding. His treatment of the Old Law, for instance, sometimes shows a keen if embryonic historical and cultural sense. Finally, we must remember that many of the apparent disharmonies Aquinas faces appear in texts, and the differences in content and point of view are clearly evident. Written traditions have replaced oral traditions in Aquinas's world; the subtle hidden transformations produced by oral traditions cannot ease his task. Neither the failures bound up with the fragile mechanisms of human memory nor the desires produced by the human need to harmonize for Aquinas, can smooth over the changes and differences in his culture's history. Indeed, Aquinas faces Augustinians in his own day who insist that sharp breaks and divisions characterize the West's history, that, for instance, pagan virtues at best are splendid vices.[13]

Aquinas's attempt to harmonize different lists of virtues, perspectives on virtue, and treatments of specific virtues, then, is a difficult task and not a simple exercise. Most important here, it rests largely on his utilization of two related ideas. The first is that a virtue can have parts. The second is that the analysis of analogical expressions underlies any attempt to harmonize or even compare apparently different virtues. With both ideas we see procedures and structures that, I think, can be of great help in the comparative philosophy of human flourishings.

Nevertheless, Aquinas normally uses both of these ideas to harmonize apparently divergent notions. I, in contrast, will use them to make comparisons, to find both similarities and differences. Aquinas, then, usually aims to find similarities or to create a structure in which parts relate to one another in a hierarchical fashion. I, on the other hand, may use the same ideas and procedures to identify both differences and similarities; indeed, I may use them to query some of Aquinas's own conclusions.

Aquinas's ideas about analogical expressions are without question the more significant and basic of the two ideas, and examining them will be my main concern. The idea that virtues have parts, however, also can play a key role in comparative analyses, and therefore I need to consider it. The idea was discussed at length earlier, and here I need only to review it quickly, focusing on how it can help us to compare different thinkers' ideas on virtues.[14] Aquinas argues that a virtue can have three parts. First are the qualities, the component parts, that help shape a single virtue's action; for example, memory and foresight in prudence. Second are those distinct virtues, allied virtues, that share the essential characteristic of the primary virtue but fail to express it fully, even if they may express other qualities of the primary virtue more fully than it does; for example, the wit to judge when exceptions to rules are needed (*gnome*). Third are those separable and substantially different activities of a virtue, the types of a virtue, that appear when the virtue operates in distinct spheres of life; for example, military and political prudence.

Aquinas uses these ideas to organize into one systematically articulated whole the panoply of virtues and ideas about specific virtues that he inherits. Augustinian ideas about patience, for example, can be seen as component or allied parts of courage, even though courage largely is defined in Aristotelian terms; Cicero and Aristotle's different accounts of magnanimity can be "synthesized" and fitted into courage's hierarchical structure. I need not review here my discussion of the insights and distortions that appear in Aquinas's accounts of particular virtues.

What is important is seeing how the general notion allows us to compare accounts of virtue that seem to have little in common. In comparing Mencius and Aquinas's different lists of virtues and different formulations of possibly similar virtues, I faced one problem constantly. Given the apparent differences in their accounts, I had to find a way to relate systematically the range of possible activities a single virtue might cover, the various actions and dispositions with which it is concerned. Mencius, for example, never analyzes courage in the way Aquinas does. However, he does examine a variety of admirable qualities, such as the character of true self-esteem or of a proper attitude toward fate, that we can see as parts of courage. We can relate Mencius's ideas on the proper approach to fate to Aquinas's ideas on patience and Mencius's ideas on appropriate self-esteem to Aquinas's ideas on magnanimity, vanity, and pusillanimity. Mencius, then, may seem to lack an account that is prominent in Aquinas. But utilizing the idea that virtues have parts allows me, as discussed at length, to compare productively the two thinkers' accounts and establish systematic relationships that preserve both similarities and differences.[15]

The same situation also was evident when I started from a virtue in Mencius that appears to resemble no virtue in Aquinas; for example, Mencius's ideas on yielding and its consummation in the virtue of propriety (*li*). If we look in Aquinas for allied virtues of Mencius's propriety, however, we find various candidates. One candidate, for instance, are all those related virtues that cover relationships in which people incur unfulfillable debts, such as in their relationships to their parents. Moreover, what Aquinas calls social virtues, a significant group of qualities for him, also can be seen as component parts of Mencius's propriety. The notion that virtues have parts provides, then, a conceptual structure that helps to establish relationships among various qualities or virtues. It allows us to both make comparisons between the two thinkers and highlight features of each thinker that we might otherwise miss.[16]

The idea that virtues have parts, as well as most other aspects of Aquinas's attempt to harmonize different thinkers' ideas on virtues, rests on one major foundation: the theoretical procedures or performances involved in the analysis of analogical predication. In the final two sections, I develop the general implications of these procedures. I also examined earlier how Aquinas employs them in his analysis of specific virtues and in his development of expansions and semblances of virtue. Here, however, I want to focus on a few especially revealing instances of how Aquinas utilizes analogical analyses at precisely these places where he seems to face contrasting formulations. His aim is to harmonize not compare. Nevertheless, evaluating his successes and failures helps us to understand better his approach and to see how we can both use his method and must change it.[17]

Let us start with two brief examples that illuminate well how Aquinas operates and the problems and possibilities in his approach. At one place, Aquinas accepts Augustine's definition of virtue (the definition was actually Peter of Poitier's), which contains prominently the idea that "God works [virtue] in us without us." Aquinas is deeply committed to the principle that grace does not replace nature, as the definition claims, but rather presupposes and perfects it. He, however, can utilize the definition by unraveling the contexts to which different features of the definition respond, the senses of efficacy it employs, and the aspects of virtue with which it is concerned. At another place, Aquinas accepts Aristotle's notion that courage concerns primarily death in warfare. Aquinas is fully aware that an important distinction exists between facing possible death in actual battle to protect the city-state and facing possible death in martyrdom to serve God. But he can accept the notion by widening the normal meanings of both death and warfare. In both cases, Aquinas's synthetic efforts rest on his attempt to specify how apparent differences can include similarities, and apparent similarities, differences. He works, then, by attending to the analogical character of key terms, to the contexts in which their focal and secondary meanings operate, and to how they can be systematically related.[18]

The analysis he gives in each example contains problems, of course, but the problems are of different sorts and magnitudes. The definition of virtue fits within Aquinas's general perspective only if we overlook its rather clear meaning and see it as a statement about God's role in the ultimate causation of all virtues. Similarly, Aquinas's analysis does not correspond exactly to Aristotle's. But that analysis can be said to follow faithfully, even to develop, the implications of Aristotle's account. In the first case, then, we can say that, at best, Aquinas's use of analogy allows him to establish minimum grounds for comparison, even if it fails to bring the harmonization of views he seeks. In the second case, his use of analogy generates real and revealing resemblances.

Other examples show us still other facets of the problems and possibilities that accompany Aquinas's employment of the procedures involved in examining analogical expressions. Many of the most illuminating examples appear when Aquinas attempts to relate St. Paul and Aristotle, probably the two most important and most evidently dissimilar figures to whom he responds. (Indeed, the two discourses on virtue I have been comparing in this book appear, at times, to differ no more than the discourses of those two thinkers.) Aquinas's success in bringing them together, however, often is remarkable, even startling. Aristotle's magnanimous man, for instance, is confident about his excellence and distant from most other people. He hardly seems to be a good candidate to harmonize, or even compare, with St. Paul's ideal person, a person who exemplifies humility and service to others. Aquinas's analysis shows us, nevertheless, some striking similarities.[19]

Despite this, we are still unconvinced by aspects of Aquinas's account. We see strains between Aristotle's magnanimity and St. Paul's humility that Aquinas either fails to highlight or slides over too easily. In other instances, moreover, we may see more than just strains. Aquinas's Aristotelian reading, for example, of St. Paul's statement in Romans about his inability to do the good he desires and avoid the bad he wants to avoid, especially at first glance, probably would convince few people. Recognizing such strains or failures is instructive. These recognitions help us see those places where real differences in perspective make impossible the kind of harmonization that Aquinas pursues. In accepting such instruction, we must remember, however, that Aquinas himself does believe that some views cannot be harmonized. He often underlines, for example, the differences between Stoic and Christian views on the role of emotions in the perfected person. Nevertheless, Aquinas usually aims to harmonize, and we must remain alert to those cases where his account fails or is less than fully convincing. The attempt to harmonize that fails can reveal much of importance to us as comparativists.[20]

Even more revealing, however, can be the recognition that what initially appeared to be a complete failure may in fact be a partial success. In such cases, we see how the process Aquinas employs can uncover relationships, and thus make possible comparisons, that seemed to be inconceivable. Aquinas, for instance, highlights the analogical character of terms like *magnanimity* and *humility* when he compares St. Paul and Aristotle's ideals. That helps us both to see how some notion of a higher good must be revered by the magnanimous man and recognize how self-confidence and a sense of personal nobility may not only fit with humility but even be a necessary part of it. We, then, correctly may see strains that Aquinas did not. But his enterprise also can help us recognize similarities within differences that we missed.

Examining the strains, failures, and partial successes in Aquinas's procedures also leads us to understand another significant matter. They provide us with good examples of how Aquinas's desire to harmonize and not just compare leads him to engage imperfectly in those philosophical performances that inform the analysis of analogical predication. His analysis of Aristotle and St. Paul's positions on the failure to act as one wants to act illustrates this point well. (I examined this point from another perspective, one that stressed tensions in his thought, when I discussed Aquinas's understanding of why humans fail to become virtuous.) If we use Aquinas's own ideas about grace's instrumentality in a way he did not, we can say that Aquinas ought not simply posit a similarity between Aristotle's modified acceptance of the idea that to know the good is to do the good and Paul's rejection of that idea. Rather, he should have presented a similarity within a difference or a difference within a similarity. By focusing on the analogical character of terms like *will*, *knowledge*, and *ability* and by relating the different notions of causation (and perhaps even levels of being) to which the analogical predications refer, he could have related the two apparently disparate thinkers even if he could not harmonize them. That is, a more thoroughgoing use of Aquinas's own procedures shows how they can allow us to make comparisons we otherwise would have been unable to make, even if they cannot produce the similarities that Aquinas aimed to produce.[21]

When examining virtues, Aquinas almost always analyzes analogical expressions with one of two goals in mind. He aims either to uncover similarities or to build a structure in which parts relate to each other in a hierarchical fashion. Aquinas, then, usually is too ready to focus on the similarity aspect of the similarity in difference that constitutes analogy. This leads him, at times, to fail to highlight significant distinctions, to overlook subtle differences, and to establish imperfectly the bases for comparison, if not similarity, present.

Nevertheless, recognizing Aquinas's startling successes, evaluating why successes or failures occur, and seeing how apparent failures can be reworked into partial successes shows us the remarkable productivity of his approach. His ideas about analogical predication and the analytic procedures it spawns, I think, point toward an excellent way to do the comparative philosophy of human flourishings. Let us turn from our examination of Aquinas to a general discussion of the main features of that process.

V. Analogical Expression, Focal and Secondary Terms, and the Comparative Philosophy of Human Excellences

I believe we need to approach comparative studies through those performances that arise from examining and using analogical expressions. Through analyzing the ordered relationships among analogical terms we can preserve both clarity and textured diversity, and thereby fully articulate similarities in differences and differences in similarities. We, then, can uncover resemblances among distinct phenomena at the cost of neither variety nor similarity.[22]

The fact that this approach involves ongoing operations, continuing performances, is extremely important. It does not rest on applying a static structure or a fixed theory to material, and therefore it cannot produce the desired results as would a mechanical implement. Some comparative methods resemble such mechanical implements, and all are liable to being used in that way. That is, they can be used in a way that resembles the use of a machine to turn raw material into the desired result. This approach, in contrast, involves utilizing imaginative processes, subtle skills, and other personal qualities or excellences. Indeed, as I will discuss in the final section, the character of these qualities and the justification for their results can be difficult to specify with all the precision that some people might demand and all would hope possible.

My main business in this section is to examine this approach or method, using examples from my analysis and concentrating on the construction and relation of focal and secondary meanings. Before doing this, however, we need to see how it utilizes but differs from two related approaches. An approach based on analogy steers between the poles represented by approaches to comparative studies that rest on the primacy of either the *univocal* or the *equivocal*, speaking with a single voice and producing only similarities or speaking with many voices and producing only differences. On the one side is the claim to almost complete adequacy characteristic of univocal predication. A Freudian study that focuses only on the Oedipal complex or a theological study that focuses only on the idea of compassion can exemplify this approach. In comparative studies, this procedure sacrifices variety and thins out the thickness of the specific phenomena studied. On the other side is the claim to almost complete diversity characteristic of equivocal predication. Proponents of this position aim to explicate richly textured particulars that stand in relationships defined by contrast or even incommensurability. An anthropological study that focuses on the distinctiveness of a preliterate culture or a theologically informed analysis that explicates a single religion's supposedly unique message can exemplify this approach.

To my mind, neither the equivocal option nor the univocal option, used alone, provides a satisfactory basis for comparative studies of virtue or probably for any illuminating cross-cultural studies. The former option, equivocity, makes such studies virtually impossible. Without some common reference, we cannot even know what to contrast much less compare. The latter option, univocity, can help us clarify significant, common features, but it also produces a uniformity, often a deadening uniformity, that leaves little room for actual comparison and usually presents us with abstract, untextured ideas.

The ideas of equivocal and univocal predication have important roles to play in establishing comparisons. They should function, however, as adjuncts to, or even aspects of, the examination of analogical predications. That is, candidates for equivocal and univocal predication always will appear when we compare. These candidates must be respected and examined closely because they help us establish the appropriate context in which to do comparisons. Candidates for equivocity will appear whenever we compare significantly different figures or cultures. Psychophysical energy (ch'i) in Mencius and God (Deus) in Aquinas, especially when they appear as parts of secondary theories, are good examples of such candidates. We may find minimal grounds for comparison with these and other candidates. But we must always keep in mind just how minimal, and how tenuous, are those grounds; some comparisons are best described as being not quite equivocal. Indeed, if such notions are absolutely central to the subjects investigated, we may not be able to find real similarities in differences and differences in similarities. If, however, they only help define the context within which other elements are present, we can productively compare those other elements. We, nevertheless, must continue to refer back to the equivocal features of the context, and they always ought to generate in us both caution and tentativeness. The comparison of Mencius and Aquinas's ideas on the operation of perfected courage and the character of religious endurance, I think, illustrates how to proceed in such a situation.[23]

Candidates for univocity also will appear in any comparison. Indeed, some singleness of voice or reference must underlie any comparison. Most such candidates, however, fall into the category of what I earlier called *real but thin resemblances*, such as the ones that appear in the realm of injunctions. Common characteristics are present, but to focus only on them is to overlook significant kinds of diversity and texture. A notion of ethical obligation appears in both Mencius and Aquinas, but it is embedded in extremely different cultural contexts and relates to, or even allies with, significantly different kinds of ideas.

Recognizing candidates for equivocal and univocal predication is important. But even more important is dealing well with these candidates. With candidates for equivocity, we must pursue possible relationships but not overlook differences. Most important, we must decide just how deeply, and in just what ways, they affect the comparisons on which we focus.

When virtue is the subject, the distinction between secondary and practical theories often informs these decisions in a critical way. (I argued earlier, for example, that neither *ch'i* nor *Deus*, as conceptual parts of the respective secondary theories, is that central when we focus on most aspects of Aquinas and Mencius's practical theories.) With candidates for univocity, we must remember that they undergird any comparisons we make and yet they usually produce only thin and often finally unrevealing results.

Our main focus, however, always should be on skillfully employing the processes involved in analogical predication. Most notable is the process of articulating ordered similarities in differences. By means of this process we can "solve" or, more accurately, carefully and continually work through one of the most central and vexing problems in comparative studies: the choice of which categories to employ when we do comparisons and how best to use them. The notion that analogical terms have systematically related focal and secondary meaning gives us a productive approach to that problem.

The business of identifying and relating focal and secondary terms almost always is a difficult one. People will argue about whether the meanings are systematically connected or even truly related; that is, they will argue about whether we really have not analogy but ambiguity or even equivocity. Many will agree that the notion of "health" belongs in a distinctive, focal way to the idea of a human being, and that healthy food refers to a cause of human health and healthy urine to a sign of human health. Other notions, however, will generate substantial disagreements. For example, some will argue that "love," even if defined as an activity of persons, either has no evident focal meaning or that its various uses show no evident relationships. What, they will ask, relates my love of my wife, my children, my country, Shakespeare, and good wine. Which of them can we legitimately call focal and which secondary, and on what grounds?

Perhaps the basic problem I faced in this study is how to develop focal and secondary meanings when I dealt with discourses that are as different as my twentieth-century English, Mencius's fourth-century-B.C.E. Chinese, and Aquinas's thirteenth-century-C.E. Latin. The problem is a substantial one, but I think good reasons exists for my *initially* deriving the focal meaning of most key terms from contemporary English usage; that is, from my understanding of the terms. I must *adjust* those chosen focal terms as the comparison proceeds, as I will discuss. But let me note first why I made such an initial choice and what implications follow from it.

I am most familiar with the idiosyncrasies and nuances of contemporary English, my home discourse. It is the discourse the intricacies of which I have come to appreciate through using it and through the work of those philosophers and theologians I have read most consistently and carefully. Moreover, most of my readers will best understand it, as their experience resembles mine. Choosing it, however, does have one inevitable and important consequence for my comparative studies. My focal terms, at least initially, almost always will be closer to Aquinas's terminology than to Mencius's terminology. Were I a native speaker of Chinese, and especially were I writing for other native speakers of Chinese, the reverse would be true. I would have just as good reasons to derive my focal meanings from ideas, for example, like psychophysical energy (*ch'i*) or heart-mind (*hsin*). In that case my initial focal terms would be closer to Mencius than to Aquinas.[24]

I think that I have excellent reasons initially to select my focal meanings from the discourse with which I and my readers feel most at home. Nevertheless, dangers, and even grave temptations, accompany the selection. They are unavoidable, but a self-consciousness about their character increases my vigilance, extends my sympathies, and improves my analyses. The most critical of them will be my first topic of discussion, and then, using material from this book, I can examine the general character of the process of analyzing focal and secondary meanings.

The choice of focal terms from a home discourse may be reasonable, but people who are unclear about the processes involved in analogical predication can see in it a simple imposition of categories. In fact, many of the difficulties that arise when comparativeness from different cultures or even subcultures interact (either talk with each other or read each other's works) occur because the focal terms utilized normally are drawn from the comparativist's home discourse. In the most damaging situations, this leads one group of people to think another group of people are just imposing alien categories on their culture. Conversely, the other group may think the first group's ideas exhibit naiveté, cultural chauvinism, or even unreflective superstition. The opposing groups then may label the offending categories or focal terms in ways that just deepen rancor or misunderstanding. Labels like unsophisticated or imperialistic may be used. *Ch'i* is declared an example of primitive science; grace, an example of Western colonialism.

The situation can begin to look like the interchange, much beloved by some analytic philosophers, in *Through the Looking Glass*, between Alice and Humpty Dumpty. Humpty Dumpty says:

"There's glory for you."
"I don't know what you mean by 'glory', Alice said.
Humpty Dumpty smiled contemptuously. "Of course you don't —
till I tell you. I meant 'there's a nice knock-down argument for you!'"
"But glory doesn't mean 'a nice knock-down argument',", Alice
objected.
"When I use a word," Humpty Dumpty said, in a rather scornful
tone, "it means just what I choose it to mean — neither more or less."

"The question is," said Alice, "whether you *can* make words mean
so many different things."
"The question is," said Humpty Dumpty, "which is to be master —
that's all."[25]

Humpty Dumpty thinks that meanings always are or must be legislated,
and that such legislation depends on who has power. This notion may be
philosophically confused when we discuss some linguistic forms and many
linguistic forms within a commonly held discourse. But it clearly has considerable bite when we discuss interchanges where substantial cultural differences are evident and at issue. Who has the power to set focal terms
may seem to be the crucial question.

Recognizing this can lead some people to a gentler, more irenic but
still unsatisfactory posture. They, in conversation or writing, either will
keep a respectful distance or allow a panoply of undiscussed focal terms to
be used. Either strategy, in practice, purchases peace at the price of substantial intellectual interchange. Moreover, each posture resembles one that
relies on either equivocal or univocal predication and therefore suffers from
the problems that accompany such a reliance. The latter posture, allowing a
panoply of terms to be used, resembles a position that assumes equivocal
predication is the best for which we can hope; and the former posture,
maintaining a respectful distance, often relies on accepting univocal predications. Neither helps move forward the comparative enterprise or produce
more productive conversations among people from different cultures.

All these difficulties are exacerbated by historical circumstances
beyond anyone's control, difficulties that make painfully relevant Humpty
Dumpty's question about which is to be master. Our common history has
features that we overlook at our peril; for example, the presence of colonial
and anti-colonial movements in the recent past and the rise in the West of
a particular kind of critical reflectiveness that has been venerated by many
and excoriated by some. Even if these obstacles were not present, however,
we would still face significant difficulties. The intellectual and personal
problems involved in such intercultural exchanges are both too numerous
and too complicated to allow us to hope for any easy solution.

Despite this, I think that specific intellectual problems (and even
some of the other problems) can be ameliorated by a better understanding
of how the processes of analogical predication work. Especially important
is grasping how they rely on the use of systematically related focal and secondary meanings. We must recognize that focal terms will, for good reasons, initially be drawn from the interpreter's home discourse, as noted.
More important, we also must understand that analysis based on these processes will *modify* the chosen focal terms, will *facilitate comparisons*, and will

involve a *constructive* or normative dimension. Grasping the dynamic character of this process, then, allows us better to see how comparisons (and ideally conversations) between different ideas, cultures, and peoples can be produced. Furthermore, it also helps us recognize that such processes have constructive implications. Examples drawn from preceding chapters can illustrate well, I think, the crucial features of the process.

My use of the ideas of dispositions and of practical reason illustrates how comparative analysis may *modify* substantially the chosen focal terms. The term disposition does differ from the *habitus* of Aquinas, but it surely fits more easily into Aquinas's conceptual world than into Mencius's in which no evident equivalent can be found. Despite this, as discussed earlier, the idea of dispositions enables us to comprehend more fully a range of notions in Mencius and grasp more firmly his theory of virtue. Moreover, understanding Mencius's reasoned disquiet about some kinds of automatic reactions led me to reformulate constructively the idea of dispositions and distinguish among intelligent dispositions, habits, propensities, and invariant reactions. That normative reformulation, in turn, both established new focal and secondary meanings for the term and led me to see Aquinas's ideas in a new light.[26]

The development of the idea of practical reason may show even more clearly how examining Mencius's ideas affects the analysis of a focal term drawn initially from contemporary English usage. My constructive development of the idea owes much to my study of Mencius's intelligent awareness (*chih*). Furthermore, utilizing Mencius's ideas to develop focal and secondary meanings also led me to see more vividly how the contemporary idea of practical reason differs from Aquinas's practical wisdom (*prudentia*). Mencius's notion of *chih*, then, helped to shape my constructive enterprise, informed my interpretation of Aquinas's ideas, and allowed me to see how both thinkers resemble and differ from many contemporary understandings of practical reason.[27]

Another example, my analysis of courage, illustrates how establishing focal and secondary meanings helps to *facilitate comparisons*. Almost all agree that courage is both a general human virtue and a significant term in the Confucian tradition. Courage, however, has received considerably more theoretical analysis in Western thought than in Chinese thought, and this fact, as discussed, might reveal something important about the role of the martial spirit, or the warrior ideal, in the two cultures. In any event, Mencius and Aquinas's treatments of courage surely differ. Courage is one of Aquinas's four cardinal virtues and receives a complex, extended analysis by him. Courage neither receives an extended analysis by Mencius nor functions as one of his four central virtues. My response to this problem clarifies, I think, how the use of this method can facilitate the comparisons we make.

I initially set courage's focal meaning through Western analyses, including the one found in Aquinas. I then used the idea of secondary meanings (and even parts of courage) to interpret Mencius's account, and this enabled me to relate to courage qualities such as having an appropriate attitude to self-esteem and fate. The process of comparative analysis, however, did not stop at that point. Mencius's treatment reveals important things about both courage and Aquinas's analysis. Mencius does not focus as centrally on courage as Aquinas and can be said to separate out its various aspects more clearly. Most notably, he highlights that transformation of courage from a martial to a general and religiously important virtue that also is present but less evident in Aquinas. When we see how Mencius extends courage into the religious realm and focuses unremittingly on semblances of courage, we can understand courage more fully and also better grasp important features of Aquinas's account. Moreover, utilizing the complex and extensive analysis of courage in Aquinas enables us, in turn, to probe even further into Mencius's account.[28]

Using the processes involved in the analysis of analogical predications to compare these two accounts of courage enabled me to reach several goals. Although it initially seemed that, at best, only minimal grounds for comparison were present, I found I could compare them in illuminating ways. Moreover, comparing them also helped me to see more clearly important features in each thinker's account. Finally, the whole process led me to construct a more adequate account of the notion of courage. These examples (dispositions and practical reason, on the one hand, and courage, on the other hand), then, illustrate how developing and relating focal and secondary terms helps us do comparative studies of virtue.

Moreover, reviewing those examples also highlights one facet of the process about which I have said little so far. A *constructive* or normative dimension appears when I rework my initial focal meanings in light of those materials that inform my comparison. A kind of constructive, theoretical inquiry, then, occurs when I develop focal meanings. The comparativist works both with a contemporary understanding of ideas and with that understanding of ideas provided by the figures being compared.

The comparativist, as each of these three examples shows, aims to give a true account. The account arises, however, not just from reflection on one's own language, ideas, and experience, as is the case with much modern Western philosophy. It also arises from reflection on the language, ideas, and experience of those thinkers from different cultures with whom one deals. Comparative philosophers of religions may not examine (usually for reasons arising from considerations about space and genre) all the problems they would were they attempting only to present a convincing theoretical argument. They aim to produce a true account, nevertheless, and to use materials from traditions and thinkers that may differ sub-stantially from their own. An approach based on the idea of analogical expressions, and thus of focal and secondary meanings, has constructive implications, then, and a normative dimension.

This approach also provides tools to steer between the poles repre-sented by perspectives that rely on simple univocity or equivocity. As dis-cussed earlier, we must both utilize and mediate between each of these perspectives. Doing this, however, is very difficult. (Indeed, another nor-mative feature of this kind of inquiry, as discussed, involves developing the virtues that enable us to do it well.) To pursue the ideal of working with similarities in differences and differences in similarities is to attempt a taxing balancing act. Practitioners of this approach always face the dan-ger of slipping, easily and almost imperceptibly, toward one of the poles between which they attempt to negotiate.

Manifold reasons underlie the tendency to move toward untextured uniformities or sheer diversity. The reasons will vary from person to per-son, from discipline to discipline, from culture to culture, and from histori-cal period to historical period. I will focus, in the next section, on how the tendency arises from questions that many moderns have about the sensible-ness of embracing a procedure that relies on imaginative processes. Let me note briefly here, however, two other contemporary sources of the pressure to abandon the activities involved in the analysis of analogical predication.

We all face intense pressures today to see cross-cultural studies in terms of the sheer diversity of equivocity. Such pressures, in the intellectual world, usually arise from the social sciences or the more radical forms of humanistic hermeneutics, and often they also are accompanied by a power-ful political agenda. These pressures normally are reinforced by most peo-ple's legitimate desires both to depict those cultural experiences that often were neglected in standard accounts and to depict them in terms that reflect their distinctive characters. The pressures may be abating somewhat, as it has become clearer that to focus on radical diversity makes impossible not only comparative studies but even most studies of any culture that differs from one's own or the purportedly dominant culture. Nevertheless, the pull of equivocity remains strong for both intellectual and social reasons.

Subtle pressures also exist to move comparative studies toward the easy likeness of mere commonality, toward an overly facile harmony or an even more deadening uniformity. Some proponents of such a move produce only popular accounts, and they seem to have little extensive knowledge of tradi-tions other than the ones to which they belong. More effective are the pres-sures that arise from people in another group, with not only deeply held reli-gious commitments but also the concomitant, and commendable, desire to refuse to divide the world into those who are saved and those who are not.

All can sympathize with the desire to reject simple divisions into those who flourish religiously and those who do not. Nevertheless, few sophisticated students of religion would argue, for reasons noted earlier, that a univocal approach can operate well in comparative studies generally or in the comparative philosophy of religions more particularly. A variant of a univocal approach, one that concentrates on specific religious experiences or, perhaps, formulations of the sacred might possibly work. I remain hesitant about even it, however, especially if the focus is on abstract metaphysical formulations. Comparisons of those formulations, as discussed earlier, usually are unable to produce textured resemblances, and such comparisons often fail to deal seriously enough with differences in secondary theories.[29]

Most important to us is another reason for the tendency of many modern Western intellectuals and some traditional scholars, from various cultures, to reject the analogical and embrace instead either the univocal or the equivocal approach to comparative studies. This reason rests on an uneasiness about, or even positive distrust of, those imaginative processes that underlie a procedure that focuses on analogical predications. Let us, then, consider the role of imagination in the comparative philosophy of human flourishings. This topic is an especially propitious one with which to end, as it also allows us to consider several other significant, general issues.

VI. The Analogical Imagination and the Comparative Philosophy of Religions

The specification of analogies is in significant part a product of the imagination. The ability to spot the similar in the dissimilar and the dissimilar in the similar are marks of the imagination. Moreover, most of the capacities that allow us to develop the ramifications of those insights rest in the imagination. We can clarify the form of these imaginative processes, it is true; we even can show how they relate to and resemble common rational processes. But they remain imaginative processes.

Western scholars, especially hard-headed Western scholars, often are wary about following imaginative processes. At the least, they are wary about relying on them too much. That wariness remains even if the idea of imagination is purged of many of its more dramatic Romantic connotations and even if the wary scholars are not wed to an overly simple model of humanistic inquiry. This dissatisfaction also appears, if in a different guise, with many scholars from cultures outside the West who represent modes of scholarship that are traditional in their culture. (In some fields these traditional modes of scholarship, of course, also have deeply influenced Western scholars.) Although I will focus here only on Western scholars, the analysis given, *mutatis mutandis*, is applicable to these traditional scholars. Indeed, when problems arise in intercultural understanding, and even conversations, issues about the role of the imagination often are crucial.[30] The dissatisfaction of Western scholars with relying on the imagination often rests on their judgments about how best to understand the vocation of modern humanistic scholarship. Especially important are their judgments about what canons of verification should operate. Recent years have seen the emergence of serious disagreements about how best to justify interpretations or adjudicate among different interpretations. Questions about whether the notion of truth or reference has a place in truly humanistic scholarship often have been a central issue, and the appropriate role of the imagination often has been a significant topic. Many features of these disagreements represent a modern version of that age-old battle in the West (which can be traced to Plato but has taken different forms at different times) between the poets and the philosophers. More traditional scholars often assume both the mantle and the arguments of the philosophers. Their hesitancies about a reliance on the imagination, then, often are grounded in beliefs about the character of intellectual inquiry and even the ethical ends it must serve. These beliefs, and the deep commitments they generate, are both understandable and commendable.

Despite this, I think it clear that comparative studies of human flourishings must engage in a process that necessarily involves us in a form of imagining, in the utilization of the analogical imagination. To say we must use the imagination is not also to say that standards dissolve; it is not to join forces with some of the more radical forms of humanistic scholarship. Imaginative processes involves standards for judging interpretations and rules that can be followed well or badly. The possibility of error remains, and (as I will discuss) theories about why errors arise can be constructed.

Nevertheless, the processes involved are imaginative ones. They depend, for example, on the interpreter's sensibilities, they may evoke rather than demonstrate, and they produce inventions. The operations of the imagination, then, are rule-governed and liable to specifiable forms of error, but they produce personally formed, evocative kinds of invention. Moreover, these inventions have the power to give a new form to our experiences. The imaginative redescription produced challenges our normal experience of the contemporary world in which we live and the often distant worlds we study.

We ought not underestimate the disturbing challenges such imaginative redescriptions can generate for our understanding both of our own world and of the worlds of those people we try to understand. Mencius and Aquinas came to look very differently to me as my comparative analysis proceeded. Such a process can be distressing, especially as one's scholarly identity in part, is linked to having a correct understanding of specific figures or cultures. Even more distressing, my understanding of human excellence, and even of those abstract categories (like dispositions) that I used was changed or called in question as I proceeded. Perhaps, I thought, I was bound more by my culture than I had previously believed, say, in my sense that practical rationality must involve calculation or my idea that courage must involve at least some martial aspect. Perhaps I had unknowingly domesticated both Aquinas and Mencius's ideas about why transhuman forces are needed if human excellence is to be achieved. The constructive drive to make sense out of what arises from the comparative process, and therefore also to reformulate my own normative ideas, became a necessary part of the whole enterprise. But it often was a disturbing and even painful process.

The presence of such challenges to one's understanding of both one's self and others can make very appealing the safe harbor presented by either univocal or equivocal formulations. This appeal helps to explain the liability we all have to slip back into those more comfortable kinds of rational operations, where either just similarities or just differences are highlighted. When similarities are highlighted, no real challenges appear. When differences are highlighted, the challenges that appear are too remote to be real confrontations, they are so alien that we understand we cannot really engage them and still remain ourselves. The new constitutions of experience that the analogical imagination produces can be distressing, then, and we may avoid them for that reason. They involve us in the process of making alien the familiar, they force us to become explorers in our homeland, and this is an extremely difficult process. They also give us a gift of inestimable value, however. We can see ourselves and what we study in a new light or even in a series of new and changing lights.[31]

The light produced, however, is one that we ourselves cast, and some people may find that recognition difficult to accept. The recognition need not raise substantial problems when the constructive side of the project is being prosecuted, unless one accepts a position in which theoreticians add nothing to the inquiries they make. My desire to produce a better account of a concept by using both my own culturally informed notions and those found in Aquinas and Mencius necessarily involves me centrally in the process. But the recognition understandably makes people uneasy when the project is to produce an accurate comparison of Mencius and Aquinas's ideas. Nevertheless, if we use the analogical imagination, the locus of comparison must exist in the scholar's mind and not in the objects studied. That fact, the reasons for it, and implications of it must be accepted.

Mencius and Aquinas neither knew each other nor read each other's work. Moreover, neither thinker probably could even have imagined the genre or much of the contents of the other thinker's work. Indeed, when representatives of each thinker's ideas finally did meet, they often found grasping the other position extremely difficult; problems about the choice of focal terms were legion, for example. That is, the misunderstandings between early Catholic missionaries and Confucians were sometimes comic, and occasionally tragic, even though Neo-Confucianism contains more similarities to Catholic Christianity than does classical Confucianism.[32]

Furthermore, even if Mencius and Aquinas had met their accounts would differ from what occurs when we as comparativists bring them together. In examining Aquinas's procedure for harmonizing divergent views, for example, we saw that his procedures (although helpful to us) aim not at comparisons but at similarities or hierarchical harmonies. The results of his endeavor would differ substantially from the results of our attempt to analyze, compare, or even harmonize the diversity that appears when thinkers come from substantially different cultures. Unlike what either Mencius or Aquinas would do, for instance, I recognize radical differences in their respective secondary theories and therefore focused on their practical theories.

To stress that the locus of comparison exists in the scholar's mind, of course, is not to argue that we ought not attend closely to the objects studied. Indeed, we must always try to understand each thinker both initially, and as we proceed, in his own terms. This enterprise helps us avoid the possible distortions the comparative enterprise may introduce. Nevertheless, the very idea of understanding each thinker "in his own terms" is transmuted, and even productively challenged, by the process of comparison. The construction of focal and secondary terms, for instance, affects deeply the terminology used to describe and analyze a thinker.

Close attention to the actual texture of each thinker is crucial, but we must never forget that the comparison itself is an imaginative construction. As comparativists we manipulate the different and the common as we work. We choose which to highlight and which to neglect, and we choose when to relate them. We must work from similarities, else we will establish only contrasts or perhaps even incommensurabilities. But even then our work is anamorphic not homologous. The similarities always are just resemblances; they live in and usually are deeply formed by sharply divergent contexts. We must also pursue differences, however, if the comparisons are to be more than just tautological exercises. If they are to be interesting, revealing, and therefore also inevitably problematic, differences must be highlighted. Neither the equivocal nor the univocal can be neglected; to focus on the analogical is to work constantly with each and between both of them.

Whitehead once said that in any sophisticated philosophy virtually all the same elements would be found; differences could be explained by which elements were in the forefront and which in the background. Taken as a comment about the character of a tradition, the statement can be seen as an exaggeration in the direction of truth. (As his famous phrase puts it, Western philosophy is a series of footnotes to Plato.) In fact, traditions are traditions just because some version of his statement is true.

When we look at thinkers from markedly different cultures, however, Whitehead's notion can be extremely misleading. The image of similar elements that can be found in either the foreground or background fails to fit, unless we define the elements at a level of abstraction so general that it conveys little of importance. With truly different cultures the questions people think important to ask, the issues they think they must solve, or the concepts and secondary theories they believe they must utilize can all differ radically. Indeed, the fundamental character of these differences is what leads me to argue that the analogical imagination must be used in the comparative philosophy of religions.

We must use our imagination, then, to examine and construct analogies, to set and reset focal and secondary meanings, and to articulate their relationships. Some may hope that the mind's imaginative capacities manifest a power that unveils deeper, universal truths about the world, truths accessible only if those capacities are activated by that power. This hope draws on sophisticated, and controversial, Romantic ideas about the imagination's character and usefulness. My reliance on, and hope for, the analogical imagination is considerably more modest. Nevertheless, I think it represents a shaping, ordering power that can enable an interpreter to see inner relationships that bind and even unify what appears only to diverge.

I see such imaginings as encompassing a variety of activities in which we suppose that some state of affairs is present. We assume, entertain, consider, and even toy with or pretend that certain constructions of experience are true. These "supposings" display sophisticated intellectual abilities and often are difficult to undertake and maintain. They are difficult to entertain because they often are at war with our ever-present inclination to idolatry. Especially opposed to them is that kind of idolatry in which we attempt to understand and control our environment by means of ideas made in our own image. To entertain such supposings, then, we must overcome a disposition to control and make habitable our world, and this takes considerable flexibility and courage.

These "supposings" also manifest a very sophisticated set of mental operations. They include, for example, a variety of intellectual skills. An especially noteworthy one is the ability to suspend normal ways of conceiving one's self and subject matter to create a new picture of the world with which to live. Processes like this are common in the writing or reading of literature and in the producing or viewing of art. They also have more common forms, however, some of which are crucial to the ethical life. My desire or need to understand other people in order to help, befriend, or work with them often involves utilizing this skill. I must be able to grasp why someone would act or react in a way that differs markedly from how I would act or react. The way to achieve such understanding often rests on my ability to suspend most of my normal notions of how I, and even others I know, normally operate. I can then imaginatively produce and inhabit another world.

With comparative studies, the impetus for these imaginative activities arises from many different sources and takes many different forms. In some cases, the impetus resembles that present in the common situations just noted; that is, we realize that we cannot really fathom why the people we study act or react as they do. We recognize, for example, that we just do not understand why a thinker continues to insist that all humans must have the capacity to perfect themselves despite all the evidence he marshalls against the idea. At other times, the impetus arises from the observations, challenges, and suggestions of the community of people with whom we talk and read. A colleague or article leads us to realize, for instance, that a thinker believes adherence to roles is far more important than we had thought the thinker did.

In still others cases, the impetus appears with the inchoate but pressing need we feel to put vague ideas into the ordered form that analogical analyses demand. In some such situations, we self-consciously and laboriously examine and test our supposings to give them an appropriate structure. At other times, however, the order seems to force itself on us by crystallizations of our knowledge of, and sense for, the thinkers studied. These crystallizations arise from powers and in ways that we only dimly understand. They also lead us to consider how mysterious and often crucial are those processes that have led many to speak of muses and some of unconscious processes.

At times, often a discouragingly large number of times, we are led to recognize that our supposings are simply wrong. The notion of matter or even energy, for instance, just cannot be the focal meaning of which pyschophysical energy (*ch'i*) is a secondary meaning, nor can Mencius's Heaven (*T'ien*) be directly related to Aquinas's God. Imaginings of the sort I describe are compatible with most kinds of skepticism about the results of our imaginings. That is, the products of these imaginings can be checked and then corrected or discarded. We come to see, after further reflection, that a formulation just leaves out too much of importance or is couched in language that can mislead. We become convinced, after more study, that a key text just will not support a certain supposing. (At times, I found myself returning over and over again, finally with sinking feelings, to texts in both Mencius and Aquinas that challenged and then destroyed some of my more treasured supposings.) Then, with help, on cool reflection, or on further study, we can spot and explain the errors that appear in our own and other people's imaginative work.

Often, however, we do not just find error. Nor are we normally led to treat the problems that arise from such imaginings as simply failed assertions or bad hypotheses. In examining these cases we employ other standards of judgment. (These cases arose for me most often when I dealt with comparisons of particular virtues in Mencius and Aquinas or aspects of their underlying theories of virtue.) We use a set of evaluative terms, I think, that also occur when we judge the operations of the imagination in other realms, realms as different as sophisticated literature and the play of children. We will say, for instance, that the imaginative constructions are deft or clumsy, appear banal or exciting, are superficial or deep, show flair or remain pedestrian, or are brilliantly inane or solidly provocative.

Criteria like these are slippery. Identifying and explaining exactly why one rather than another quality applies to the comparison can be difficult. In the most complicated cases, our judgments even resemble those we make when we examine the differing interpretations that appear in considering the climactic moments of great works of literature; for example, when we ask whether Captain Vere's judgment on Billy Budd was cruel or just, or whether Gabriel's final state in Joyce's "The Dead" is one of paralysis or of compassionate union.

Moreover, we also realize the aptness of the judgments made from such criteria rests finally on the sensibilities of the observer. We find operating here, then, a version of the "good person criterion," in either its Aristotelian or Confucian forms. The flourishing person provides us with the ultimate criterion for deciding what characterizes human flourishing in all specific situations. (Judgments about the activities of the analogical imagination, however, do resemble aesthetic judgments even more closely than the ethical judgments on which the traditional account focuses.) All these judgments rest on an idea that is clearly circular, but, I think, the circle is not a vicious one. Rather, it is a benign or even virtuous one. It rests, as discussed, on the presumption that how one knows depends on what one knows; that imprecision characterizes some subjects; and that therefore some judgments can be made only by those who have a sympathetic grasp of the subject. Using this criterion, I will finally discount the views of someone who thinks Shakespeare's late comedies are superficial, clumsy, or boring, after intense discussion of the plays. Similarly, after a corresponding conversation, I will discount the views of someone who makes comments like that about illuminating products of the analogical imagination. Such judgments need not end the interchange. I finally may be persuaded that what seemed deep was superficial or vice versa. But the grounds for making such judgments (assuming no simple error exists) will remain criteria that fit within the world of imaginings.[33]

To emphasize the significance of the operations of the analogical imagination when we compare ideals of religious flourishing is not to remove such work from criticisms that arise say, from historical, philological, or textual studies. Nor is it to say that where imagination reigns, conversation ends. But it is to recognize that these comparisons are imaginative constructions that revolve around an interpreter's creation of similarities in differences and differences in similarities. Such constructions involve overcoming our inclinations to idolatry, and they utilize subtle intellectual skills. Moreover, they have their own criteria, their own kinds of sophistication or lack of sophistication.

I hope that little in my exposition of Mencius and Aquinas is simply in error, that my comparisons satisfy the criteria imaginative constructions are judged by, and that this work can involve me and others in further inquiries and conversations. More important, I hope this book illustrates, both in results and in approach, the significance of doing that kind of comparative philosophy of religions in which we compare views of human flourishing or excellence.

My inquiry produced, I believe, three related but different results. First, and most obviously, it generated illuminating interpretative descriptions of each figure and the various relationships between them. Second, it generated some constructive conclusions about theories of virtue and analyses of particular virtues. Third, it showed how comparing thinkers who spring from different cultures is itself an important activity, and one that contains its own flourishing and stunted forms.

The last two results, perhaps particularly the last one, have the most general applicability and therefore may be the most important. We must develop those abilities that allow us to compare different visions of the world, and we must engage in the normative analysis that such comparisons involve if we are to thrive, or perhaps even survive, in the present world. We live in a world where we often find radically diverse ideals of human flourishing. Some of these ideals differ as markedly from our own as do the ideals that appear in Mencius and Aquinas. To meet the challenges and opportunities of our new situation, I think, we must want to engage in activities that resemble what I do in my comparison of Mencius and Aquinas. Moreover, and more important, we must be able to carry out that enterprise as well as we can. My whole inquiry rests, then, on the belief that we need a particular set of intellectual skills and virtues to do the comparative philosophy of human flourishings and that acquiring them is critical if we are to meet the personal and social challenges we all face.

Notes

Chapter 1. The Comparative Philosophy of Religions and the Study of Virtue

1.   The relationship of the constructive and descriptive enterprises is discussed generally in Chapter Five, see especially Sections III and IV. For constructive treatments of courage, see Chapter Four, Sections I, III, IV, and VII; on the second topic, see Chapter Three, Sections VIII and IX; on semblances and expansions of virtue, see Chapter One, Section V; Chapter Three, Sections IV, VI and IX; and Chapter Four, Section III.

I will, incidentally, use the terms *religious flourishing* and *human flourishing* interchangeably as these two thinkers (and I) assume each involves the other. This usage is not uncontroversial, of course.

2.   On the distinction between notional and real confrontations, see Williams 1985; pp. 160-167. Williams never discusses those confrontations that seem to fit neatly into neither category, and he may even question either their existence or their importance. For a further discussion of this issue, see Yearley, forthcoming "Conflicts."

3.   Three earlier articles of mine examine aspects of these differences at length: see Yearley 1982, 1983a, and 1985c. I will return to this topic and other scholars' treatment of it.

This book employs the Wade-Giles romanization. Lists at the end of the book contain the Wade-Giles romanization, the *Pinyin* romanization, and the Chinese character or characters. One list contains terms in the text, a second names and titles, and a third long quotations.

4.   MacIntyre (1988) presents this argument well, if usually by means of an exposition of thinkers rather than by means of a theoretical argument; see pp. 164-208, 401-403.

5.   For a more extensive discussion of these three kinds of theory, see Chapter Five, Section III.

6.   The quote from Bentham appears in Flemming 1980, p. 587; on the Kohlberg quote see Kohlberg 1971, p. 77; also note Meilaender's (1984), justifiably critical treatment of Kohlberg's whole enterprise, pp. 85-95.

7.   See Yearley 1990c, for a review essay on contemporary work on virtue in the areas of philosophy, Christian theology, and public philosophy. For specific studies of virtue in various traditions, see most articles and the bibliography in Hawley 1987, and Lovin and Reynolds 1985, pp. 1-66, 203-327.

8.   For a position that resembles in broad outline the one presented here, see Hampshire 1977, especially pp. 15-17, 55. For a criticism of the "idea of morality," see Williams 1985, pp. 175-196. On the issue of morality's definition, see Wallace and Walker 1970.

    Ethical, I think, is an analogical term and possesses both focal and secondary meanings (see Chapter Five, Section V, for an extended discussion of the idea of analogical prediction). Unlike the term *white,* it does not signify some single quality that is universally present in all instances of the phenomenon; unlike the term *bat,* however, it is not simply an equivocal term. Systematic ambiguity is present, then, but clear relationships among the different uses of the term can be identified. We can specify focal meanings to which a variety of secondary meanings relate, even if they lack something the central instances contain. For example, ethical action, clearly occurs when I act to alleviate the pain of a person who has been assaulted, and it is only slightly less evident when I act to relieve someone's psychic distress. But secondary meanings emerge when I write an article on aesthetics aimed at helping people appreciate Donatello.

9.   Williams 1985, p. 153. I also share Williams's doubts that reflection can provide beliefs that are both action-guiding and world-guided in the ways necessary for such beliefs effectively to guide this important class of actions. See Williams 1985, pp. 148-155; also note pp. 54-70; 110-117.

10.   The influence of ways of life is illuminated if we examine how Nagel's ideas on five kinds of commitment might be evaluated in different cultures; for example, meditational virtuosity might be seen as a perfectionist goal in one culture and only an acceptable private project in another (see Nagel 1979, pp. 128-141).

11.   The approach I advocate here probably fits most closely with what is called an *empirical* approach in the introduction to Lovin and Reynolds 1985, pp. 18-20, although their concern is not with virtues. Most of the essays in that volume, however, focus on ways of life.

    With ethicists, my first approach is best exemplified by Green 1978 and 1988; the second by Little and Twiss 1978; and the third by Donagan 1977, pp. 34-35. The introduction to Lovin and Reynolds presents the first two, pp. 12-18. Conversations with John Reeder helped me clarify distinctions among these approaches.

12.   On the general issue of the diversity of goods that different ways of life present, see Hampshire 1983, pp. 20-26, 32-43, 127-169; Nagel 1979, pp. 128-141; and Rosenthal 1987, pp. 41-47.

13. Roberts (1984) presents well the differences between these two kinds of virtue, but Pincoffs (1986) raises important questions about aspects of the distinction; see, for example, Pincoffs 1986, pp. 73-100. I will discuss (especially in Chapter Three) questions about the role of practical reason in virtue, but note here that it underlies rather than fits into the two categories; it forms virtue and therefore is distinctive.

As noted in note 7, Yearley 1990c covers contemporary work on virtue in three areas. An overview of contemporary philosophical work on virtue appears in Pence 1984 and a review of evident problems in the approach in Louden 1984. For an appreciative but critical treatment of the Western virtue tradition, especially in its Aristotelian form, see Williams 1985, pp. 35-36; 174-196. Three influential and interesting attempts to reconstruct that tradition are Wallace 1978; Foot 1978, pp. 10-18, and 1983; and Hampshire 1977. MacIntyre's work has brought to prominence ideas in that tradition all would agree are helpful, but his reformulations of it have satisfied only a few of even his most sympathetic critics; see especially the criticisms by Bernstein 1984; Scheffler 1983; Schneewind 1982, 1983; and Wartofsky 1984. Shklar 1984 argues, if briefly, that Kant not Aristotle ought to be our starting point when thinking about virtue (pp. 232-237); on this subject see O'Neill 1984, Loudon 1986, and Hill 1973.

Finally, positive motivation rather than the absence of negative motivation is primary in most accounts, and surely fits Mencius and Aquinas's account. Brandt (1970) disagrees however; for a cogent criticism of his position, see Hudson 1980, Roberts 1984, and Wallace 1978, pp. 60-61.

14. For further discussions of the good person criterion, see note 26 in Chapter Three and the text to which it refers, as well as the analysis at the end of Section VI of Chapter Five.

15. On the question of differences between ascription and deliberation, see Williams 1985, pp. 10-11, and for the significance of regret, see Williams 1981b, pp. 27-28. My ideas on virtue's relationship to duty and consequences were clarified by Becker 1986, for example, pp. 30-72, 145-150. Note, however, that to focus only on cases involving conflict is to miss much of what is important in the concept of virtue; on problems with "quandary ethics," see Pincoffs 1971 and 1986.

16. On the need to combine approaches and deal with different genres, see the end of the second section of Yearley 1990c, pp. 4-5. That essay contains extensive bibliographic references, but note that in the first area illuminating and representative treatments appear in Baron 1984, Becker 1975, Foot 1983, Herman 1981, Stocker 1976, and Wallace 1978; in Sidgwick 1981, see, for example, pp. 217-230, 320-336. Some examples of excellent work in the second area are Dent 1984, Hunt 1985, MacDowell 1979, Roberts 1984, Rorty 1988, and Watson 1984.

17. For an overview of some issues in the third area, see Findlay 1970. Also note Evans 1979; Gadamer 1986; Pincoffs 1986, pp. 101-114; and Williams 1985, pp. 1-5, 18-32, 152-155 and the discussions about the diversity of goods referred to in note 12. Illuminating interchanges on this subject appear between Wolf 1982 and Adams 1987, pp. 164-173, and MacIntyre (see especially 1984b and 1984a, pp. 218-222) and Bernstein 1984 and Schneewind 1983. Hartmann's (1975) work contains a fascinating historical overview of shifts in the ideal of excellence.

18. Many contemporary religious thinkers are concerned with virtue, and their work often reflects similar themes; for example, Hauerwas 1981a and b, Herms 1982, Gustafson 1981, 1984, McClendon 1986, Meilaender 1984, and Sokolowski 1982, pp. 69-86.

19. Foot 1978, pp. 8-14, develops virtue's corrective character, but see Slote's (1984) comments, pp. 32-59, and Roberts's (1984) criticisms; also note Nowell-Smith 1954, p. 250, for the relation of this idea to "possible worlds."

20. Hare 1963, pp. 149, 155, 187-191, has developed such an argument, and Geach (1977) has responded, if in a sometimes problematic fashion; see especially pp. 150-155. A. Rorty (1988) has the most balanced analysis and develops well the problems that arise with virtue's expansionism; see pp. 299-313. Also note MacIntyre's (1984a) evocative if perhaps mythic portrait of a Greek heroic age, pp. 121-130. A fascinating account of the characteristics of a later Western version of such an age and why it passed is found in Hirschmann 1977, pp. 9-47.

21. From James 1985, pp. 265-266.

22. Aphorism 405 in *Mixed Opinions and Maxims* [1879], found in Nietzsche 1967.

23. Milosz 1968, p. 70. He refers here only to Catholic doctrine.

24. Irwin 1977, pp. 173-174. Note that stressing choice can imply a valuation of personal autonomy and thus personal rights that, in turn, generate difficulties for the pattern of thinking present in many traditional virtue theories; for example, it may lead one to argue that prudential and ethical objectives are very different. See Irwin's discussion of this, pp. 284-285.

Reliability in the "production" of praiseworthy acts, of course, is an important part of why virtuous activity is prized; but intent, manner of performance, and character are also crucial. Aristotle puts the point succinctly when he says preference or decision "is thought to be most closely bound up with virtue and to discriminate character better than actions do" (*N. E.* llllb4-6).

25. Irwin 1977, pp. 240-241; also see pp. 160-163, 173-174, and 282; and note Aristotle's *N. E.* 1169a22-25. Little contemporary work has been done on either counterfeits or semblances of virtue, but see Scheman 1979 on the shamming of sympathy; Hunt's 1980 analysis of courage; and MacIntyre's comments on simulacrums of virtue (for example, 1984a, pp. 171, 182-183, 224, 239-243). Langan 1979 and McClendon 1986, pp. 124-126 examine theological aspects of the idea.

Chapter 2. The Context for Mencius and Aquinas's Ideas of Virtue

1. Senior and distinguished examples of such scholars are A. Graham, D. Munro, D. Nivison, and B. Schwartz. As will become clear, I have learned much (however imper-

fectly) from all of them, whatever may be my disagreements with specific features of each one's accounts. Despite their differences, they (and those they have influenced) display, I think, an approach to the period that manifests many substantial similarities.

Two further, brief comments are in order. First, in all studies of past thinkers the claim that an interpretation is ahistorical *can* manifest fundamental differences about, for example, how best to understand the coherence or power of an abstract argument or how best to judge whether a thinker is blindly or reflectively following a tradition. The issue, then, can be differences in interpretation not attention or lack of attention to historical context.

Second, the interpretative principle of charity functions differently, I think, when we examine each of the three kinds of theories; see Chapter 5, Section III. Moreover, at least the precept of unavoidable charity in interpretation, at times, is opposed to the idea of partitioning the mind, an idea that is necessary if we are to give a full account of rationality; see Davidson 1982, especially p. 302. This can cause serious problems, some of which I discuss in Chapter 3, Section VII, and Yearley 1985.

2.   My desire to keep this inquiry focused and my recognition of the limitations of my own competencies are important reasons why little is done with later commentators. But the decision also rests on my belief that a critical difference is made by the distinctions in secondary theories. (Chu Hsi's interpretation of *tuan* as thread-end rather than sprout exemplifies just how crucial that difference can be; see Graham 1958, p. 54 and Ivanhoe 1990.) For a further discussion of this see Chapter 3, Section II — especially note 10 — and Yearley 1985c. Also note the extended discussion of aspects of this subject in Ivanhoe 1990, for example, pp. 3-4, 47-48, 89-90, 113-114.

For my views on Mencius's relationship to his close successors, see Yearley 1980 and the forthcoming pieces on Hsün Tzu and Chuang Tzu. The latter piece focuses on features of the *Chuang Tzu* that relates much more closely to Mencius than do the features that I highlighted in Yearley 1983b.

3.   See especially Chapter 3, Section V, for Aquinas's relationship to his successors. Examples of modern scholars who query important features of traditional understandings of Aquinas are Burrell 1973 and 1979, D'Arcy 1953, Finnis 1980, Gustafson 1984, Lonergan 1967b, 1971, and MacIntyre 1988.

4.   See Chenu 1964, pp. 128-136, on the role of authority in Aquinas and Kenny on how the terminology can harm rather than help his analysis (1980, pp. 33-43). On the issue of his impersonal and sparse style and the characterization of him as "being in a hurry," see the *Summa Theologiae*, volume 27, p. xv, and volume 35, pp. xiv-xvii. Lonergan 1985, pp. 35-54, presents a particularly balanced, general account of the differences and similarities between Aquinas and modern thinkers.

In what follows, references to the *Summa Theologiae* are noted by arabic numerals punctuated by periods. For example, 1.92.1.2 refers to Part 1, question 92, article 1, response to the second objection or query; if the reference was just to the body of the response, it would be 1.91.1; 2-1 refers to the first part of Part 2, 2-2 to the second part. The Eyre and Spottiswood-McGraw-Hill Latin text and translations are used, at times I will refer to the introductions, appendices, or notes of that edition, referring to them by volume number. Other of Aquinas's texts that I refer to are noted at the beginning of the Selected Bibliography, but my main source will be the *Summa Theologiae*.

With Mencius, references are made by book, part of the book, and particular passages: for example, 1a7 is Book 1, part A, passage 7. Unless otherwise noted, translations are from Lau. Various translations of Mencius are listed at the beginning of the Selected Bibliography, and the *Harvard-Yenching Institute Sinological Index Series Supplement* no. 7 Chinese text is used. On problems in the translation of Mencius, see Nivison 1980c and Richards 1932.

5.   2-1.65.2; also note 2-1.63.2 and 65.3; on divinization, see, for example, 2-1.51.4. Sokolowski 1982 presents an excellent if brief analysis of both the significance of the infused virtues and their relationship to the natural virtues; see pp. 69-86, especially pp. 77-81. On both the character of God's action and the need for it, Lonergan's (1971) account remains a classic one; see pp. 41-55; 77-84; 109-112; and 112 ff. also Lonergan 1967a, pp. 54-67. For especially important, for our purposes, texts on this issue, see 2-1.109.3, 110.2.11.2 and 3, and 113.1. On grace and the Old Law, see 2-1.106.1 and 107.1 and 1.2. Note, however, both Aquinas's account of the difficulties in experiencing the signs of grace (see 2-1.112.5) and his analysis of how and why it may fail to inform all of a person's actions, 2-1.65.3.2 and 3.

6.   For the character of the Gifts, see especially 2-1.68.4. On how they complete the actions of the theological virtues see 2-1.68.4.3; completion is needed because human reason is formed "only after a fashion and imperfectly" by the theological virtues (2-1.68.2). For a different understanding of "prompting," see Milhaven 1968, p. 283. Wadell treats the Gifts at length (1985, pp. 169-193) and also note O'Connor's analysis in *Summa* 1964 ff., volume 24.

7.   See Chapter 5, Section IV, but also note Sections V and VI.

8.   For various examples of how these shifting standards work, see 2-1.66.1.4; 1.4.1; 4; 6; and 6.1.

9.   Although Aquinas dutifully attempts to deal with many traditions and most traditional issues, he does consider some more important than others; for example, the "Neoplatonic" ladder of virtues is treated but never informs his analysis; see 2-1.65.5.

Moreover, the intricacies of the schemes to organize virtues, in fact, may be one of his lesser interests. I am indebted to, if not always agreeing with, MacIntrye's comments on the problems that arise in Aquinas's structuring of the virtues, see 1984a, pp. 178-179. See Chapter 5, Section IV for a further discussion.

10.   We also can question whether traditional claims even can deal adequately with the various strands in their own traditions. For a defense of the idea that we should embrace the concept of conflicts among ideals of human flourishing, see Yearley forthcoming "Conflicts."

11. 2a6; also see 6a6. I have changed Lau's "dutifulness" to "righteousness" and his "wisdom" to "intelligent awareness." For an excellent philosophical treatment of Mencius's ideas on virtue see Shun 1986, a work to which I am much indebted. On *tuan* as sprouts, see note 2.

12. For important examples of propriety's use in Mencius, see 3a2; 4a17, 18, 26; 5a2, 4-6; 6b1; 7a39; 46; and note 4b28. The relationship of propriety to ways of life, including the issue of their normative force, will be discussed later; see Chapter 2, Section VI and Chapter 3, Section II. For an examination of an important tension in Mencius's ideas on this subject, see Yearley 1985a.

Schwartz has a very balanced treatment of early Confucian ideas about propriety, but also note Graham 1989, pp. 10-15, 22-25 and Fingarette's (1972) analysis; see especially Schwartz 1986, pp. 72-82. Cua discusses at length the role of propriety in Hsün Tzu, and in so doing treats various points that are also relevant to an understanding and evaluation of Mencius's ideas; see, for example, Cua 1985, pp. 10-14, 78-87, 98-101, 160-163. Also note Fehl 1971 and my treatment of Hsün Tzu in Yearley 1980 and Yearley forthcoming, "Hsün Tzu."

Unlike the other virtues, propriety's seeds are described differently at different places: *jang*, "yielding" or "deference," and *tz,u*, "declining," are featured in 2a6; and *ching*, "reverence," and *kung*, "respect," in 6a6. All these terms have rich histories; for example, on *jang* in Confucius, see Schwartz 1986, p. 73. For later uses of *ching* see Graham 1958, pp. 67-73. The original reference may have been to the appropriate attitudes to have during sacrifices to ancestors.

13. I drew "intelligent awareness" from Irwin's (1977) translation of Aristotle's *phronesis* in *N. E.*; he gives his rationale on pp. 411-412. On *ch'üan*, see 7a26 and note 3b9. Cua develops in interesting ways what he calls the doctrine of *ching ch'üan*, "the normal and the exigent," and applies it to 1b8 and 4a17; see Cua 1978, pp. 72-76. *Chih* refers almost exclusively to ethical knowledge, although occasionally it also refers to intelligence or the ability to learn; for example, 6a9.

Although no intellectual faculties are noted in Mencius that correspond to the kinds of theoretical reasoning identified by Aquinas, sophisticated intellectual inquiry does appear. We find, for example, procedures that resemble the Socratic *elenchus* and versions of the definitional question, and issues about the possible misuses of language are often prominent. See Schwartz 1986, pp. 88-96, for an eloquent statement on the presence of such inquiry in Confucius, but also note Hansen's (1983) different approach and the detailed studies in Graham 1989; for example pp. 389-423, and Lau 1963b.

14. Especially important references to shame are 3b1, 4b33, 6a12 but also see 2a9, 5a2, 5b1, 6a16. On aversion, they are 1a4, 2a9, 3b3, 4a3, 6a10. On the difference of *yi* from *jen*, see 7b31 and note 6a11; I will discuss differences between *li* and *yi* in the next section. (Translating *yi* as "dutifulness" or "justice" involves using ideas that often are related only tangentially to Mencius; using "propriety" often is awkward or leads to awkward forms, and it usually today refers only to conventional standards.)

The difference between the evaluative and motivational in *yi* and *chih* resembles, I think, the distinction between agent and spectator perspectives. Note, however, Munro 1969, pp. 75-76; he differs from me on the ideas of the evaluative and motivational in *yi* and *chih*.

Mencius's position may have been affected by discussions of *yi* in the *Mo Tzu*. The focus there is on doing, not being good; acts that manifest *yi* are the results of analytic thinking about what will benefit the most people (see Schwartz 1986, pp. 146-147, 157; and Graham 1978, pp. 45, 270, 450-451).

15. Legge wrote: "It can hardly be questioned in England that the palm for clear and just thinking belongs to Bishop Butler, but it will presently be seen that his views and those of Mencius are, as nearly as possible, identical. There is a difference of nomenclature and a combination of parts, in which the advantage is with the Christian prelate. Felicity of illustration and charm of style belong to the Chinese philosopher. The doctrine is the same in both" (1895, pp.56-57 in the introduction to Legge's translation of Mencius; also note pp. 58-69). We easily can be irritated by Legge granting to Mencius the cold comfort of "charm of style," but he is right to point to some striking resemblances. Differences also need to be noted, however; for example, the role of conscience in Butler and the relation of *jen* to other parts of the self in Mencius.

16. 7a45 speaks of the three levels; note that Dobson's (1963) translation of this passage is considerably clearer than is Lau's (1970). Unlike Confucius, where *jen*, at times at least, is the overarching, all-inclusive virtue — and thus can be translated by Waley (1955) as the "Good" — *jen* for Mencius is a specific virtue. On *jen* generally, see 2a6, 6a6, 7b31; as specified especially by familiar relations see 1a1, 3a5, 4a27, 5a3, 6b3, 7a15.

Understanding the exact mechanisms of graded love presents difficulties. A major question is whether Mencius sees qualities such as the ability to think, relate to others, and feel pain as universals; see 7a45, noted earlier, and the attitude to the ox seen and lamb unseen in 1a7.

17. *Hsin*, which also play a prominent role in the *Analects*, also may relate to what Mencius at 2a2 calls one of his two strengths, insight into words. For the Neo-Confucian transformation of the idea, see Graham 1958, pp. 54-56.

18. On benevolence and beneficence, see 2-2.31, especially 2-2.31.4 Aquinas's use of the term follows Aristotle's and probably can be translated as "kindness." Note that one might argue Aristotle never fully develops the meaning implicit in his description of the action, a description that moves the term closer both to Mencius's benevolence and Aquinas's charity; see *N. E.* Book 9, Chapter 7. The role that benevolence assumes in early modern thought in part is explicable as an attempt to meet the challenge Hobbes presents, without using many traditional religious ideas.

19. For the general notion of locative and open religions, see Smith 1970; he makes no reference to China. Ideas resembling yielding also appear in places other than Aquinas's analysis of justice, of course; for example, in his treatments of charity and prudence.

20. See Chapter 4, Sections VIII and IX for an extended discussion of this subject. On the relationships among the three kinds of theory, see Chapter 5, Section III.

21. 7a33; Lau (1970) translates *jen/yi* as "moral." The reference to the sages appears in 2a2. On the need to act immediately, see 3b8; also note Nivison 1979, p. 428. Mencius echoes many modern Western accounts in arguing that negative injunctions take precedence over positive ones; see 7b31.

22. 5b7; a version of the incident also appears in 3b1. The gamekeeper reacts to an insult and therefore his act resembles the one described in 6a10 where propriety is not evidently important. Nevertheless, my point here is that the violation of a rule of propriety can generate this intense a reaction. Note that Mencius recognizes the problems with people who do not take death seriously enough; see 4b23; 30.

23. On the case of the sister-in-law, see 4a17. For more problematic cases, see (in addition to the previously mentioned examples in 5b7 and 3b1) Mencius's failure to give condolences to a bereaved person because it would violate the propriety of the court (4b27) and his attitude to Shun's possible surrender of his benevolent rulership to protect his father, if the father killed someone (7a35). Also note the discussions in 4a19; 6b1; 7b31, 33. I will discuss other facets of this subject in treating Mencius's position on semblances of virtue in Chapter 3, Section IV.

24. Yearley 1985a discusses at length this tension in Mencius. Recognizing the presence of this tension in Mencius, I think, is of the upmost importance, as it allows us to see the ways in which he does and does not simply accept the saving significance of a past, perfect social order. Mencius does seem, however, never adequately to have focused on these questions and worked them through. He is less interested in the subject of propriety than was Confucius, for example, and he does have doubts about the *Book of History*; see 7b3. On the more general problems these tensions illustrate, see MacIntyre's three possible ways of conceiving virtue; 1984a, pp. 183-185.

25. On "timeliness" see 5b1 and 3b10; on stages in self-cultivation, see 2a2; both ideas will be discussed at length in Chapter 3.

At 1a7 Mencius says only "officials (*shih*) can have a constant heart without a constant means of support"; also note 3a3, 4. Mencius also makes harsh judgments about Kuan Chung, a "pragmatic politician"; see 2a1, 2b2, 6b15. His attitude is striking given Confucius's admiration for him; see *Analects* 14: 16, 17 and note Schwartz 1986, pp. 109-112.

26. 7a41. I do not mean to preclude the possibility that the "perfectionism" evident in much virtue theory can co-exist with at least some kinds of, say, contractarianism; public policy and private ideas of excellence do not need to be the same.

27. Possible exceptions to normal social rules often appear, for Aquinas, in situations where God's direct intervention means that more than just another way of life is involved. The Israelite's stealing goods from the Egyptians or God's command to sacrifice Isaac are two such instances. Finnis argues Aquinas never really develops an adequate account of the process that puts the rules of natural law into

effect (see 1980, pp. 281-286), but note Donagan's 1977 attempt to describe and defend such a procedure and Stout's examination of it (1983b, pp. 179-185).

28. 2-1.100.1; the context is Aquinas's treatment of the decalogue. The first quote is from 2-1.57.2. Milhaven 1968 contains a painstaking analysis of many of the relevant passages and discusses, for example, the character of the principles, the problem of applying them, and how dispensations may be made with regard to the second but not the first tablet.

29. Donagan 1984, p. 293.

30. See especially 2-1.100.3.1 and 2-1.100.3.11.1. On the noncontradictory character of the guides, see 2-1.19.2.2, but note how the idea of velleity operates to allow for real conflicts (for example, 2-1.13.5.1) and see the analysis of penance.

Donagan (1977) argues (in an analysis to which I am much indebted) that emphasizing that the goal is treating human beings not human goods avoids several subtle difficulties and captures well the intent of both Aquinas's philosophical formulations and his understanding of the biblical injunction. Note, however, Stout's (1983b) critical analysis of Donagan, and Finnis (1980, 1983) and Grisez's (1969) somewhat different approach. We will examine further aspects of this question in Chapter 3, Sections V and VI.

31. Donagan puts a similar point well when he defends both the integrity and the limits of a rationalist morality against those moderns who want to make the amalgamation Aquinas rejects (1984, pp. 308-309): "In many situations, the considerations I may have to weigh in answering the question, What shall I do? are irreducibly multiple: considerations of desire, convenience, affection, indignation, and courtesy — along with those of morality. The rationalist position is that, in most cases, moral considerations do not suffice to answer the question, What shall I do? What they do suffice to answer is the very different question, What conditions are imposed by practical reason on what I may do?" Practical reason here is used, more in a Kantian than a Thomistic sense, however, and moral refers to what I have been calling injunctions.

For an exposition that fills out important aspects of this general idea, see Adams's (1987, pp. 164-173) response to Wolf 1982. Questions remain about possible conflicts among different possible human perfections, but Aquinas never really treats that issue.

Chapter 3. Mencius and Aquinas's Theories of Virtue

1. See Chapter 5, Section V for a discussion of this.

2. On the notion of *te*, see Boodberg 1952-53; Nivison 1980a; and Graham 1989, pp. 13, 190-191, 282; and Munro, pp. 63, 101-107, 125-126, 185-197. For an example of a use of *te* from a somewhat later time that carries few ethical overtones, see the *Chuang Tzu* (Graham 1981), Chapter 5, and note Graham's comments on it.

3. 3a2; see *Analects* 12: 19; also note 7a13, on a gentleman's transforming influence. On people submitting themselves to virtue, see 2a3; on the sage transforming others, see 7b25; on virtue enabling one to function well in bad times, see 7b10; on virtue's link to character and its role in friendship, see 5b3 and 2a6. Mencius also believes virtues are manifest physically, see 4a15, 7a21, 24, 38. The link of virtue to forces such as *ch'i* and Heaven will be discussed more fully later. See Ivanhoe 1990 for Mencius as someone who demystifies virtue, pp. 35, 58-59, 151-152, 157.

4. The first quote is from Aquinas 1965 (*On the Virtues in General*), p. 88; the second from p. 76; the Aristotle quote appears on p. 88 and comes from *N. E.*, 1106a15-19. Note that virtue can translate either of two Greek words: *arete* ("excellence") or *dunamis* ("power").

5. The literature on analogy and the processes it spawns in Aquinas and the Thomistic tradition is immense. See Tracy 1981, pp. 438-439 for a succinct review of it. On the general procedure in Aquinas, see especially Burrell 1973 and 1979; Finnis 1980, pp. 277 ff., 364-366; and Ross. McInerny, 1968, pp. 24-29, discusses its application to the idea of virtue. For more general treatments of the background and use of the idea, see Farrer 1972, pp. 64-90; Hardie 1968, pp. 59-67; Wallace 1978, pp. 27 ff.; and Tracy 1981, pp. 405-456.

6. The first quote is from 2-1.55.4; the second from 2-1.50.2; on the general issue of dispositions also see especially, 2-1.50.3.3.2 and 3.3.3, and 2-1.49.4.3, and note my later discussion of the general idea. Although Aquinas draws on Aristotelian ideas about dispositions, he expands the notion, especially in regard to infused virtues, and it can begin to resemble power or ability; see Sokolowski 1982, pp. 79-81.

7. On the two positions and Confucianism's relationship to them see 3b9, 7a26, 7b26. We do not know enough about Yang Chu's ideas to specify them with exactitude: he in fact may have advocated calculating attempts to preserve one's self; see Graham 1989, pp. 53-64, 170-172. Later Taoist movements, notably strains in the *Chuang Tzu*, stress "naturalness" and may represent "developments" of the position. Graham 1981 argues that Chuang Tzu may have started as a Yangist; see pp. 117-118, 221-223.

8. 6a7. For discussions of the framework Mencius uses in analyzing human nature, see Lau 1953 and 1963; Graham 1967; and Shun 1986, pp. 77-121, 182-192. Graham argues that Mencius looks to external criteria in formulating his view of nature. I agree but also think that internal observation of the self is crucial, as I will discuss; see Shun's 1986 criticism of Graham on this point.

9. The relationship of this model to a metaphysical teleology or biology is discussed in MacIntyre 1984, p. 196; Williams 1985, p. 44; and, from a different perspective, in Schneewind 1984. For more general discussion see Williams 1985, pp. 35-36, 174-196, and the references to MacIntyre and others in note 13 of Chapter 1; also see the discussion of this issue in Yearley 1990c.

10. Neo-Confucian interpretations of Mencius usually are set within the context of searching for an "enlightenment" that lets an underlying Mind shine forth. (This discovery model, incidentally, resembles the model found in many parts of the Ch'an tradition.) One might argue that these commentators "develop" notions implicit in

Mencius's account, but many presuppositions do differ; see Graham 1958, pp. ix-x, 53-55, 64-66, 96-107, and note 2 of Chapter 2 above. Ivanhoe 1990 examines in detail the differences between Mencius and Wang Yang-ming in a convincing fashion.

11. 6a6. The meaning of Mencius's idea that human nature is good has been much discussed by both traditional and modern scholars. Excellent general discussions of the issue occur in Lau 1953; Graham 1958, pp. 44-60, 1967, 1989, pp. 117-132; and Shun 1986, pp. 182-193. Aquinas 2-1.49.4.3 discusses differences between the capacity for and disposition to do good and evil in a way that resembles Mencius's point. Mencius, I think, can be said to argue that what is most peculiarly human is good, and then to stipulate that those qualities constitute human nature.

12. 2a2. The translation follows Riegel 1979, but I have corrected "rice" to grain.

13. The translation is from Shun 1986 who discusses the passage and later interpretations of it at length (see pp. 145-151).

14. 2a6.

15. 1a7. The translation is from Nivison 1979, p. 420. This is an extremely voluntaristic statement, and Mencius does modify it elsewhere. See Chapter 3, Section VII, and the end of Chapter 3, Section IX, for discussions of Mencius's voluntarism.

The "single" process of extension is described in various ways in Mencius, as Shun notes; see 1986, pp. 157-158. In 1a7 Mencius speaks of extending (*t'ui*) a compassionate reaction. But Mencius also speaks of making the basic reactions reach (*ta*) in 7a15, 7b3, and of expanding them to the full (*k'uo ch'ung* or *ch'ung*) in 2a6, 7b31. The more technical notion or vocabulary of "filling the categories" (*ch'ung lei*) occurs in 3b10, 5b4, and a similar notion appears elsewhere; see 7a17, 7b1. The starting points for extension are noted as *tuan* only in 2a6, but reactions of various sorts are noted in 1a7, 3b3, 4a27, 6a10, 6b1, 7a15, 7b31. Finally, *t'ui* has technical overtones; it is a term in Mohist logic for using what is the same in that which an opponent does not accept and that which he does accept in order to propose the former. (For the Mohist reference, see Graham 1978, p. 438; and note Nivison 1980b, pp. 746, 753.)

16. The relation between thinking and getting is in 6a15 and Lau's translation has been modified; on thinking the four virtues are unnatural, see 6a6; on misunderstanding the exalted, see 6a17; on misdirecting energies, see 6a13.

Understanding exactly what *ssu* refers to is difficult. For references that imply directing attention to something, see 2a2, 2a9, 4b29, 5a7, 5b1. But note that it also can connect to the desire to do what one thinks about (for example, 3a5, 6a9) and thereby can refer to incipient actions or desired future states. (Also note 3a6, 4b24, 5a2, and 7b37.) Mencius thinks that people's lack of virtue is due to their not "*ssu*ing" when they could (6a6, 6a13, 17) and that people become virtuous if they *ssu* (6a15, cf. 6a6, 7a3). 6a7 also describes how our senses pursue certain objects as is stated in 6a15; also note 7b24. My understanding of *ssu* was helped considerably by the work of Frank Gramlich 1980, pp. 145-170. Also see Nivison 1973, p. 13. For *ssu*'s relation to concrete observation in the *Analects*; see Waley 1955, pp. 44-45 and Schwartz 1986, pp. 88 ff.

17. 7b31; also note 3b3, 6b1. The translation is from Nivison 1979, p. 424. Also note 7b1 where Mencius describes a particularly horrible extension of ruthless behavior; my thanks to P. J. Ivanhoe for pointing out this passage.

18. On the difficulty of describing second-order rules, an important issue in the "virtue-duty" debate, see Herman 1981. Deliberations that apply rules and those that use resemblances share many characteristics, of course. But the number and complexity of the rules that we need in many situations means that rules, I think, can be only of limited help to beings that have our limited capacities; see the discussion in Section VIII. The difference in the two procedure's ability to motivate people is treated in what follows.

Mencius's engagement in this argument — features of which we will return to in Chapter 4, Section VII — brings him closer to many arguments found in contemporary Western discussions (where proponents of virtue theory oppose neo-Kantian or utilitarian ideas) than most of the arguments in which Aquinas is engaged. Note, however, that rules and deductions from them play an important role for Aquinas in the realm of injunctions.

19. See Murdoch 1971; Newman makes the distinction in his *Grammar of Assent*. For a discussion of how Mencius's agent acts that differs somewhat from mine in its stress on voluntaristic action, see Nivison 1980b, p. 756. Serious disagreements exist about whether anything resembling a modern notion of the individual is present in Mencius, in other traditional Chinese thinkers, or even in traditional Western thinkers like Aquinas (see, for example, Munro 1977, pp. 1-8, 15-25; and Munro 1985).

Mencius does not stress personal differences as we do, but he does tailor his appeal to individuals and some striking portraits of individuals do appear. I think, then, it is an overstatement to claim he lacks a sense of the individual and would emphasize only the description of roles or general categories.

Aquinas also does not have a modern sense of the individual. But he makes a clear distinction in 2-1.63.1 between our individual nature, with its distinctive inclinations, and our specific nature as rational beings, which is shared by all. Also note 2-1.46.5, where he distinguishes among the generic, specific, and individual in relation to anger.

20. 4a17. I discuss as aspects of this question in Yearley 1985a, pp. 319-322.

21. 7b37; see *Analects*, 11: 26 and note 11: 23; 17: 11; 17: 16; as well as 5: 23, and 13: 21. J. Ware 1960 provides the alternative translation of *hsiang-yüan*. The term has a rich history in China; see Metzger 1977, pp. 40, 156, 186, 213, and 250, note 50.

22. 7b11 contains some fascinating comments on the case of someone who does apparently generous things to be thought generous; also see 4a16. Also note Mencius's apparently empirical claim that to focus on satisfaction or "profit" is inevitably to be led to value one's superficial desires too much; see, for example, lal and Mencius's other discussions with that king.

23. 4b19; Nivison's translation 1979, p. 423.

24. 4b11; the translation follows Nivison 1980a, and I am especially indebted to his second lecture. The first quote is from 4b6; note, however, the picture that appears in 6b12 and also see 3b8 and 7a33. Relevant to this is the striking passage (1b8) where Mencius says regicide is not the question if one kills someone who fits into the heinous category of "outcast."

25. Chapter 38, *Tao Te Ching*; trans. D. C. Lau 1963a, p. 99.

26. 5b1; see 2a2 for the quote on Confucius's uniqueness and for other references to those sages and Confucius, see 2a9, 5b1, 6b6, and 2a2, where he is described as acting "according to circumstances" (2a2 describes their inability to do a wrongful deed; 6b6 concerns their benevolence). On Confucius as "timely," see Schwartz 1986, p. 112, and *Analects*, 18: 8; also see Schwartz, pp. 83- 84, on the importance of dyads in Confucianism. Shun's work on this issue has helped me considerably; see 1986, pp.37-40.

The classic Western statement of the "good person criterion" appears in Aristotle's *N. E.*: see 1176a10-29 for a clear formulation and note 1176b9-1177a10 for an indirect one; also note 1140b5. The idea rests on the procedure announced at 1094b13-1095a11 and 1095b1-14. Note Aquinas's commentary on these passages; *In Ethics.*, especially pp. 831 and 898 and see his treatment of connatural knowledge in, for example, 1.1.6.3, 2-1.22.2, 2-2.27.4.1. Also see Irwin 1977, pp. 45-46, 239-241, 280-285, for an exposition of ideas that underlie the criterion. I examine features of this criterion at length in Yearley, forthcoming "Conflicts."

27. 7b26 speaks of the movement from Mohism to Confucianism. For an imperfect middle way between the two, see 7a26; for Mencius's fullest statement about the threat they pose, see 3b9. (Yearley, forthcoming "Chuang Tzu" presents a notion of rational control that is closer to Mencius than to the Mohists.) For the mysterious type, the *shen*, see 7b25 and note Graham 1989, pp. 100-105, 241.

The phrase "inertial tendency toward goodness" comes from Schwartz 1986, p. 299. I am indebted to Schwartz's analysis of the role of deliberation in early Confucianism, but I think he makes an overly sharp distinction between the normal and the sagely; see pp. 190, 208, 274 ff. He sets up his analysis in terms of *yu-wei* and *wu-wei* models.

28. 2-1.17.5.2 in Donagan's translation; on this point see Donagan 1981, p. 654. Aquinas's main explication of the human soul and its actions occurs in 1.75-89 and 2-1.6-17. In what follows I will make a sharp distinction between the general criteria that operate in theoretical and practical reason. The distinction recently has been queried by many in Aristotle's case, and a somewhat similar situation may hold for Aquinas; for an account of the debate regarding Aristotle, see Nussbaum 1986, pp. 240-263, 290-317. Also note Yearley 1990b.

29. Wiggins 1978, p.150. Aquinas and Aristotle differ on this subject, but they agree one cannot deliberate about or question everything, at least at the same time. For the quoted definition of will, see 2-1.6.2; also note 2-1.8.1 and see Donagan 1981, p. 644. For an excellent treatment of the difficulties in translating certain key terms, for example, *appetitus* and *passiones animae*, see D'Arcy's introduction to volumes 19 and 20 of the *Summa*, 1964 ff., pp. xxiii-xxviii, and his notes.

30. See Finnis 1980 on the structure and history of what I am calling *Stoic* readings of Aquinas, pp. 45-48, 337-343, 374-378; also note Verbeke 1983. Many of the most important interpretative issues appear in the disagreement between McInerny, Finnis, and Grisez 1967; see, for example, McInerny's account, 1982, pp. 40-62, 128.

O'Connor (1967) exemplifies someone who reads Aquinas by means of the Stoic picture and then criticizes him; for a succinct outline of the "fact-value" debate, see Williams 1985, pp. 123-131. See Boswell 1980, pp. 318-332, for an especially illuminating example of how Aquinas's own accounts can display tensions or confusions.

31. On sin's character as involving a withdrawal from reason, see 2-1.18.5; 64.2.3, and 71.2. Donagan 1969 has an excellent treatment of the thwarting of natural ends, and Finnis analyzes difference between the various hierarchies, some more natural than others, that Aquinas uses; see 1980, pp. 94-95, 398-403.

32. The question of conscience presents difficult interpretative issues; for an outline of the controversy see McInerny 1982, pp. 105-116; also see Finnis 1980, pp. 77-78, 133; Pieper 1965, p. 11 and 1967, pp. 63-78; Potts 1982, pp. 678 ff.; and Gilby, *Summa* 1964 ff., volume 18, appendices 15 and 16. Important analyses in the *Summa* are 1.79.13 and 2-1.19.5 and 6. On *synderesis*, see, for example, 1.79.12; 2-1.94.1.2; and *On Truth*, xvi, 1; the topic engendered considerable debate at the time.

33. The first quote is found in 2-1.18.1; the second in 2-1.18.5; the third in 2-1.18.8; for the hierarchy reaching from good to failure, see 2-1.21.1 and 2.

34. For especially relevant texts on the idea of revelation in this context, see 2-1.100.1 and 2; also note 2-1.21.1, 2-1.19.4, and 19.4.3; also note *On Truth*, xiv, 1. The fixity of the directives revelation produces is a matter of controversy and relates closely to the questions about practical wisdom I discussed. I think Aquinas has a remarkably sophisticated picture of what we can draw from revelation; see 1.1.9 and 10 for a schematic presentation and note some of his more probing statements on faith; see for example, 2-2.1.6 and 7, 2.1, 2.7.3, and 4.8. As noted, however, his treatment of the role of ethos in such judgments is problematic, and he obviously differs greatly from any modern interpreter; see Aquinas 1966, pp. 3-27.

35. 2-1.63.1 Aquinas describes positions that resemble the purest forms of my discovery and development models and then argues a third intermediate model is best in 2-1.63.1 and Aquinas 1965 (*On the Virtues in General*), pp. 92-94. For a fascinating piece relevant to this issue, see Wolterstorff 1986.

36. 2-1.27.3.4. The reference to seeds appears in 2-1.63.2.3; for other reference to seeds, see 2-1.63.1 and 2-1.51.1.

37. 2-1.58.4.3. The other quote on natural tendency appears in 2-2.123.1.3; also note 2-1.63.1.

38. Both quotes are from 2-1.65.1. Aquinas discusses counterfeit virtues in 2-2.11.1.2 and presents another hierarchy in 2-2.123.12.

39. See 2-2.55.3. In 2-2.47.13 Aquinas claims, using these distinctions, that four kinds of practical wisdom or prudence exist: false prudence, two forms of genuine but incomplete prudence, and complete prudence. (For examinations of Aquinas on practical wisdom, see MacIntyre 1988 and O'Neil 1955.) As I will discuss in the next chapter, he complicates this structure when he introduces practical wisdom's more clearly religious dimension; see 2-2.55.6.

40. See the discussion of beneficence in Chapter 2, Section V, and the references in note 18 of that chapter; for the relevant treatment of courage, see Chapter 4, Section III.

41. 2-1.56.4.3. Note 2-1.56.4 where a less satisfactory image appears: the craftsman's relationship to his tools. Aquinas's thought, unfortunately, often is dominated by this latter image, and it causes various problems in his analysis. (The issue here relates to modern debates about the significance of virtue; see, for example, the disagreement between Stocker 1976 and Baron 1984, and note the discussion in Section VIII of this chapter.)

For Aquinas's general treatment of the relationship of emotional states to virtues, see 2-1.60.2. Perhaps the single most interesting example is anger, which I will discuss in Chapter 4, Section III; see 2-1.46.4 and 6-7. For a careful and interesting analysis of Aquinas's treatise on the passions, see Harak 1986, pp. 67-117; also note Baker 1941, Jordan 1986a, and Lottin 1949-1954.

42. The quote on the importance of the good not the difficult appears, for example, in 2-2.123.12.2; and the quote on doing not just good but doing it well appears, for example, in 2-1.65.4. The quote on the need for more than aptness appears in 2-1.56.3. (Aquinas uses these ideas to help distinguish between moral virtues and both intellectual virtues and skills; see 2-1.57.1, 57.4, 57.5, and 2-1.21.2.3.)

43. For a treatment of Mencius's views on the origin of evil see Ivanhoe 1990, pp. 49-60, 71-72. For an interesting treatment, if drawn from a much later time, of how evil's presence is dealt with in an organismic cosmology, see Graham 1958, pp. 23-30, 127-130. Aspects of the more theoretical problems that surround this issue are treated in Chapter 4, Section IX, and Chapter 5, Section III.

44. See the introduction to Legge's translation of Mencius, pp. 71-72; the italics appear in the original. Note that some of the differences between Mencius and Confucius on the subject may be due to the fact that they often taught or advised different kinds of people.

45. In Aquinas's normal usage *peccatum* ("sin") refers to the failure of any activity to achieve its purposes whereas *culpa* ("fault") refers only to failures arising from voluntary activity, from choice and reason. This reverses most modern English usage where fault is a broader term than sin, but I will follow contemporary usage. (Also note that evil [*malum*] usually refers to anything that lacks the goodness it should have, and vice [*vitium*] to an ethically evil disposition.)

46. A general theoretical treatment of sin's character is found in 2-1.71-89, but Aquinas usually treats each of these sins as excesses or deficiencies of a mean state; that is, he follows Aristotle structure. For them as capital sins, see 2-1.84. For vanity or vainglory see 2-2.132; for envy see 2-2.36; for anger, see 2-2.158 but note 2-

1.46-48; for avarice, see 2-2.118; for gluttony, see 2-2.148; for lust, see 2-2.154; for *acedia*, see 2-2.35 and note 2-2.136 and 2-1.35-39; for pride, see 2-2.162. Note that *acedia* often, and for Aquinas mistakenly, can be combined with *tristitia*, "sorrow, sadness, grief, or dejection." For modern treatments of these, see Capp's (1987) theological treatment and Lyman's (1978) sociological and literary one.

47. See 2-1.85; also note 2-1.49.4.3, where Aquinas discusses differences between the capacity for and disposition to do good and evil in a way that resembles Mencius.

48. See, for example, 1.50-64, 2-1.80. Aquinas argues the human will can be moved by an object that attracts it, by someone offering or proposing an object, or by someone who persuades another an object is desirable. The devil or demons may act in the last two ways, but even then the human will is not moved by necessity. As purely mental thoughts and not physical realities, the devil or demons are "thinking thoughts" (*intelligibilia intelligentia*), they are finite and cannot directly implant new conceptions.

49. On the coherence of the virtuous life and chaos of its opposite, see 2-1.73.1. For Mencius's account of equilibrium, see Chapter 4, Section IX.

50. See his treatments of the daughters of spiritual apathy, 2-2.35.4. Pieper 1986 develops these ideas in an evocative fashion.

51. On the relation of the Old and New Laws, see 2-1.106.1, 107.1, and 1.2; also note 2-1.63.3 and 114.1, and 2-2.24.10. As I will discuss in Chapter 4, Section V (note 33 especially), Aquinas thinks a Christian ought not just find joy in good but also possess a sadness that rises from an acute sense of the evil present in both persons and the world; patience is the virtue that manifests the appropriate balance of both attitudes.

52. For a typical treatment see 6a15; for an illuminating example of his discussions with kings see 1a7 and the kings' mention of his "supreme ambition." Our understanding of Mencius clearly is affected by the fact that we have numerous detailed examples of his interactions with people in power and relatively few examples of his treatment of, say, disciples. Despite this, we can still evaluate how Mencius treats those who do not seem to display cruder deformations.

53. The quotation from Legge is found on p. 72 of the introduction to his translation of Mencius. Aristotle's treatment of weakness of will is found in *N. E.* 1145b8-1148b14; for Aquinas's treatment of continence, see 2-2.155 and 156.

54. The subject of weakness of will and the problems that surround it have been discussed much by contemporary philosophers. For representative treatments of the subject both as a purely theoretical issue and as it appears in Western thinkers, see Davidson 1982 and the articles in Mortimore 1971.

55. For Aristotle's account, see the opening of Book 7 of the *N. E.*; the placement would be especially important if Aristotle, in fact, is starting his analysis anew at that place. Also note how Aquinas explains problems with holy people's character in terms of the inability of infused virtues to form the whole personality; see 2-1.65.3 and 3.2, and see his treatment of ignorance in 2-1.76.2-4. I will examine

several features of Aquinas's treatment of the subject from another perspective at the end of Section IV of Chapter 5.

56. See, for example, 3a4 and 3b9, but also note 6b15 and 7a18. On the need for minimal material support, see 1a7.

57. The image of Ox Mountain appears in 6a8; the passage Legge notes is 4a10. I examined Mencius's ideas about the abilities to know and do the good in Sections II and especially III of this chapter, and I will discuss other aspects of those ideas at the end of Section IX. I return to that subject, focusing on the example of courage, in Chapter 4, Section VII and analyze how Mencius counsels people to deal with failures to reach the goods they seek in Chapter 4, Section IX.

Worth noting here, however, are the various reasons why people fail that Mencius does present. (Also note the treatment of ability in 1a7 and the extravagant statement at 6b2 that may be ironical.) 3b9 discusses how incorrect ideas block *jen* and *yi*; also see 2a2 and 6a1 on the role of erroneous ethical or general beliefs and Riegel 1979, p.442. Other causes for failure can be uncontrolled desires (see 1a7, 1b3, 5, 4b30) and the already noted unreflective operation of the senses; see 6a15. More mysterious sources also are noted: for example, *ch'i*, apparently, if incorrectly cultivated, can reinforce certain errant desires and lead people to be driven in ways they did not intend; see Schwartz 1986, pp. 179-184, 270-274. Finally, it is unclear just how many people may fit within his category of the nonhuman (*fei jen*); see, for example, 2a6 and note 1b8.

Responses to these general questions appear in other thinkers in the period, of course: see, for example, Chuang Tzu's idea on how fate determines people's possible fulfillment (pp. 78-79 in Graham's translation) and Hsün Tzu's nuanced criticism and qualification of Mencius's position in Section 23 of the *Hsün Tzu*.

58. See Lonergan's 1971 account of grace and free will (especially pp. 41-55, 77-84, and 109 ff.) and Sokolowski 1982, pp. 69-86; also note the references in note 5 of Chapter 2. Aquinas's ideas about the character of human sinfulness also rest on his views about people's need to relate appropriately to God whenever they act, and the difficulty in doing that, a topic I will discuss in considering semblances of courage in Chapter 4, Section III. This general subject, of course, is an immensely complicated one, but Aquinas can be said to accept an Aristotelian position on the importance of dispositions and yet to reject Aristotle's notion that at best only a select few can be brought up in a way that will enable them to be virtuous. The tension in Mencius between his more and less voluntaristic sides reflects a similar concern. Also see Williams 1985, who focuses, in the two opening chapters and throughout, on the closely related questions of whether one can persuade those people who most need to be persuaded.

59. See the discussion of Mencius's voluntarism at the end of Chapter 3, Section IX. The constructive issue here is an especially thorny one, even if we leave aside the question of possible human immortality. Neither Mencius nor Aquinas doubt people can be fundamentally transformed, and if we think of such transformations as "conversions" in, say, Lonergan's extended sense, such transformations do, I think, occur (see the references in note 70 of this chapter).

The issue of how best to explain them remains, however. Mencius and Aquinas present the general outlines of what, to my mind, are the two most viable positions. (Versions of these two positions also appear in various other traditions; for example, Ch'an and Pure Land Buddhism). Nevertheless, filling in the outlines, much less deciding between them, involves tackling various complicated issues, many of which fit within secondary theory.

60. Williams specifies well a number of the major difficulties in the "Aristotelian project" in an account that is appreciative of the project's integrity; see 1985, pp. 35-36, 174-196. For critical descriptions of a prominent modern view that opposes a picture like this one, see Murdoch 1971, pp. 4-7, 24-28, 47-54, 76-82; and C. Taylor 1985a, pp. 14-76, 97-113, and 1985b, pp. 134-151, 248-288; also note section two of Yearley 1990b.

61. For a modern treatment of emotions to which I am especially indebted, see C. Taylor 1985a, pp. 45-76, 101-114, 188-191, 196-203; also note Dent 1984, Evans 1975, Fortenbaugh 1975, and Lyons 1980. Note that any use of the idea of unconscious emotions would greatly complicate this position. This position can lead toward but need not imply an evalative theory of the emotions — such as Scheler or Brentano's — where the claim is that emotions provide us with an important kind of knowledge; see Findlay 1970 for an exposition, pp. 16-36, 57-66.

62. D'Arcy makes this point strongly, perhaps too strongly, in relation to Aquinas see his introduction to volume 19 of the *Summa* 1964 ff., pp. ix-xi. For an example of someone who argues for the subtlety and usefulness of the scheme, see Reid's lengthy appendices in volume 21 of the *Summa* 1964 ff.

63. My analysis of virtue's expansionistic propensities is indebted to A. Rorty's 1988 work on courage; see pp. 299-313. Note that different virtues will have different tendencies to excess; courage seems especially prone to excess whereas practical reason's excess appears only in some of its operations; for example, in considering matters too closely when an immediate decision is required; see section five of Yearley 1990b.

The traditional form of this question has been to ask about the unity or connectedness of virtue. The answers have been many but none, I think, are fully satisfying in all details. Irwin 1977 examines the problem in its classical forms (pp. 86-90, 207, 304-306; Langan 1979 analyzes a classical theological treatment of how charity connects the virtues, and Watson 1984 has a fascinating modern discussion. Foot 1978 defends a version of the claim but has received serious criticism; see Roberts 1980 and Flemming 1984. For examples of why people abandon the idea, see Wallace 1978 and MacIntyre 1984a, pp. 162-163, 179-180; MacIntyre now, incidentally, thinks his criticism of Aquinas on this subject was simply mistaken, see 1988, p. x.

64. Nussbaum 1986, p.299; the context is a description of Aristotle. She later writes (p. 304) that "when there is not *time* to formulate a full concrete decision, scrutinizing all the features of the case at hand, it is better to follow a good summary rule then to make a hasty and inadequate concrete choice. Furthermore, rules give constancy and stability in situations in which bias and passion might distort judgment." Mencius and Aquinas's positions are not as "anthropocentric" as Aristotle's, at least as it is painted by Nussbaum, in part because of how they view injunctions.

65. Wiggens 1980a, p. 237; italics are in the text. (A shorter version of this paper appears in Raz 1978, pp. 144-152.) Wiggin's analysis arises from an interpretation of Aristotle, but it has been extended by other people. For a striking defense of the idea, see McDowell 1979, who is indebted to Murdoch 1971. He also leans heavily on Cavell 1976 to answer questions about how to ground the judgments and explain the impossibility of codification. For a critical evaluation of aspects of McDowell's account, see Williams 1985, pp. 217-218.

66. On the general idea, see Taylor 1985a, pp. 15-44; I question his emphasis on the significance of the capacity to reform judgments, however. His work draws on Frankfurt 1971 and is illuminated by Watson 1982.

67. I first encountered the idea of the command and weighing models in Wallace 1978, but I have changed them considerably. Incidentally, the problems that arise for this position, if we focus on unconscious deformations in weighing, can hardly be overestimated. See the comments on Davidson's (1982) ideas about partitioning the mind in note 1 of Chapter 2.

68. My treatment differs from but draws on Burnyeat (1980) and Kosman's (1980) examination of the classical Greek picture of indirect formation and Robert's (1984) treatment of both kinds of formation from a modern perspective. Even with indirect formation, the interaction of reason and emotion need not always be smooth, as cases (discussed in Section VII) of weakness of will and spiritual apathy show; cases of self-deception display the difficulty even more clearly.

69. I find implausible the extreme voluntarism found in, say, Mohism and at least parts of Sartre. I might decide firmly, upon painful reflection, for example, that most humans function best without deep human attachments. But the power or form of my previous emotional reactions would not change as soon as I made that decision. In a few cases, sudden changes may occur; a sudden, or apparently sudden "flash of recognition" about a person's character may radically change my emotional attitudes. In still other cases (and perhaps with some kinds of people), only indirect formation may work: Freud's work presents us with many such examples; see Yearley 1985b.

70. See 1a7 and possibly 6b2 for examples; on Aquinas, note, for example, how Lonergan uses the idea of conversion and relates it to Thomistic ideas of grace to explain some such changes; see 1971, pp. 121-125; 1972, pp.130-132, 241-243, 267-270, 283-284; and 1985, p. 52.

71. For accounts of classical notions of dispositions, see Irwin 1977, pp. 45-47; Lonergan 1971, pp. 41-55; and Kenny's translation of and commentary on 2-1.49-54, especially pp. xix-xxxix, in *Summa* 1964 ff. Roberts 1984 presents a balanced account of the modern philosophical debate on this topic. For an influential but, I think, flawed modern account, see Brandt 1970; note the criticisms by Hudson 1980, Wallace 1978, and Roberts 1984. Ryle's (1949) account remains a classic one, despite its now well-discussed difficulties. None of these authors are responsible for my breakdown of dispositions.

72. For a more precise technical rendering of this distinction, see Irwin 1977, pp. 45-46; however, questions exist about his use of cause. Also note von Wright 1963 on the general question, and see Irwin 1977, pp. 162-163 and 280, 283 on how this relates to differences between crafts and virtues; Wallace 1978 presents a somewhat different viewpoint, see pp. 45-55.

Chapter 4. Mencius and Aquinas's Conceptions of Courage

1. For a discussion of the issue of courage's social location, see the opening of Section V of Chapter 1.

2. Pears, Roberts, and Wallace are modern philosophers who, as will become evident, have influenced my thinking on the general concept of courage. The only book-length contemporary treatment of courage is by Walton, and some comment is needed on how my treatment differs from his. Walton 1986 focuses on individual acts of courage in a way I do not, and his analysis relies on a picture of practical reasoning, which usually differs markedly from the picture I present (see pp. 13-14, 76-95, 116-120, 140-149).

Most important, much of the form, as well as force, of his analysis arises from two factors. First is his desire to link the idea of courage, by way of the concept of supererogation, with analyses of morality that rely on universalizability and duty; see pp. 10-12, 20-24, 180-181. Neither Mencius nor Aquinas fits easily with this picture of morality; both, for example, would reject any attempt to see their idea of virtue as an example of simple personal aspirations (see pp. 154-157). Moreover, Mencius lacks an idea of supererogation and Aquinas's differs from the one Walton presents.

Second, Walton doubts the usefulness of the notion of dispositions, although at times he so modulates his position that it becomes unclear (see pp. 32 and 197-215, especially pp. 198-199, 206-207, 213-215, 219-220). Dispositions, however, are crucial to Mencius and Aquinas's accounts. Furthermore, my understanding of dispositions differs from Walton's particularly on the role in them of rationality and the importance of reason's formation of emotions. He, nevertheless, has identified well difficulties that exist with a dispositional understanding of some forms of courage (see pp. 4-5, 197).

3. The analysis of different goals is drawn from Pear's (1980) study of Aristotle, but note Duff's 1987 often different understanding and Garver's 1980 criticism of his treatment of the relation of external and internal goals, especially p. 174, note 31. See Irwin 1977, pp. 239-241, on expressive and acquisitive motives. For a more formal description of courage, see Wallace 1978, pp. 60-81, and Flemming 1980.

The question of different goals, which relates to the unity of virtues issue, also is treated by Walton, but his position is unsatisfying to me (see 1986, pp. 27, 52-55, 76-89, 133). I think his distinction between definitions of courage that rest on practical reason and those that rest on an ethical matrix, between bravery and courage, states but does not resolve the issue. (An interesting avenue into the unity of virtues question that he does not pursue is provided by his account on pp.

103-104 of Gray's distinction between soldiers who are occasional cowards and those who are constitutional cowards; see Gray 1970, pp. 111 ff.)

4.   Slote 1984 argues, correctly, I think, that a loss of at least a temporary sort occurs for even the just because their well-being is damaged in the sense that it could be better than it now is; see pp. 66-68, 112-119. His point does not, however, affect the general distinction.

5.   See Kenny 1963 and Kelly 1973, who applies his distinction to courage; also note Garver 1980. The distinction between kinds of activity is Aristotle's; for example, the difference between *kinesis* and *energia*. Aquinas makes a similar distinction between *motus* and *operatio*; see 2.1.31.1 and 2. Note, however, that this kind of analysis easily can overlook the pleasure that can come from adherence to the internal goal. On the general notion of pleasure in Aristotle, an analysis largely accepted by Aquinas and implicit in Mencius's account of at least ethical activity, see Urmson 1967 and W. D. Ross 1959, p. 200.

6.   The role of skills in courageous activity can produce two phenomena that cannot occur with normal virtues. People may excuse themselves by declaring their actions intentional, and they may let their skills get rusty. Neither can happen with normal virtues. On the issue of virtues and skills in relationship to courage, see Roberts 1984; also note Wallace's 1978 account, pp. 44-59.

7.   2-2.123.12 and 12.3; also note the definition in 2-1.61.4. The first quote is from 2-2.123.1 and the second from 2-2.123.3; the third quote on virtue's concern with the good, comes from 2-2.123.12.2.

Jaffa's book on Aquinas's commentary on the *Nicomachean Ethics* (an "unduly neglected minor modern classic" according to MacIntyre 1984a, p. 278) is germane to my inquiry in that he aims, in part, to examine Aquinas's relationship to the "natural" ethics of Aristotle (see Jaffa 1952, p. 196, note 20 as an example). His analysis, much of which focuses on the example of courage, often is helpful. Moreover, I agree that Aquinas's procedure for analyzing the *Nicomachean Ethics* obscures how Aristotle well may be describing only natural and moral virtues in Books 1-6 and describing the highest and strict virtues, heroic virtues, in Books 7 and following (see Jaffa 1952, pp. 36, 64, 69, 73, 93-98). That distinction is especially important with courage because Aristotle treats it in Book 3 and again in Book 9 (see, for example, 1169a18-35). I think, however, that Aquinas's treatment of courage in the *Summa*, on which I focus, often presents a markedly different picture than the treatment in his commentary.

I also disagree with some features of Jaffa's understanding of Aquinas's general approach. Compare, for example, my own and Jaffa's understandings of *synderesis* (Jaffa 1952, pp. 114-115) and of the idea of virtue's specification of its highest degree of power (ibid., p. 72). Such disagreements lead me to different conclusions about Aquinas's relationship to Aristotle's natural virtues and to an often different picture of his relationship to Mencius. Many of these differences may be displayed most clearly by comparing my analysis of semblances of courage and Jaffa's treatment of heroic virtues (pp. 67-115). For other differences, see my analysis in Yearley 1971.

8.   For the idea of imprinting one's own likeness on the world, see 2-2.123.7 and note 2-2.123.8. On the subject of courage illustrating in exaggerated form three common characteristics of virtue, note the following passages: On the relation of courage to act categories, see 2-2.140.2.3. On the relation to pleasure see 2-2.123.8.2, but note the nuanced treatment of pleasure and especially intense physicial pain in 2-2.123.8.1, 9, and 9.3; also note his distinctions among kinds of pleasure at 2-1.31.3. On the relation of skills to courage, see 2-2.123.1.2 and 2-2.128.1.7.

9.   For a good study of this problem in Aristotle, see Urmson 1980; Pears 1980 also comments well on it. For relevant texts in Aristotle, see *N. E.* 1107a28 ff.; 1115a6 ff.; and *E. E.* 1220b39; 1228a1-23 ff.

10.   2-2.123.3. Aquinas's account can be read to highlight the differences (see 2-2.127.2.3), but confusions do exist; see, for example, 2-2.126.2.3.

I do not find persuasive either Walton's account of the relationship of fear and courage or his distinction between the cowardly and the courageous (see 1986, pp. 89-92), largely because he never gives a detailed analysis of the character of an emotion (see ibid., pp. 65-66, 82, 94, 134-140). At least at times, he seems to reject a cognitive view of the emotions or to focus only on situations where it is less applicable. (His argument might have been strengthened by pursuing Aquinas's account, as he implies on p. 94; also see pp. 137-138.) The discussion of how courage and cowardliness are contraries and not contradictories is helpful, however; see pp. 178-179.

11.   For Aquinas's description of the problems and attempt to work them through see 2-2.126.1-2; also note 2-2.64.5. *Intimiditas* is usually used by Aquinas but *impaviditas* appears in 2-2.126.2. *Timiditas* normally covers, in my terms, both timidity and cowardliness. For examples of the extension of the meanings of words in scholastic Latin, see 2-2.123.2, 129.3; also note 125.2.

12.   See 2-1.45.4 and note 2-2.127.2.3. For two major accounts of daring, see 2-1.45.2 and 2-2.127; also note the relation of fear and love developed in 2-2.125.2. Acts of daring can be specified definitely, then, only after they have failed. Nevertheless, we can be reasonably sure about our predictions if we know enough about both the people and the situations they will encounter.

13.   2-2.123.1.2. Aquinas gives somewhat different treatments in various places in both the *Summa* and *In Ethics*. Note that in 2-2.128.1.7 he says that "though they unite in the act of courage, their motives are different. . . . So they are defined not as parts, but as modes, of courage *(fortitudinis modi)."*

As Walton notes (1986, p. 117), Nevin develops certain semblances of courage: the fanatic, the person with an erratic temperament, and the inveterate objector. Gray 1967 also presents a rich picture of the different sorts of motives that operate with soldiers.

14.   2-2.128.1, the seventh objection; see Hunt's (1980) analysis of this phenomenon.

15.   On both semblances, see 2-2.128.1.1.

16. For a definition of anger, see 2-1.46.1-3; for its relation to justice, see 2-1.46.4 and 6. The interactions of reason and anger are very complex, and Aquinas's attempt to chart them conceptually is not always successful. He, for example, will employ an overly rigid temporal sequence to clarify the point; see *In Ethic.* 1964, 575, p. 254. More penetrating analyses occur in 2-1.46.4 and 6-7. Also note 2-1.46.5, where Aquinas distinguishes among the generic, specific, and individual levels. Generically, desire is more natural than anger but specifically, given reason's presence, revenge is more human than gentleness. Finally, individual temperaments underlie the predisposition to anger, and they differ considerably.

Aquinas's account of this semblance is further complicated by the fact that the category he uses, "impulses of passion" (*impulsum passionis*), refers in his Greek sources to *thumos*, "spiritedness." This concept has a remarkable if often mysteriously wide range of meanings: it is one of the three parts of the soul for Plato and a crucial if difficult to specify motivating factor for Aristotle.

17. 2-2.55.6, also note 2-2.55.1 and 4; Matthew 6:31 is the reference. Aquinas claims such solicitudes has two forms. The first resembles "prudence of the flesh" in that people's special effort to gain temporal rewards or pleasures makes them unduly perturbed about the world. It thereby impedes their teaching about or pursuing of spiritual matters. On this general issue, see Donagan 1985.

18. For the reference on planning, see 2-2.55.7.3; on taking no thought for the morrow, see 2-2.55.7; Matthew 6:34 is the reference. On the role of the final good for the whole of life, see 2-2.47.13. The general position here is another illustration of Aquinas's insistence that grace does not destroy nature but presupposes and perfects it.

19. The question of how to divide the parts of courage was a major issue in Aquinas's day; see Gauthier 1951. Various technical problems appear in Aquinas's account, some of which I noted in Chapter 2, Section III; see, for example, 2-2.140.2.2, 2-2.128.1, and the preface to 2-2.129.1. Note that courage has no kinds or types, the third part of a virtue, and, in a sense, the semblances function as its types; see 2-2.128.1.7.

Some of what Walton delineates as courage's "outer edges," for example, determination, relates to what Aquinas calls courage's *parts*; see 1986, pp. 97-115, 133-134. Aquinas's analysis, however, ranges far more widely than Walton's and therefore helps us deal with the vexing question of those acts that relate to courage but are not simply identical with it.

20. 2-2.123.2; for other passages on this topic, see, for example, 2-2.123.5 and 6; 2-2.139.1; 2-2.141.3; 2-2.186.1.

21. 2-2.123.5. Aquinas's expansion of the conception of martyrdom illustrates how he widens the meaning of facing death; see 2-2.124.3 and 5 and 5.1.

22. 2-2.123.4. On the two aspects of the second idea, see 2-1.55.1 and 2-2.129.2.

23. For an example of the use of such an "Existentialist" framework to interpret Aquinas's ideas on courage, see Pieper 1965, pp. 117-141; also note how Rahner 1961 uses a similar mix of ideas, pp. 26-31, 56-78, 81-119. Tracing the exact con-

nections between a change in horizon and any specific act can be impossible. The approach, however, does capture conceptually the clear difference that appears, for example, between how different people approach life and how a single person faces different stages or changes in his or her own life.

24. Aquinas's main statement of the arguments for his claim occurs in 2-2.123.6, but also note 2-2.123.6.2, and 2-2.123.7.3, and 2-1.45.2. On the significance of endurance, see 2-2.123.6 and 2-2.128.1; also note 2-2.123.6.2 and 2-2.123.11.

25. Forbearance (longanimity or "long sufferings") combines two quite different concepts; enduring lengthy labors and, from the New Testament, enduring injuries because one has much to be forgiven; see 2-2.136.5 and 2-1.70.1.2. Two revealing relationships are between perseverance (steadfastness or persistence) and constancy (see 2-2.137.3) and between perseverance and obstinacy (see 2-2.138.2.2).

26. For an examination of the significance of the idea of being "on the way," see Pieper 1986, pp. 9-21. Pieper's analysis of hope in that book has interesting resemblances to my analysis of patience; indeed, the relationship between patience and hope can be close. For a treatment of patience as an ideal of religious life in a slightly later time, see Kieckhefer 1984, pp. 50-88.

27. 2-2.136.1. The first quote is from 2-2.136.4.2. On the importance of patience's more natural form, see 2-1.66.5.2. On the relation to pain (dolor), see 2-2.136. 3 and 4.2; on the relation of pain to sorrow, see 2-1.35.2.

Treatments of patience were a stock procedure in the ethical treatises of the twelfth and thirteenth centuries, but Aquinas's major examination is skimpy, only one question in five articles. He did not work out all of the implications of his analysis or problems in it, I think. For example, sorrow is an impulse emotion and yet patience is treated with courage that deals with contending emotions. More important, Aquinas also argues that patience is not the highest virtue if some standards are used, such as the need to fight against evil; see 2-1.66.5.2, 2-2.72.3-4, 2-2.108.1.2, 2-2.136.2 and 4.2. This situation exemplifies how hierarchical judgments depend on the criteria used, but it also relates to the notion that patience has both natural and supernatural forms.

28. Tristitia can be translated by sadness, grief, sorrow, dejection and related words; it gives rise to anxiety, torpor, resignation, and even collapse; see Deferrari 1960 for the range of meanings. Aquinas devotes five questions and twenty-five articles to an often brilliant analysis of the concept; see 2-1.35-39.

29. For comments on the Beatitude about the just, see 2-1.69.3 and 3.4 and 4; for the quote on those who mourn, see 2-1.69.3.3. The reference to the example of Christ's suffering is found in 3.34.6.2. Aquinas takes very seriously the injunction that one is sent as a sheep among wolves; when dealing with Christ's example, he argues that people often may have simply to bear afflictions without harboring bitterness against their attackers; see Pieper's (1965) analysis of these ideas.

30. 2-2.136.4.2; on spiritual apathy, see 2-2.35.1.4. Spiritual apathy is closely linked to "sadness" and in some accounts of the seven sins even replaces it; see

Chapter 3, note 46. Aquinas, unfortunately, never gives a full account of the relationship between spiritual apathy and patience.

31. 2-2.136.2.2; I take uproot to refer only to those aspects of emotions that improperly trouble the soul.

32. 2-2.136.3; on the general point, also see 2-2.136.3.1. and 3.3.

33. 2-2.28.2. Although patience is not categorized as one of the inward or outward effects of charity in the analysis of charity, it clearly is an effect in the sense noted in this and the previous quotation. The point is important in that it underlines the degree to which Aquinas's thought is oriented around the pursuit of good rather than the avoidance of evil and the participation in God rather than the separation from him; see my discussion of this in Chapter 3, Section VII. Recognizing that orientation is crucial to grasping the two sides that characterize patience.

34. 2-2.139.1.1. The first brief quote is from 2-1.68.4. The second long quote is from 2-2.139.1. Confidence (*fiducia*) and security (*securitas*), freedom from anxiety, both usually are described as parts of magnanimity, and in that context they relate only to people's sense of their own natural abilities; see 2-2.129.6.3 and 2-2.129.7.2. Controversy existed about their role in courage; see note a, pp.120-121, *Summa* 1964 ff., vol. 42. Aquinas clearly is extending the normal meaning of confidence in this context.

35. For the first quote 2-1.26.3.4; for the second quote, see 2-1.27.2.2. On love's lacking its own proper vocabulary, see 1.27.4 and 36.2.

For a treatment of the complex issue of the relationship of love and knowledge, see *Summa* 1964 ff., vol. 1, pp. 124-132; also note Crowe's (1959) analysis of complacency and concern, affective consent and striving concern. On the Gift of Wisdom, see 2.2.45; 45.3 discusses the practical aspect of the gift; also note *Summa* 1964 ff., vol. 35, pp. 200-202. For a treatment of charity in Aquinas, see Scharlemann 1964; Outka 1972 analyzes modern uses of it and related ideas.

36. 2-1.69.3. The Latin phrase can be taken to mean either that the gifts make a person immune to the contending passions for such is God's will or that the gift make a person as immune to them as God wills the person to be (see note 1 on p. 53 of vol. 24 of the *Summa* 1964 ff. for a brief discussion of the translation of the problem). The latter interpretation fits best with Aquinas's general picture, but the former may be intended here. In the same passage Aquinas declares that although virtue restrains a person in following the impulse emotions, "the Gifts, however, spurn them totally if necessary." Moreover, in 2-1.63.4 Aquinas makes a strong statement about the difference between infused and acquired virtues.

37. *Analects* 17: 23; the reference in the *Chung Yung* is 20, 8. For the linking of the three in the *Analects*, see, for example, 9: 29 and 14: 28; note that 1b3 in the *Mencius* contains a similar connection. Lai 1985 contains an account of courage in the early Confucian tradition that often differs from the one presented here.

38. See Section V of Chapter 1 for the critique of courage as a virtue.

39. 6b15; 7a18 expresses the same idea without a mention of Heaven. As P. J. Ivanhoe pointed out to me, the use of *tung* ("agitation") in this and other passages casts an interesting light on the unmoved mind (*pu tung hsin*) in 2a2, a notion I will examine later.

40. 5b1; see Section IV of this chapter for Aquinas's distinction between perseverance and forbearance.

41. One illuminating way to examine these changes is to focus on the question of what goals people need to pursue to make intelligible the sacrifice of the self. Christian theologians, for example, have argued that only an understanding of transcendental value can fully explain the self-sacrifice that Aristotle describes in *N. E.* 1169a26-36. That is, the fine or honorable (*kalos*) can provide a legitimate motive only if placed within a framework different from the one Aristotle himself provides. A similar kind of argument could be said to exist in Mencius, although the presentation of the Heaven-given germs would provide the standard. In both cases, of course, the judgments rest on controversial grounds, such as that a legitimate motive must involve more than just the pursuit of the regard of other people in the society. On the general issue of the role of subjectivity in the Chinese thought of this period, see Graham 1989, pp. 95-105.

42. I will treat certain of these positions at more length in examining Mencius's position on perfected courage; our earlier examination of semblances of virtue also dealt with them.

43. 6a16; the first quote is from 6a17; on the general issue, also see 6a11-14. Other people saw self-respect in terms of not receiving insults. As is said in a roughly contemporary text, the *Mo Tzu*: "Men will fight to the death over one [insulting] word, which is valuing honor (*yi*) more than life"; see Graham, 1967, p. 239.

44. 1b3.

45. 2a2. I use Riegel's 1979 translation here and in what follows and have been much influenced by his excellent study of the passage. However, I have changed *yi* from propriety to righteousness, *chih* from inclination to will, and follow Nivison's (1973) interpretation of *yen*.

 Chih refers to a direction of the mind and can cover both a person's general aims in life and, occasionally, more specific intentions; see 2b12,14; 4a10; 6b8,9; 7a24. *Will* in the general sense that Aquinas uses it, probably is a reasonably good equivalent and not prone to the difficulties that Riegel states, see pp.441, 454 note 27.

46. 2a2. For descriptions of the two kinds of courage, as exemplified by Pei-kung Yu and Meng Shih-she, see the opening of 2a2.

 Chao Ch'i takes *so* to mean moral rightness and Shun follows him (1986, p. 243 note 18). Whereas Riegel takes it, if hesitantly, to refer to a "tension or tightness (either physical or mental) due *not* to nervousness but rather to the absence of nervous trembling or agitation. . .[that relies on] one's own feelings of inner steadfastness and self-satisfaction" (1979, pp. 438-439). The character is not used elsewhere in Mencius or, for example, in the *Analects* or the *Mo Tzu*.

47. Finding an equivalent for *ch'i* is a classic example of the problems involved in establishing commensurability between truly different systems of thought. For good if varying treatments of it, see Riegel 1979, pp. 453-454; Waley 1934, pp. 28, 46-49, 57-58; Schwartz 1986, pp. 179-184, 270-274; Graham 1989, pp. 101-104, 117-119; Ivanhoe 1990, pp. 155, 160; and Lau's 1970 translation of Mencius, pp. 24-25. Graham's study of it in later thinkers explicates well many of the general problems that arise in finding appropriate equivalents; see 1958, pp. 31-43.

A key issue that appears in Mencius's use of the term (especially in 2a2 but also, say, in 6a8) is finding formulations that preserve the notion that *ch'i* is pervasive and continuous and yet also show that the fullest expression of human *ch'i* differs from and transcends most normal manifestations of *ch'i*. I discuss aspects of this issue in Section IX of this chapter.

48. 2a2; Riegel's translation, 1979; also note Ivanhoe's (1990) alternate translation, p. 76.

49. See Section III of Chapter 5 for a further discussion of this. Although we can only speculate, there are fascinating possible resemblances between Mencius's *ch'i* and Aquinas's *spiritedness*, and the *thumos* it draws on, especially when courage is the subject (see note 16 of this chapter). The way in which this kind of empowerment operates and is understood at the levels of practical and secondary theory links the three ideas.

50. 6a10; Nivison's translation, 1980b, pp. 751-752. 6a11-14 contains examples of a similar kind of reasoning and we discussed its general form at length in Chapter 2. Also note 4a27, where a striking if cryptic picture is drawn of the joy that virtuous action can produce.

51. 3b9 discusses how incorrect ideas block *jen* and *yi*; see 2a2 and 6a1 on the role of erroneous ethical or general beliefs and Riegel 1979, p. 442. See note 56 in Chapter 3 for a more extended discussion of texts that speak of reasons for failure.

52. See the earlier analysis of the role of training and dispositions in Chapter 3, Sections II, III, and IX, as well as the treatment of failure in Chapter 3, Section VII. Aspects of the discussion in this section could be said to produce a more nuanced account of why people fail than Mencius himself presents, but, as noted, I am developing Mencius's practical theory in a way that he himself does not.

53. See the earlier treatment of Mencius's voluntarism at the end of Chapter 3, Section IX. Extension, I think, is a fully self-conscious process only for an undeveloped person or someone facing a new and difficult situation. Mencius articulates and emphasizes the conscious characteristics of the process mainly to explain it to beginners or to justify actions. His ideal person is moved by intelligent dispositions rather than by a fully conscious process of extension, voluntaristically activated, that works by means of resemblances. (Mencius's desire to reject a Mohist calculation of "profit" and application of rules also makes him wary of talking in too voluntaristic a fashion.)

54. See especially the discussion of virtues in locative and open religions in Section V of Chapter 2.

55. 2a2. The passage continues to note that Tzu-kung said "not to tire of learning is wisdom (*chih*) [and] not to tire of teaching is benevolence." A less complete version of this text appears in *Analects* 7:33.

56. 4b14. The first quote is from 4b28; Lau's translation has been changed somewhat; see Graham's rendering, 1967, p. 268. In 4b14, the phrase *tzu te* also may involve the sense of "getting it one's self," and the ability to draw deeply upon it may relate to being able to trust it; see Sellmann's (1987) work on *tzu te*. For an examination of another pre-Han Confucian's ideas on equanimity, Hsün Tzu's, see Yearley 1980.

57. 3b2; Lau's translation has been changed slightly; also note 7a9 and 6a10. The first quotation is from 4a27.

58. 2a4; the context of the remark is such that the older idea of virtue seems to be the reference.

59. 7a1; Shun's (1986) translation, pp. 50-51. Controversy surrounds the question of how Mencius sees *ming*; for an outline of the different positions see ibid., pp. 184-188. Clearly, however, *ming* in 7a3 refers to the quality of being outside human control whereas in 7a2 it is said to reside in human action. It is linked with *li* and *yi* in 5a8: "Confucius went forward in accordance with propriety (*li*) and withdrew in accordance with what was right (*yi*) and in matters of success and failure said 'There is the Decree' (*yu ming*)."

Evidence exists, mostly in polemics found in the *Mo Tzu*, that some Confucians were fatalists who made little attempt to better society or self and focused their energy only on ritual and music. Mencius may be reacting against such people with his dual emphasis on both fate's place and the need for human action; see *Mo Tzu*, Chapter 48; and Schwartz 1986, pp. 138-142, 122-127; also note Munro 1969, pp. 85-88.

60. 5a6. For the use of *T'ien ming*, see 4a7-8. The idea of the Heavenly Mandate (*T'ien ming*) reflects an early myth in which a "high God" acts to replace a corrupt ruler with a good ruler; see Creel 1970a, pp. 82-87, 93-100, 493-506.

On Heaven's desires, see 2b13; on it giving responsibility, see 6b15; on it as a source of political power, see 5a5; on people fearing, serving, and recommending rulers, see 1b3, 7a11 and 5a6; on Heaven causing things not in human control, see 1b14,16. For other important references on heaven, see 2a7, 3a5, 6a6, 6a15, 6a16, 7a1, 7b24. On the uses of *T'ien* and *ming* in the *Analects*, see Lau 1979, p. 29.

61. 2b13; see Nivison's discussion of this point in 1980c, pp. 107-108. Chu Hsi puts a similar point well in commenting on this passage: "We see in this how the sage's grief for the world can co-exist harmoniously with an honest delight in Heaven." For an extended and fascinating analysis of this passage, see Ivanhoe 1988.

62. For the religious character of this, see Yearley 1975a. Foot discusses the issue of what one would most fear to lose, without referring to religion, in arguing against Frankena 1970; see Foot 1978, pp. 157-189. Also note the later idea that Mencius's idea of goodness was an expression of admiration; see Graham 1958, p. 45.

63. 1b14. The quote comes from a discussion with a duke and the presence of ideas about lineage may modify the general point.

64. 7a3; the translation by Shun (1986, pp. 185-186) is slightly revised; also note 1b14, 5a8, 7a1, 7a2, 7a21, and 7b24.

65. 7a2; see Graham's 1967 rendering of this, p. 256.

66. This position manifests what can be called Mencius's *practical type* of religious thought. See Yearley 1975c, although I do not in that article differentiate the three kinds of theory evident in Mencius. Also note Shun's (1986) argument that chosen definitions of human nature also play a role (pp. 183-193); 7b24 and 7a21 are crucial texts here.

Chapter 5. Conclusion

1. Many of these differences are noted briefly in preceding chapters, but three earlier articles of mine examine aspects of them at length: see Yearley 1982, 1983a, and 1985c.

2. For accounts of their theories of virtue see Chapter 3, especially Sections II through VI; for resemblances in their conceptions of the self see Sections VIII and IX. For their ideas on semblances of virtue and expansions of virtues, see Chapter 1, Section V, Chapter 3, Sections V and VI, and Chapter 4, Sections V, VII and IX.

3. Examinations of this topic appear in Chapter 2, Section IV, and Chapter 4, Section IX.

4. See the treatment of courage, for example, in Chapter 4, Sections III, VI, VIII, and IX; on practical reason see Chapter 3, Section VIII.

5. See Horton 1982, especially pp. 216-217, 227-238; Horton's revision of his formulations owes much to M. Hesse's work. The article discusses his earlier work and the subsequent controversy.

6. For Aristotle's general approach, see, for example, *N.E.* 1094b13-1095all, 1095b1-14, and 1145b3-9. Also note, however, those places at which this approach is modified by what I called the *good person criterion*; for example, 1168a25-1169b2 and 1179a33-1180a6. Contemporary thinkers like Gadamer 1986, of course, have developed aspects of this approach and applied it to a wide range of areas, and the differences between practical theory and Aristotle's approach, I think, will become clear as we analyze practical theory's character.

7. See MacIntyre 1984a, pp. 187-191, and McClendon 1986, pp. 162-177.

8. See Chapter 2, Section V and Chapter 4, Sections IX and especially VIII; also note in Chapter 3, Section VII the role of practical and secondary theories in the explanation of failures to be virtuous.

9. See, for example, my discussion in Chapter 2, Section I, Chapter 3, Sections IV and V, and Chapter 4, Section IX.

10. For the discussion of how Mencius does not develop the idea of disposition, see the end of Section VI of Chapter 3. For the discussion of development and discovery models, see Section II and V of the third chapter. For the constructive analysis of dispositions, see Chapter 3, Section IX; for the idea of dispositions and Mencius, see, for example, Chapter 3, Sections II, IV, and VII.

11. With Mencius, for example, note his account of Confucianism's relationship to Mohism and Yang Chu, as discussed at various places, and the kinds of analysis he uses in treating, say, the expression of the four virtues through familial relationships. (Incidentally, the way in which other synthetic traditions, for example, Vedanta, deal with apparent differences is, I think, a very productive area of inquiry.)

12. See the treatment in MacIntyre 1988, for example, pp. 164-208, 401-403. MacIntyre emphasizes the importance of J. H. Newman's work on this topic; on Newman, also see Yearley 1978.

13. I discussed these issues in, for example, Chapter 2, Section I, and Chapter 3, Section V. On the distinction between oral and literary traditions, see the use made of Watt and Goody's work by Horton 1982, pp. 206, 250-256.

On Aquinas's historical understanding, see, for example, how he treats the case of the kid boiled in his mother's milk (2-1.102.6.4) and note Bourke's analysis of his historical sense in volume 29 of the *Summa Theologiae* 1964 ff., pp. xviii ff. On the general question of Aquinas's differences from moderns, see Lonergan 1985, pp. 35-54.

14. See the discussion in Chapter 2, Section III.

15. See the discussion in Chapter 4, Sections VI and IX.

16. See Chapter 2, Section V.

17. See the discussion especially in Chapter 3, Sections I and VI, and Chapter 4, Sections III and V. Also see note 5 of Chapter 3 for references to the immense literature on Aquinas's idea of analogy. I am especially indebted to Burrell's work (1973, 1979) and his emphasis on how Aquinas does not present a doctrine or theory of analogy but a philosophical activity or performance; see, for example, 1979, pp. 55-67. Also note Farrer's (1972, pp. 69-81) evocative discussion of the need to extend the idea beyond its traditional uses, and Tracy's (1981) examination, for example, pp. 405-456.

18. For the definition of virtue see 1-2.55.4; for the analysis of death, see Chapter 4, especially Section IV but also Section III.

19. For a good example of his treatment of this aspect of magnanimity, see 2-2.129.3. For Aristotle's treatment of magnanimity, see *N.E.* Book 4, Chapter 3.

Aquinas, as noted earlier, never analyzes fully the idea that some virtues cannot be harmonized in a single life; for example, the virtues needed for decent citizenship and for revolutionary life. Nevertheless, aspects of his overall perspective seem to allow for this possibility as we see in his treatment of different religious vocations and practices.

20. For the reading of St. Paul, see 2-1.10.3; also note the treatment of incontinence at 2-2.156. For an example of Aristotle's treatment, see *N.E.* 1145b8-1148b14. On the issue of Stoic views of the emotions, see 2-1.59.2 and 3.

21. As discussed in Chapter 3, Section VII, there are significant questions about the coherence of Aquinas's own utilization of a modified version of the principle that to know the good is to do the good.

22. I am much indebted to Tracy's (1981) work on the idea of the analogical imagination, but I use that idea in what follows for purposes that often differ from his; for example, my focus is less theological and I do not highlight the notion of participation and critique. (Also note W. Lynch's work on this idea, although he focuses on literature and often employs a very traditional Thomistic metaphysics; see 1980, pp. 118-193, especially 136-160.) As noted earlier, Burrell's work (1973, 1979) on analogical expression also has helped me greatly, although I will use it here for purposes that often differ from those on which he focuses.

23. See especially Sections VIII and IX in Chapter 4.

24. People, of course, can work between different languages; see, for example, Shun's (1986) use of modern Western ideas and Cua's use of *ching ch'üan*, the doctrine of the normal and the exigent (1978, pp. 72-76). Also note the issue of how choices of focal terms create hierarchies but hierarchies that shift as the criteria employed change; see my treatment of this subject in Aquinas in Chapter 2, Section III.

25. See L. Carroll 1971, p. 163 (the passage is from Chapter 6 of *Through the Looking Glass*). Pitcher's (1971) article in the volume illustrates how philosophers have used this passage; see pp. 395-398.

26. I examined the secondary uses of the idea in the third section of this chapter; see Chapter 3, Section IX for a more extended discussion and note 10 of this chapter for further references. For an analysis of how disposition differs from the *habitus* of Aquinas, and the terms related to it, see Kenny's discussion in volume 22 of the *Summa Theologiae* 1964 ff. Other distinctions between Aquinas's language and contemporary language are discussed by D'Arcy in the introductions to volumes 19 and 20.

27. See especially the discussions in Chapter 3, Sections IV, V, and VIII.

28. See Chapter 4, especially Sections I, VI, VIII, and IX.

29. The most sophisticated analyses, about which I know, of problems in approaches based on radical diversity appear in the articles in Hollis and Lukes

1982; also note Davidson 1985. The contemporary treatment of mysticism by virtually all sophisticated scholars exemplifies, I think, how almost all agree that simple univocal predication is inadequate.

30. My use of the idea of "imagination" relates to some of Aquinas's uses, but I am not here employing it in the more technical senses that he does when he draws on Aristotle's *De Anima*. For a critical evaluation of Aquinas's ideas, see Kenny 1980, pp. 77-79; for an evocative presentation of some of its more general implications, see White 1961, pp. 125-157, especially 142.

The role of the imagination in literature, philosophy, and Christian theology, of course, has been much discussed. Little, however, has been done with its role in comparative religion; for work in that area from which I have learned much, see Smith 1982. Also note Ryle's still evocative comments on the various activities that fit under the idea of imagination, see 1949, pp. 245-279; and see Lovibond 1983, especially pp. 190-200. Finally, Yearley 1990b sets out a general context within which to place the intellectual excellence that is imagination.

31. Wittgenstein, among others, writes powerfully about the difficulties of this kind of exploration; see, for example, *Philosophical Investigations* 1968, No. 206. See the earlier discussion of real and notional confrontations in Chapter 1, Section I, noting note 10.

32. Early Roman Catholic responses, especially Ricci's have been examined at length, but also note Gernet's (1986) depiction of Chinese responses to the first Catholics they met; those encounters were between Neo-Confucians and Roman Catholics. Legge's introduction to his translation of Mencius, pp. 56-73, also contains, as noted earlier (see Chapter 3, Section VII), a fascinating example of a later contact.

33. See note 26 in Chapter 3 and the discussion surrounding it for a brief examination, with textual references, of the good person criterion.

Chinese Terms

Wade-Giles	Pinyin	
ai	ai	愛
ch'i	qi	氣
chih ("intelligent awareness")	zhi	智
chih ("will")	zhi	志
ch'in	qin	親
ching	jing	敬
ching ch'üan	jing quan	經
ch'ing	qing	情 權
ch'üan	quan	權
chün tzu	junzi	君 子
ch'ung	chong	充
ch'ung. . . lei	chong. . . lei	充 類
erh	er	貳
fei jen	fei ren	非 人

Wade-Giles	Pinyin	
fu ssu	fu si	弗思
hao jan chih ch'i	hao ran zhi qi	浩然之氣
hsiang yüan	xiang yuan	鄉原
hsiao	xiao	孝
hsin ("fidelity")	xin	信
hsin ("heart," "mind")	xin	心
hsiu	xiu	羞
jang	rang	讓
jen	ren	仁
jen yi	ren yi	仁義
kung	gong	恭
k'uo. . . ch'ung	kuo. . . chong	擴充
lei	lei	類
li ("ritual," "propriety")	li	禮
li ("profit")	li	利
li ming	li ming	立命
ming	ming	命
pu ssu	bu si	不思
pu tung hsin	bu dong xin	不動心
shen	shen	神
shih ("official")	shi	士
shih ("actuality")	shi	實
shih/fei	shi/fei	是非
so	suo	縮

ssu	si	思
ta	da	達
tao	dao	道
te	de	德
te chih	de zhi	得 之
T'ien	Tian	天
T'ien ming	Tian ming	天 命
ts'e	ce	惻
ts'u	ci	辭
tuan	duan	端
t'ui	tui	推
t'ui en	tui en	推 思
tung	dong	動
tzu te	zi de	自 得
wu	wu	惡
wu wei	wu wei	無 為
yen	yan	言
yi ("righteousness," "morality")	yi	義
yin	yin	隱
yu ming	you ming	有 命
yu wei	you wei	有 為
yung	yong	勇

Names and Titles

Wade-Giles   Pinyin

Analects (=Lun Yü, q.v.)

Wade-Giles	Pinyin	
Ch'an	Chan	禪
Chao Ch'i	Zhao Qi	趙 岐
Chou	Zhou	周
Chu Hsi	Zhu Xi	朱 熹
Chuang Tzu	Zhuangzi	莊 子
Chuang Tzu	*Zhuangzi*	
Chung Yung	*Zhong Yong*	中 庸
Confucius (=K'ung Tzu)	Kongzi	孔 子
Hsüan (a king)	Xuan	宣
Hsün Tzu	Xunzi	荀 子
Hsün Tzu	*Xunzi*	
Kao Tzu	Gaozi	告 子
Kuan Chung	Guan Zhong	管 仲
Kung-sun Ch'ou	Gongsun Chou	公 孫 丑
Liu-Hsia Hui	Liuxia Hui	柳 下 惠
Lun Yü	*Lun Yu*	論 語
Mencius (=Meng Tzu, q.v.)		
Meng Shih-she	Meng Shishe	孟 施 舍
Meng Tzu	Mengzi	孟 子

Meng Tzu	*Mengzi*	
Mo Tzu	Mozi	墨子
Mo Tzu	*Mozi*	
Pei-kung Yu	Beigong You	北宮黝
Po Yi	Bo Yi	伯夷
Shun (a sage-king)	Shun	舜
Sung	Song	宋
T'ang	Tang	唐
Tao Te Ching	*Dao De Jing*	道德經
Tzu-kung	Zigong	子貢
Wang Yang-ming	Wang Yangming	王陽明
Wen (a king)	Wen	文
Wu (a king)	Wu	武
Yang Chu	Yang Zhu	陽朱
Yao (a sage-king)	Yao	堯
Yi (a famous archer)	Yi	羿
Yi Yin (a sage)	Yi Yin	伊尹

Long Quotations

Wade-Giles	*Pinyin*	
chih ming che	zhi ming zhe	知 命 者
hsiu shen yi ssu chih	xiu shen yi si zhi	修 身 以 俟 之
mo fei ming yeh	mo fei ming ye	莫 非 命 也

pi yu shih yen,
  erh wu cheng;
  hsin wu wang,
  wu chu chang yeh
	bi you shi yan,
	  er wu zheng;
	  xin wu wang,
	  wu zhu zhang ye
		必 有 事 焉
		而 勿 正
		心 勿 忘
		勿 助 長 也

shun shou ch'i cheng	shun shou qi zheng	順 受 其 正

ta jen che yen pu pi hsin,
  hsing pu pi kuo,
  wei yi so tsai
	da ren zhe yan bu bi xin,
	  xing bu bi guo,
	  wei yi suo zai
		大 人 者 言 不 必 信
		行 不 必 果
		惟 義 所 在

t'ui ch'i so wei	tui qi suo wei	推 其 所 為

yu jen yi hsing,
  fei hsing jen yi yeh
	you ren yi xing,
	  fei xing ren yi ye
		由 仁 義 行
		非 行 仁 義 也

Selected Bibliography

Sections A and B refer to the translations of Mencius and works of Aquinas that were consulted. Section C lists works cited in the notes or found to be of particular importance.

A. Translations of the Meng Tzu

CHAI, CH'U, AND CHAI WINBERG. 1965. *The Sacred Books of Confucius and Other Confucian Classics*. New York: University Books.

DOBSON, W. A. C. H. 1963. *Mencius: A New Translation Arranged and Annotated for the General Reader*. Toronto: University of Toronto Press.

LAU, D. C. *Mencius*. 1970. Baltimore: Penguin Books.

LEGGE, JAMES. 1895. *The Works of Mencius*, 2d ed. *The Chinese Classics*, vol. 2. Reprinted New York: Dover, 1970.

LYALL, LEONARD A. 1932. *Mencius*. London: Longmans, Green and Co.

WARE, JAMES. 1960. *The Sayings of Mencius*. New York: New American Library of World Literature.

B. Translations and Works of St. Thomas Aquinas

1951. *On the Virtues in General*, trans. J. P. Reid. Providence, R. I.: Providence College Press.

1952-54. *On Truth [Quaestiones Disputatae de Veritatae]*, trans. R. W. Mulligan and others. Chicago: Henry Regnery.

C. G. On the Truth of the Catholic Faith [Summa Contra Gentiles], trans. A. C. Pegis and others. New York: Doubleday, 1955-57.

De car. On Charity [De Caritate], trans. L. H. Kendzierski. Milwaukee: Marquette University Press, 1960.

1964 ff. *Summa Theologiae*, 60 vols., general eds. T. Gilby and T. C. O'Brien. London: Eyre and Spottiswode; New York: McGraw-Hill.

In Ethic. Commentary on the Nicomachean Ethics [In X Libros Ethicorum], trans. C.I. Litzinger. Chicago: Henry Regnery, 1964.

1965. *Selected Writings of St. Thomas Aquinas: The Principles of Nature, On Being and Essence, On the Virtues in General, On Free Choice*, trans. R. P. Goodwin. Indianapolis: Bobbs-Merrill Co.

1966. *Commentary on Saint Paul's Epistle to the Ephesians*, trans M. L. Lamb. Albany, N.Y.: Magi Books.

C. General

ADAMS, ROBERT. 1985. "Involuntary Sins." *Philosophical Review* 94, no. 1: 3–31.
————. 1987. *The Virtue of Faith and Other Essays in Philosophical Theology.* New York: Oxford University Press.

ANSCOMBE, ELIZABETH. 1958. "Modern Moral Philosophy." *Philosophy* 33: 1–19.

ARISTOTLE. *N. E.* 1985. *Nicomachean Ethics*, trans. T. Irwin. Indianapolis, Ind.: Hackett.
————. *E. E. Eudemian Ethics.*
————. *C. W.* 1984. *The Complete Works of Aristotle: The Revised Oxford Translation*, 2 vols., ed. Jonathan Barnes. Princeton, N. J.: Princeton University Press, Bollingen Series.

AUDI, ROBERT, AND WAINWRIGHT, WILLIAM, eds. 1986. *Rationality, Religious Belief, and Moral Commitment: New Essays in the Philosophy of Religion.* Ithaca, N. Y.: Cornell University Press.

BAKER, RICHARD. 1941. *The Thomistic Theory of the Passions and Their Influence upon the Will.* Ann Arbor, Mich.: Edwards Brothers.

BARON, MARCIA. 1984. "On the Alleged Repugnance of Acting from Duty." *The Journal of Philosophy* 81, no. 4: 197–220.

BAUER, WOLFGANG. 1976. *China and the Search for Happiness: Recurring Themes in 4,000 Years of China Cultural History*, trans. M. Shaw. New York: Seabury Press.

BECKER, LAWRENCE. 1975. "The Neglect of Virtue." *Ethics* 85: 110–122.
———. 1986. *Reciprocity*. London: Routledge and Kegan Paul.

BERGER, PETER. 1983. "On the Obsolescence of the Concept of Honor." In S. Hauerwas and A. MacIntyre, eds., *Revisions: Changing Perspectives in Moral Philosophy*, pp. 172–181. South Bend, Ind.: University of Notre Dame Press.

BERNSTEIN, RICHARD J. 1984. "Nietzsche or Aristotle?: Reflections on Alasdair MacIntyre's *After Virtue*." *Soundings* 67: 6–29.

BODDE, DERK. 1939. "Types of Chinese Categorical Thinking." *Journal of the American Oriental Society* 59: 200–219.
———. 1955. "On Translating Chinese Philosophical Terms." *Far Eastern Quarterly* 14: 231–243.

BOODBERG, PETER. 1952/53. "The Semasiology of Some Primary Confucian Concepts." *Philosophy East and West* 2: 317–332.

BOSWELL, JOHN. 1980. *Christianity, Social Tolerance, and Homosexuality: Gay People in Western Europe from the Beginning of the Christian Era to the Fourteenth Century*. Chicago: University of Chicago Press.

BOURKE, VERNON. 1966. *Ethics in Crisis*. Milwaukee: Bruce Publishing Co.

BRANDT, RICHARD. 1970. "Traits of Character: A Conceptual Analysis." *American Philosophical Quarterly* 7: 23–37.
———. 1981. "W. K. Frankena and the Ethics of Virtue." *The Monist* 64: 271–292.

BURNYEAT, M. F. 1980. "Aristotle on Learning to Be Good." In A. O. Rorty, ed. *Essays on Aristotle's Ethics*, pp. 69–92. Berkeley: University of California.

BURRELL, DAVID, CSC. 1973. *Analogy and Philosophical Language*. New Haven, Conn.: Yale University Press.
———. 1979. *Aquinas: God and Action*. London: Routledge and Kegan Paul.

CAPPS, DONALD. 1987. *Deadly Sins and Saving Virtues*. Philadelphia: Fortress Press.

CARROLL, LEWIS. 1971 [1896]. *Alice in Wonderland*, ed. D. J. Gray. New York: W. W. Norton and Co.

CAVELL, STANLEY. 1976. *Must We Mean What We Say?* Cambridge: Cambridge University Press.

CHENU, M. D., OP. 1964. *Toward Understanding St. Thomas,* trans. A. Landry and D. Hughes. Chicago: Henry Regnery.

CHING, JULIA. 1977. *Confucianism and Christianity: A Comparative Study.* New York: Kodansha International.

CIKOSKI, JOHN. 1975. "On Standards of Analogical Reasoning in the Late Chou." *Journal of Chinese Philosophy* 2: 325–357.

CLARK, STEPHEN. 1975. *Aristotle's Man: Speculations upon Aristotelian Anthropology.* Oxford: Clarendon Press.

COOPER, JOHN. 1975. *Reason and Human Good in Aristotle.* Cambridge, Mass.: Harvard University Press.

CREEL, H. G. 1953. *Chinese Thought from Confucius to Mao Tse-Tung.* New York: The New American Library.
———. 1970a. *The Origins of Statecraft in China,* vol. 1. *The Western Chou Empire.* Chicago: University of Chicago Press.
———. 1970b. *What Is Taoism and other Studies in Chinese Cultural History.* Chicago: University of Chicago Press.

CROWE, FREDERICK, SJ. 1959. "Complacency and Concern in the Thought of St. Thomas Aquinas." *Theological Studies* 20: 1–39, 193–230, 343–381.

CUA, A. S. 1978. *Dimensions of Moral Creativity, Paradigms, Principles, and Ideals.* University Park: Pennsylvania State University Press.
———. 1985. *Ethical Argumentation: A Study in Hsün Tzu's Moral Epistemology.* Honolulu: University of Hawaii Press.

D'ARCY, M. C. 1953. *St. Thomas Aquinas.* London: Burns, Oates and Washbourne.

DAVIDSON, DONALD. 1982. "Paradoxes of Irrationality." In R. Wollheim and S. Hopkins, eds., *Philosophical Essays on Freud,* pp. 289–305. Cambridge: Cambridge University Press.
———. 1985 [1973/74]. "On the Very Idea of a Conceptual Scheme." In J. Rajchman and C. West, eds., *Post-analytic Philosophy,* pp. 129–144. New York: Columbia University Press.

DEFERRARI, ROY. 1960. *A Latin-English Dictionary of St. Thomas Aquinas.* Boston: Daughters of St. Paul.

DENT, N. J. H. 1981. "The Value of Courage." *Philosophy* 56: 574–577.
———. 1984. *The Moral Psychology of the Virtues.* Cambridge: Cambridge University Press. .

DONAGAN, ALAN. 1969. "The Scholastic Theory of Moral Law in the Modern World." In A. Kenny, ed., *Aquinas: A Collection of Critical Essays*, pp. 325–339. Garden City, N. Y.: Doubleday and Company.
———. 1977. *The Theory of Morality.* Chicago: University of Chicago Press.
———. 1981. "St. Thomas Aquinas on the Analysis of Human Action." In N. Kretzmann, A. Kenny, and J. Pinborg, eds., *The Cambridge History of Later Medieval Philosophy*, pp. 642–654. Cambridge: Cambridge University Press.
———. 1984. "Consistency in Rationalist Moral Systems." *Journal of Philosophy* 81, no. 6: 291–309.
———. 1985. *Human Ends and Human Actions: An Exploration in St. Thomas' Treatment.* Milwaukee: Marquette University Press.

DUBS, HOMER. 1959/60. "Theism and Naturalism in Ancient Chinese Philosophy." *Philosophy East and West* 9: 163–172.

DUFF, ANTHONY. 1987. "Aristotelian Courage." *Ratio* 29: 2–15.

ECO, UMBERTO. 1988 [1970]. *The Aesthetics of Thomas Aquinas*, trans. H. Bredin. Cambridge, Mass.: Harvard University Press.

EVANS, DONALD. 1979. *Struggle and Fulfillment: The Inner Dynamics of Religion and Morality.* Philadelphia: Fortress Press.

FALK, W. D. 1969 [1963]. "Prudence, Temperance, and Courage." In J. Feinberg, ed., *Moral Concepts*, pp. 114–119. London: Oxford University Press.

FARRER, AUSTIN. 1972. *Reflective Faith: Essays in Philosophical Theology*, ed. C. Conti. London: SPCK.

FEHL, NOAH. 1971. *Rites and Propriety in Literature and Life: A Perspective for a Cultural History of Ancient China.* Hong Kong: Chinese University of Hong Kong.

FUNG YU-LAN. 1952. *A History of Chinese Philosophy*, vol. 1, trans. D. Bodde. Princeton, N. J.: Princeton University Press.

FINDLAY, J. N. 1970. *Axiological Ethics.* London: Macmillian and Company.

FINGARETTE, HERBERT. 1972. *Confucius: The Secular as Sacred.* New York: Harper and Row.

FINNIS, JOHN. 1980. *Natural Law and Natural Rights*. Oxford: Clarendon Press.
————. 1983. *Fundamentals of Ethics*. Washington, D.C.: Georgetown University Press.

FLEMMING, ARTHUR. 1980. "Reviving the Virtues." *Ethics* 90: 587–595.

FOOT, PHILIPPA. 1978. *Virtues and Vices*. Berkeley: University of California Press.
————. 1983. "Utilitarianism and the Virtues." *Proceedings and Addresses of the American Philosophical Association* 57: 273–283.

FORTENBAUGH, W. W. 1975. *Aristotle on Emotion*. London: Duckworth.

FRANKENA, WILLIAM. 1970. "Prichard and the Ethics of Virtue." *The Monist* 54: 1–17.

FRANKFURT, HARRY. 1971. "Freedom of the Will and the Concept of a Person." *Journal of Philosophy* 68, no. 1: 5–20.

FRENCH, P.; UEHLING, T., Jr.; and Wettstein, H., eds. 1988. *Ethical Theory: Character and Virtue*. Midwest Studies in Philosophy, vol. 13. Notre Dame, Ind.: University of Notre Dame Press.

GADAMER, HANS-GEORGE. 1986. *The Idea of the Good in Platonic-Aristotelian Philosophy*, trans. P. C. Smith. New Haven, Conn.: Yale University Press.

GARVER, EUGENE. 1980. "Aristotle on Virtue and Pleasure." In D. DePew, ed., *The Greeks and the Good Life*, pp. 157–176. Indianapolis, Ind.: Hackett Publishing Company.

GAUTHIER, R.A., OP. 1951. *Magnanimité*. Paris: Vrin.

GEACH, PETER. 1969. *God and the Soul*. London: Routledge and Kegan Paul.
————. 1977. *The Virtues*. Cambridge: Cambridge University Press.

GEERTZ, CLIFFORD. 1973. *The Interpretation of Cultures*. New York: Harper and Row.

GERNET, JACQUES. 1968. *Ancient China: From the Beginnings to the Empire*, trans. R. Rudorff. Berkeley: University of California Press.
————. 1986 [1982]. *China and the Christian Impact: A Conflict of Cultures*, trans. J. Lloyd. Cambridge: Cambridge University Press.

GERT, BERNARD. 1966. *The Moral Rules: A New Rational Foundation for Morality*. New York: Harper and Row.

GILLIGAN, CAROL. 1982. *In a Different Voice*. Cambridge: Harvard University Press.

GILSON, ETIENNE. 1956 [1948]. *The Christian Philosophy of St. Thomas Aquinas*, trans. L. K. Shook. New York: Random House.

GIRARDOT, NORMAN. 1976. "The Problem of Creation Mythology in the Study of Chinese Religion." *History of Religions* 15, no. 4: 289–318.

GRAHAM, ANGUS. 1958. *Two Chinese Philosophers: Ch'eng Ming-tao and Ch'eng Yi-chuan.* London: Lund Humphries.
———. 1959. "'Being' in Western Philosophy Compared with *shih/fei* and *yu/wu* in Chinese Philosophy." *Asia Major* n.s. 7: 1–2, 79–112.
———. 1964. "The Place of Reason in the Chinese Philosophic Tradition." In R. Dawson, ed., *The Legacy of China*, pp. 28–56. Oxford: Oxford University Press.
———. 1967. "The Background of the Mencian Theory of Human Nature." *Tsing Hua Journal of Chinese Studies* n.s. 6, nos. 1–2: 215–271.
———. 1978. *Later Mohist Logic, Ethics, and Science.* Hong Kong: Chinese University Press.
———. 1981. *Chuang-tzu: The Seven Inner Chapters and Other Writings from the Book Chuang-tzu.* London: George Allen and Unwin.
———. 1989. *Disputers of the Tao: Philosophical Argument in Ancient China.* La Salle, Ill.: Open Court.

GRAMLICH, FRANK. 1980. "Mencius's Moral Philosophy." Dissertation, Stanford University, Department of Philosophy.

GRANET, MARCEL. 1934. *La Pensée Chinoise.* Paris: Editions Albin Michel.
———. 1977 [1922]. *The Religion of the Chinese People*, trans. M. Freedman. New York: Harper and Row.

GRAY, J. GLENN. 1970 [1959]. *The Warriors: Reflections on Men in Battle.* New York: Harper and Row.

GRISEZ, GERMAIN. 1969. "The First Principle of Practical Reason." In A. Kenny, ed., *Aquinas: A Collection of Critical Essays*, pp. 340–382. Garden City, N. Y.: Doubleday and Company.

GREEN, RONALD. 1978. *Religious Reason: The Rational And Moral Foundations of Religious Belief.* Oxford: Oxford University Press.
———. 1981. Review of David Little and Sumner B. Twiss, *Comparative Religious Ethics.* In *Journal of Religion* 61: 111–113.
———. 1988. *Religion and Moral Reason: A New Method for Comparative Study.* New York: Oxford University Press.

GUSTAFSON, JAMES. 1981. *Ethics from a Theocentric Perspective*, vol. 1. Chicago: University of Chicago Press.
———. 1984. *Ethics from a Theocentric Perspective*, vol.2. Chicago: University of Chicago Press.

HAMPSHIRE, STUART. 1977. *Two Theories of Morality.* Oxford: Oxford University Press.

———. 1978. "Morality and Pessimism." In S. Hampshire, ed. *Morality and Pessimism,* pp. 1–22. Cambridge: Cambridge University Press.

———. 1982. "Morality and Convention." In A. Sen and B. Williams, eds. *Utilitarianism and Beyond,* pp. 145–158. Cambridge: Cambridge University Press.

———. 1983. *Morality and Conflict.* Cambridge: Harvard University Press.

HANSEN, CHAD. 1972. "Freedom and Responsibility in Chinese Ethics." *Philosophy East and West* 22, no. 2: 169–186.

———. 1983. *Language and Logic in Ancient China.* Ann Arbor: University of Michigan Press.

HARAK, G. SIMON, SJ. 1986. "The Role of Passions in the Formation of Character." Dissertation, University of Notre Dame, Department of Theology.

HARDIE, W. F. R. 1968. *Aristotle's Ethical Theory.* Oxford: Clarendon Press.

HARE, R. M. 1963. *Freedom and Reason.* Oxford: Oxford University Press.

HARTMANN, NICHOLAI. 1975 [English, 1932; German, 1926]. *Ethics,* 2 vols., trans. S. Coit. Atlantic Highlands, N. J.: Humanities Press.

HAUERWAS, STANLEY. 1981a. *A Community of Character: Toward a Constructive Social Ethics.* Notre Dame, Ind.: University of Notre Dame Press.

———. 1981b. *Vision and Virtue.* Notre Dame, Ind.: University of Notre Dame Press.

HAWLEY, JOHN S., ed. 1987. *Saints and Virtues.* Berkeley: University of California Press.

HERMAN, BARBARA. 1981. "On the Value of acting from the Motive of Duty." *Philosophical Review* 66, no. 2: 233–250.

HERMS, EILERT. 1982. "Virtue: A Neglected Concept in Protestant Ethics." *Scottish Journal of Theology* 35, no. 6: 481–495.

HILL, THOMAS. 1973. "Servility and Self-Respect." *The Monist* 57: 87–104.

HIRSCHMAN, ALBERT. 1977. *The Passions and the Interests: Political Arguments for Capitalism before its Triumph.* Princeton, N. J.: Princeton University Press.

HOLLIS, M. AND LUKES, S., eds. 1982. *Rationality and Relativism.* Cambridge, Mass.: The MIT Press.

HORTON, ROBIN. 1982. "Tradition and Modernity Revisited." In M. Hollis and S. Lukes, eds., *Rationality and Relativism*, pp. 201–260. Cambridge, Mass.: The MIT Press.

HSU, CHO-YUN. 1965. *Ancient China in Transition: An Analysis of Social Mobility, 722-222 B.C.* Stanford, Calif.: Stanford University Press.

HSÜN TZU. 1963. *Hsün Tzu: Basic Writings*, trans. B. Watson. New York: Columbia University Press.

HUDSON, STEPHEN. 1980. "Character Traits and Desires." *Ethics* 90: 539–549.

HUNT, LESTER. 1980. "Courage and Principle." *Canadian Journal of Philosophy* 10: 281–293.

IRWIN, TERENCE. 1977. *Plato's Moral Theory: The Early and Middle Dialogues*. Oxford: Clarendon Press.

IVANHOE, PHILLIP JOHN. 1988. "A Question of Faith: A New Interpretation of *Mencius* 2b13." *Early China* 13: 153–165.
———. 1990. *Ethics in the Confucian Tradition: The Thought of Mencius and Wang Yang-Ming*. Mercer, Georgia: Scholars Press.

JAFFA, HARRY. 1952. *Thomism and Aristotelianism: A Study of the Commentary by Thomas Aquinas on the Nicomachean Ethics*. Chicago: University of Chicago Press.

JAMES, WILLIAM. 1985 [1902]. *The Varieties of Religious Experience: A Study in Human Nature*. New York: Viking Penguin.

JORDON, MARK D. 1986a. "Aquinas's Construction of a Moral Account of the Passions." *Freiburger Zeitschrift für Philosophie und Theologie* 33, no. 1–2: 71–97.
———. 1986b. *Ordering Wisdom: The Hierarchy of Philosophical Discourses in Aquinas*. Notre Dame, Ind.: University of Notre Dame Press.

KANT, IMMANUEL. 1964 [1797]. *The Doctrine of Virtue: Part II of The Metaphysics of Morals*, trans. M. J. Gregor. Philadelphia: University of Pennsylvania Press.

KELLY, JACK. 1973. "Virtue and Pleasure." *Mind* 82: 401–408.

KENNY, ANTHONY. 1963. *Action, Emotion and Will.* London: Routledge and Kegan Paul.
———. 1980. *Aquinas.* New York: Hill and Wang.

KIECKHEFER, RICHARD. 1984. *Unquiet Souls: Fourteenth-Century Saints and Their Religious Milieu.* Chicago: University of Chicago Press.

KOHLBERG, LAWRENCE. 1971. "Stages of Moral Development as a Basis for Moral Education." In C. M. Beck, B. S. Crittenden, E. V. Sullivan, eds., *Moral Education: Interdisciplinary Approaches.* New York: Paulist Press.

KOLNIA, AUREL. 1978. *Ethics, Value, and Reality.* Indianapolis, Ind.: Hackett Publishing Company.

KOVESI, JULES. 1967. *Moral Notions.* London: Routledge and Kegan Paul.

KOSMAN, L. A. 1980. "Being Properly Affected: Virtues and Feelings in Aristotle's Ethics." In A. O. Rorty, ed., *Essays on Aristotle's Ethics,* pp. 103–116. Berkeley: University of California Press.

KRAUSZ, MICHAEL, AND MEILAND, JACK, eds. 1982. *Relativism: Cognitive and Moral.* Notre Dame, Ind.: University of Notre Dame Press.

KRUSCHWITZ, ROBERT, AND ROBERTS, ROBERT, eds. 1987. *The Virtues: Contemporary Essays on Moral Character.* Belmont, Calif.: Wadsworth Publishing Co.

LAI, WHALEN. 1985. *"Yung* and the Tradition of the *Shih*: The Confucian Restructuring of Heroic Courage." *Religious Studies* 21: 181–203.

LANGAN, JOHN, SJ. 1979. "Augustine on the Unity and Interconnection of the Virtues." *Harvard Theological Review* 72: 81–95.

LAU, D. C. 1953. "Theories of Human Nature in Mencius and Shyuntzyy." *Bulletin of the School of Oriental and African Studies* 15: 541–565.
———. 1963a. *Lao Tzu: Tao Te Ching,* trans. with an Introduction. Baltimore: Penguin Books.
———. 1936b. "On Mencius' Use of the Method of Analogy in Argument." *Asia Major* n.s. 10: 173–194. [Reprinted in D. C. Lau, trans., *Mencius.* Baltimore: Penguin Books, 1970.]
———. 1969. "Some Notes on the Mencius." *Asia Major* n.s. 15, no. 1: 62–81.
———. 1979. *Confucius: The Analects,* trans. with an Introduction. Baltimore: Penguin Books.

LEAR, JONATHAN. 1984. "Moral Objectivity." In A. Brown, ed., *Objectivity and Cultural Divergence*, pp. 135–170. Cambridge: Cambridge University Press.
———. 1988. *Aristotle: The Desire to Understand*. Cambridge: Cambridge University Press.

LEVENSON, J. R., AND SCHURMANN, F. 1969. *China: An Interpretative History from the Beginnings to the Fall of Han*. Berkeley: University of California Press.

LITTLE, DAVID, AND TWISS, SUMNER. 1978. *Comparative Religious Ethics: A New Method*. New York: Harper and Row.

LITTLE, DAVID. 1978. "The Present State of Comparative Religious Ethics." *Journal of Religious Ethics* 9: 186–198.

LOHR, C. H. 1982. "The Medieval Interpretation of Aristotle." In N. Kretzmann, A. Kenny, J. Pinborg, eds., *The Cambridge History of Later Medieval Philosophy*. pp. 80–98. Cambridge: Cambridge University Press.

LONERGAN, BERNARD, SJ. 1967a. *Collection: Papers by Bernard Lonergan, S.J.* ed. F.E. Crowe, SJ. New York: Herder and Herder.
———. 1967b. *Verbum: Word and Idea in Aquinas*. South Bend, Ind.: University of Notre Dame Press.
———. 1971. *Grace and Freedom, Operative Grace in the Thought of St. Thomas*, ed. J. P. Burns. New York: Herder and Herder.
———. 1972. *Method in Theology*. New York: Herder and Herder.
———. 1974. *A Second Collection: Papers by Bernard Lonergan, S.J.*, ed. W. Ryan, SJ., and B. Tyrrell, SJ., Philadelphia: Westminster Press.
———. 1985. *A Third Collection: Papers by Bernard Lonergan, S.J.*, ed. F. E. Crowe, S.J. New York: Paulist Press.

LOTTIN, DOM ODON. 1949–1954. *Psychologie et Morale Aux XII et XIII Siècles*, 6 vols. Louvain: Abbaye du Mont Cesar.

LOUDEN, ROBERT. 1984. "On Some Vices of Virtue Ethics." *American Philosophical Quarterly* 21, no. 3: 227–236.

———. 1986. "Kant's Virtue Ethics." *Philosophy* 61: 473–489.

LOVIBOND, SABRINA. 1983. *Realism and Imagination in Ethics*. Minneapolis: University of Minnesota Press.

LOVIN, ROBIN, AND REYNOLDS, FRANK, eds. 1985. *Cosmogony and Ethical Order: New Studies in Comparative Ethics.* Chicago: University of Chicago Press.

LUSCOMBE, D. E. 1982. "Natural Morality and Natural Law." In N. Kretzmann, A. Kenny, and J. Pinborg, eds., *The Cambridge History of Later Medieval Philosophy*, pp. 705–720. Cambridge: Cambridge University Press.

LYMAN, STANFORD. 1978. *The Seven Deadly Sins: Society and Evil.* New York: St. Martin's Press.

LYNCH, WILLIAM, SJ. 1960. *Christ and Apollo: The Dimensions of the Literary Imagination.* New York: Sheed and Ward.

LYONS, WILLIAM. 1980. *Emotion.* Cambridge: Cambridge University Press.

MCCLENDON, JAMES, JR. 1986. *Ethics: Systematic Theology, Volume I.* Nashville: Abingdon Press.

MACDOWELL, JOHN. 1979. "Virtue and Reason." *The Monist* 62: 331–350.

MACHLE, E. 1976. "Hsün Tzu as a Religious Philosopher." *Philosophy East and West* 26, no. 4: 443–461.

MCINERNY, RALPH. 1968. *Studies in Analogy.* The Hague: Nijhoff.
———. 1975. *St. Thomas Aquinas.* Notre Dame, Ind.: University of Notre Dame Press.
———. 1982. *Ethica Thomistica: The Moral Philosophy of Thomas Aquinas.* Washington, D.C.: Catholic University of America Press.

MACINTYRE, ALASDAIR. 1977. "Epistemological Crises, Dramatic Narrative, and the Philosophy of Science." *The Monist* 60: 453–472.
———. 1984a. *After Virtue*, 2d ed. Notre Dame, Ind.: University of Notre Dame Press.
———. 1984b. "Bernstein's Distorting Mirrors: A Rejoinder." *Soundings* 67: 30–41.
———. 1988. *Whose Justice? Which Rationality?* Notre Dame, Ind.: University of Notre Dame Press.

MACKIE, J. L. 1977. *Ethics: Inventing Right and Wrong.* Baltimore: Penguin Books.

MANDELBAUM, MAURICE. 1955. *Phenomenology of Moral Experience.* Baltimore: Johns Hopkins Press.

MARTIN, CHRISTOPHER, ed. 1988. *The Philosophy of Thomas Aquinas.* New York: Routledge and Kegan Paul.

MASPERO, HENRI. 1950. *Mélanges Posthumes sur les Religions et l'Histoire de la Chine*, 3 vols. Paris: Civilisations du Sud.
———. 1978 [1927]. *China in Antiquity*, trans. F. A. Kierman, Jr. Amherst: University of Massachusetts Press.
———. 1981 [1971]. *Taoism and Chinese Religion*, trans. F. A. Kierman, Jr. Amherst: University of Massachusetts Press.

MEILAENDER, GILBERT. 1984. *The Theory and Practice of Virtue*. Notre Dame, Ind.: University of Notre Dame Press.

METZGER, THOMAS. 1977. *Escape from Predicament*. New York: Columbia University Press.

MEYNELL, HUGO. 1986. *The Theology of Bernard Lonergan*. Atlanta: Scholars Press.

MILHAVEN, JOHN. 1968. "Moral Absolutes and Thomas Aquinas." In C. Curran, ed., *Absolutes in Moral Theology?* pp. 154-185. Washington, D.C.: Corpus Books.

MILLS, C. WRIGHT. 1963. "The Language and Ideas of Ancient China." In I. Horowitz, ed., *Power, Politics and People: The Collected Essays of C. Wright Mills*. New York: Columbia University Press.

MILOSZ, CZESLAW. 1968. *Native Realm: A Search for Self Definition*. Garden City, N. Y.: Doubleday and Co.

MORLEY, A. 1935. "Some Ethical Ideals of the Tso-chuan." *Journal of the Royal Asiatic Society*: 274-284, 449-458.

MORTIMORE, G. W., ed. 1971. *Weakness of Will*. London: Macmillian.

MOTE, FREDERICK. 1972. "The Cosmological Gulf between China and the West." In D. Buxbaum and F. Mote, eds., *Transition and Permanence: Chinese History and Culture*. Hong Kong: University of Hong Kong Press.

MUNRO, DONALD. 1969. *The Concept of Man in Early China*. Stanford, Calif.: Stanford University Press.
———. 1977. *The Concept of Man in Contemporary China*. Ann Arbor: University of Michigan Press.
———. 1985. ed. *Individualism and Holism: Studies in Confucian and Taoist Values*. Ann Arbor: University of Michigan Center for Chinese Studies.

MURDOCH, IRIS. 1966 [1956]. "Vision and Choice in Morality." In I. Ramsey, ed., *Christian Ethics and Contemporary Philosophy*. New York: Macmillian.
———. 1971. *The Sovereignty of Good*. New York: Schocken Books.

NAGEL, THOMAS. 1979. *Mortal Questions.* Cambridge: Cambridge University Press.
————. 1980. "The Limits of Objectivity III, Ethics." In S. McMurrin, ed., *The Tanner Lectures on Human Values*, pp. 119–139. Salt Lake City: University of Utah Press.
————. 1986. *The View from Nowhere.* New York: Oxford University Press.

NAKAMURA, HAJIME. 1964 [1947]. *Ways of Thinking of Eastern Peoples: India-China-Tibet-Japan*, trans. P. Weiner. Honolulu: East-West Center Press.

NEEDHAM, JOSEPH. 1956. *Science and Civilization in China*, vol. 2, *History of Scientific Thought.* Cambridge: Cambridge University Press.

NEUHAUS, RICHARD J., ed. 1986. *Virtue: Public and Private.* Grand Rapids, Mich.: William B. Eerdmans Publishing Company.

NEWMAN, JOHN HENRY. 1891 [1870]. *An Essay in Aid of a Grammar of Assent.* London: Longmans, Green and Co.

NIETZSCHE, FRIEDRICH. 1967 [1879]. *Mixed Opinions and Maxims.* In *On the Genealogy of Morals, Ecce Homo*, trans. W. Kaufman. New York: Random House.

NIVISON, DAVID. 1973. "Philosophical Voluntarism in Fourth-Century China" (unpublished manuscript).
————. 1978/79. "Royal 'Virtue' in Shang Oracle Inscriptions." *Early China* 4: 52–55.
————. 1979. "Mencius and Motivation." *Journal of the American Academy of Religion Thematic Issue* 47, 3s: 417–432.
————. 1980a. "Investigations in Chinese Philosophy" (unpublished manuscript, the Walter Y. Evans-Wentz Lectures).
————. 1980b. "Two Roots or One?" *Proceedings and Addresses of the American Philosophical Association* 53, no. 6: 739–761.
————. 1980c. "On Translating Mencius." *Philosophy East and West* 30: 93–122.
————. 1985. "D.C. Lau, Mencius: Comments and Corrections" (unpublished manuscript).

NOWELL-SMITH, PATRICK. 1954. *Ethics.* Harmondsworth, England: Penguin Books.

NUSSBAUM, MARTHA C. 1986. *The Fragility of Goodness: Luck and Ethics in Greek Tragedy and Philosophy.* Cambridge: Cambridge University Press.

O'CONNOR, D. J. 1967. *Aquinas and Natural Law.* London: Macmillan.

O'NEIL, CHARLES J. 1955. *Imprudence in St. Thomas Aquinas.* Milwaukee: Marquette University Press.

O'NEILL, ONORA. 1984. "Kant after Virtue." *Inquiry* 26: 387–405.

OUTKA, GENE. 1972. *Agape: An Ethical Analysis.* New Haven, Conn.: Yale University Press.

PEARS, DAVID. 1980. "Aristotle's Analysis of Courage." In A. O. Rorty, ed. *Essays on Aristotle's Ethics,* pp. 171–188. Berkeley: University of California Press.

PENCE, GREGORY. 1984. "Recent Work on Virtue." *American Philosophical Quarterly* 21, no. 4: 281–298.

PIEPER, JOSEF. 1965. *The Four Cardinal Virtues,* trans. R. Winston, C. Winston, L. Lynch, and D. Coggan. New York: Harcourt Brace and World.
———. 1967 [1949]. *Reality and the Good,* trans. S. Lange. Chicago: Henry Regnery.
———. 1986 [1977]. *On Hope,* trans. M.F. McCarthy, SND. San Francisco: Ignatius Press.

PINCOFFS, EDMUND. 1971. "Quandary Ethics." *Mind* 80: 552–571.
———. 1986. *Quandaries and Virtues: Against Reductionism in Ethics.* Lawrence: University Press of Kansas.

PITCHER, GEORGE. 1971. "Wittgenstein, Nonsense, and Lewis Carroll." In D.J. Gray, ed. *Alice in Wonderland,* pp. 387–402. New York: W.W. Norton and Co.

POTTS, TIMOTHY. 1982. "Conscience." In N. Kretzmann, A. Kenny, and J. Pinborg, eds., *The Cambridge History of Later Medieval Philosophy,* pp. 687–704. Cambridge: Cambridge University Press.

PRELLER, VICTOR. 1967. *Divine Science and the Science of God: A Reformulation of Thomas Aquinas.* Princeton, N. J.: Princeton University Press.

PUTNAM, HILARY. 1981. *Reason, Truth and History.* Cambridge: Cambridge University Press.

RAHNER, KARL. 1961. *On the Theology of Death,* trans. C. H. Henkey. New York: Herder and Herder.

RAWLS, JOHN. 1971. *A Theory of Justice*. Cambridge: Harvard University Press.
————. 1980. "Kantian Constructivism in Moral Theory: The Dewey Lectures, 1980." *Journal of Philosophy* 77, no. 9: 515–572.

RAZ, JOSEPH, ed. 1978. *Practical Reasoning*. Oxford: Oxford University Press.

REEDER, JOHN, JR. 1988. *Source, Sanction, and Salvation: Religion and Morality in Judaic and Christian Traditions*. Englewood Cliffs, N. J.: Prentice-Hall.

REYNOLDS, CHARLES, ed. 1986. *Soundings*. Symposium: *Habits of the Heart* 70: 1–2.

RICHARDS, I. A. 1932. *Mencius on the Mind: Experiments in Multiple Definition*. London: Routledge and Kegan Paul.

RICKETT, W. A. 1965. *Kuan Tzu: A Repository of Early Chinese Thought*. Hong Kong: Hong Kong University Press.

RIEGEL, JEFFREY. 1979. "Reflections on an Unmoved Mind: An Analysis of Mencius 2a2." *Journal of the American Academy of Religion Thematic Issue* 47, 3s: 433–458.

ROBERTS, ROBERT. 1984. "Will Power and the Virtues." *Philosophical Review* 93, no. 2: 227–247.

RORTY, AMELIE OKSENBERG, ed. 1980. *Explaining Emotions*. Berkeley: University of California Press.
————. 1988. *Mind in Action: Essays in the Philosophy of Mind*. Boston: Beacon Press.

ROSEMONT, HENRY. 1970/71. "State and Society in Hsün Tzu: A Philosophic Commentary." *Monumenta Serica* 29: 38–78.
————. 1974. "On Representing Abstractions in Archaic Chinese." *Philosophy East and West* 24, no. 1: 71–88.

ROSENTHAL, ABIGAIL L. 1987. *A Good Look at Evil*. Philadelphia: Temple University Press.

ROSS, J. 1969. "Analogy as a Rule of Meaning for Religious Language." In A. Kenny, ed. *Aquinas: A Collection of Critical Essays*, pp. 93–138. Garden City, N. Y.: Doubleday and Company.

ROSS, W. D. 1930. *The Right and the Good*. Oxford: Clarendon Press.
————. 1959 [1923/1953]. *Aristotle*. New York: Meridian Books.

RUBIN, VITALY. 1976. *Individual and State in Ancient China: Essays on Four Chinese Philosophers*, trans. S. Levine. New York: Columbia University Press.

RYLE, GILBERT. 1949. *The Concept of Mind*. London: Hutchinson and Company.
———. 1967. "Teaching and Training." In R. S. Peters, ed., *The Concept of Education*, pp. 105–119. London: Routledge and Kegan Paul.

SCANLON, THOMAS. 1982. "Contractualism and Utilitarianism." In A. Sen and B. Williams, eds., *Utilitarianism and Beyond*, pp. 103–128. Cambridge: Cambridge University Press.

SCHARLEMANN, ROBERT. 1964. *Thomas Aquinas and John Gerhard*. New Haven, Conn.: Yale University Press.

SCHEFFLER, SAMUEL. 1983. Review of *After Virtue: A Study in Moral Theory* by Alasdair MacIntyre. *Philosophical Review* 92, no. 3: 443–447.

SCHEMAN, NAOMI. 1979. "On Sympathy." *The Monist* 62: 320–330.

SCHNEEWIND, J. B. 1982. "Virtue, Narrative, and Community: MacIntyre and Morality." *Journal of Philosophy* 79: 653–663.
———. 1983. "Moral Crisis and the History of Ethics." In P. French, T. Uehling, Jr., and H. Wettstein, eds., *Midwest Studies in Philosophy*, vol. 8, *Contemporary Perspectives on the History of Philosophy*, pp. 525–542. Minneapolis: University of Minnesota Press.
———. 1984. "The Divine Corporation and the History of Ethics." In R. Rorty and Q. Skinner, eds., *Philosophy in History*, pp. 173–192. Cambridge: Cambridge University Press.

SCHUSTER, J. B. 1933. "Von den Ethischen Prinzipien: Eine Thomasstudie zu S. Th. I-II, q. 94, a. 2." *Zeitschrift für Katolische Theologie* 57: 44–65.

SCHWARTZ, BENJAMIN. 1986. *The World of Thought in Ancient China*. Cambridge, Mass.: Belknap Press of Harvard University Press.

SERTILLANGES, A. D. 1922. *La Philosophie Morale de Saint Thomas d'Aquin*. Paris: Felix Alcan.

SELLMANN, JAMES. 1987. "Three Models of Self Integration (*tzu Te*) in Early China." *Philosophy East and West* 37: 372–391.

SHIH, JOSEPH. 1969/70. "The Notion of God in Ancient Chinese Religion." *Numen* 16–17: 99–138.

SHKLAR, JUDITH. 1984. *Ordinary Vices.* Cambridge, Mass.: Belknap Press of Harvard University Press.

SHUN, KWONG-LOI. 1986. "Virtue, Mind and Morality: A Study in Mencian Ethics." Dissertation, Stanford University, Department of Philosophy.

SIDGWICK, HENRY. 1981 [1907]. *The Method of Ethics,* 7th ed. Indianapolis, Ind.: Hackett Publishing Company.

SLOTE, MICHAEL. 1984. *Goods and Virtues.* Oxford: Oxford University Press.

SMITH, JONATHAN Z. 1970. "The Influence of Symbols on Social Change: A Place on Which to Stand." *Worship* 44: 457–474.
———. 1982. *Imagining Religion: From Babylon to Jonestown.* Chicago: University of Chicago Press.

SOKOLOWSKI, ROBERT. 1982. *The God of Faith and Reason: Foundations of Christian Theology.* Notre Dame, Ind.: University of Notre Dame Press.
———. 1985. *Moral Action: A Phenomenological Study.* Bloomington: Indiana University Press.

STOCKER, MICHAEL. 1976. "The Schizophrenia of Modern Ethical Theories." *Journal of Philosophy* 63, no. 4: 453–466.

STOUT, JEFFREY. 1980. "Weber's Progeny, Once Removed." *Religious Studies Review* 6, no. 4: 289–295.
———. 1983a. "Holism and Comparative Ethics: A Response to Little." *Journal of Religious Ethics* 11, no. l: 301–315.
———. 1983b. "The Philosophical Interest of the Hebrew-Christian Moral Tradition." *The Thomist* 47, no. 2: 165–196.
———. 1984. "Virtue among the Ruins: An Essay on MacIntyre." *Neue Zeitschrift für Systematische Theologie und Religionsphilosophie* 26, no. 3: 275–273.

T'ANG CHÜN-I. 1961/62. "The *T'ien Ming* (Heavenly Ordinance) in Pre-Ch'in China." *Philosophy East and West* 11–12: 195–218, 29–49.

TAYLOR, CHARLES. 1982. "The Diversity of Goods." In A. Sen and B. Williams, eds., *Utilitarianism and Beyond,* pp. 129–144. Cambridge: Cambridge University Press.
———. 1985a. *Human Agency and Language: Philosophical Papers 1.* Cambridge: Cambridge University Press.
———. 1985b. *Philosophy and the Human Sciences: Philosophical Papers 2.* Cambridge: Cambridge University Press.

TAYLOR, RICHARD. 1985. *Ethics, Faith, and Reason.* Englewood Cliffs, N. J.: Prentice-Hall.

TRACY, DAVID, ed. 1978. "Celebrating the Medieval Heritage: A Colloquy on the Thought of Aquinas and Bonaventure." *Journal of Religion* 58, Supplement.
———. 1981. *The Analogical Imagination: Christian Theology and the Culture of Pluralism.* New York: Crossroads.

TU WEI-MING. 1979. *Humanity and Self-Cultivation: Essays in Confucian Thought.* Berkeley: Asian Humanities Press.

URMSON, J. O. 1967. "Aristotle on Pleasure." In J.M.E. Moravcsik, ed. *Aristotle: A Collection of Critical Essay,* pp. 323-333. Garden City, N. Y.: Doubleday Anchor.
———. 1980. "Aristotle's Doctrine of the Mean." In A. O. Rorty, ed., *Essays on Aristotle's Ethics,* pp. 157-170. Berkeley: University of California Press.

VERBEKE, GERARD. 1983. *The Presence of Stoicism in Medieval Thought.* Washington, D.C.: Catholic University of America Press.

VERWILGHEN, A. F. 1967. *Mencius: The Man and His Ideas.* New York: St. John's University Press.

VON WRIGHT, GREG HENRICK. 1963. *The Varieties of Goodness.* London: Routledge and Kegan Paul.

WADELL, PAUL. 1985. "'An Interpretation of Aquinas' Treatise on the Passions, the Virtues, and the Gifts from the Perspective of Charity as Friendship with God." Dissertation, University of Notre Dame, Department of Theology.

WALEY, ARTHUR. 1934. *The Way and Its Power: A Study of the Tao Te Ching and Its Place in Chinese Thought.* London: Allen and Unwin.
———. 1955 [1938]. *The Analects of Confucius.* London: Allen and Unwin.

WALLACE, G., AND WALKER, A. D. M., eds. 1970. *The Definition of Morality.* London: Metheun and Co.

WALLACE, JAMES. 1978. *Virtues and Vices.* Ithaca, N. Y.: Cornell University Press.

WALTON, DOUGLAS. 1986. *Courage: A Philosophical Investigation.* Berkeley: University of California.

WARTOFSKY, MARX. 1984. "Virtue Lost or Understanding MacIntyre." *Inquiry* 27: 235–250.

WATSON, GARY. 1982. "Free Agency." In G. Watson, ed., *Free Will*, pp.96–110. New York: Oxford University Press.
———. 1984. "Virtues in Excess." *Philosophical Studies* 46: 57–74.

WEBER, MAX. 1951 [1920/21]. *The Religion of China*, trans. H. Gerth. Glencoe, Ill.: Free Press.

WEILAND, GEORG. 1982a. "The Reception and Interpretation of Aristotle's Ethics." In N. Kretzmann, A. Kenny, and J. Pinborg, eds. *The Cambridge History of Later Medieval Philosophy*, pp. 657–672. Cambridge: Cambridge University Press.
———. 1982b. "Happiness: the Perfection of Man." In N. Kretzmann, A. Kenny, and J. Pinborg, eds., *The Cambridge History of Later Medieval Philosophy*, pp. 673–686. Cambridge: Cambridge University Press.

WEISHEIPL, JAMES. 1974. *Friar Thomas d'Aquino: His Life, Thought, and Work*. Garden City, N. Y.: Doubleday and Company.

WHITE, VICTOR, OP. 1961 [1952]. *God and the Unconscious*. Cleveland, Ohio: Meridian.
———. 1955. *God the Unknown and Other Essays*. London: The Harvill Press.

WIGGINS, DAVID. 1976. "Truth, Invention, and the Meaning of Life." *Proceedings of the British Academy* 62: 331–378. London: Oxford University Press.
———. 1978. "Deliberation and Practical Reason." In J. Raz, ed., *Practical Reasoning*, pp. 144–152. Oxford: Oxford University Press.
———. 1980a. "Deliberation and Practical Reason." In A. O. Rorty, ed., *Essays on Aristotle's Ethics*, pp. 221–240. Berkeley: University of California.
———. 1980b. "Weakness of Will, Commensurability, and the Objects of Deliberation and Desire." In A. O. Rorty, ed., *Essays on Aristotle's Ethics*, pp. 241–265. Berkeley: University of California.

WILLIAMS, BERNARD. 1973. "Morality and the Emotions." In *Problems of the Self*. Cambridge: Cambridge University Press.
———. 1981a. "Persons, Character, and Morality." In *Moral Luck: Philosophical Papers*, pp. 1–19. Cambridge: Cambridge University Press.
———. 1981b. "Moral Luck." In *Moral Luck: Philosophical Papers*, pp. 20–39. Cambridge: Cambridge University Press.
———. 1981c. "Utilitarianism and Moral Self-Indulgence." In *Moral Luck: Philosophical Papers*, pp. 40–53. Cambridge: Cambridge University Press.

———. 1985. *Ethics and the Limits of Philosophy*. Cambridge, Mass.: Harvard University Press.

WITTGENSTEIN, LUDWIG, 1965 [1929-30]. "Wittgenstein's Lecture on Ethics." *Philosophical Review* 74: 1.
———. 1968 [1953]. *Philosophical Investigations*, trans. G. E. M. Anscombe. Oxford: Basil Blackwell and Mott Ltd.

WOLF, SUSAN. 1982. "Moral Saints." *Journal of Philosophy* 89, no. 8: 419-439.

WOLLHEIM, RICHARD. 1984. *The Thread of Life*. Cambridge, Mass.: Harvard University Press.

WOLTERSTORFF, NICOLAS. 1986. "The Migration of Theistic Arguments: From Natural Theology to Evidentialist Apologetics." In R. Audi, W. Wainwright, eds., *Rationality, Religious Belief, and Moral Commitment: New Essays in the Philosophy of Religion*, pp. 38-81. Ithaca, New York: Cornell University Press.

WONG, DAVID. 1984. *Moral Relativity*. Berkeley: University of California Press.

YEARLEY, LEE. 1970. "Karl Rahner on the Relation of Nature and Grace." *Canadian Journal of Theology* 16, nos. 3 & 4: 219-231.
———. 1971. "The Nature-Grace Question in the Context of Fortitude." *The Thomist* 35: 557-580.
———. 1975a. "Mencius on Human Nature: The Forms of His Religious Thought." *Journal of the American Academy of Religion* 43, no. 2: 185-198.
———. 1975b. "Toward a Typology of Religious Thought: A Chinese Example." *Journal of Religion* 55, no. 4: 426-443.
———. 1978. *The Ideas of Newman: Christianity and Human Religiosity*. University Park: Pennsylvania State University Press.
———. 1979. Review of Confucianism and Christianity: A Comparative Study by Julia Ching. *Philosophy East and West* 29, no. 4: 509-512.
———. 1980. "Hsün Tzu on the Mind: His Attempted Synthesis of Confucianism and Taoism." *Journal of Asian Studies* 39, no. 3: 465-480.
———. 1982. "Three Ways of Being Religious." *Philosophy East and West* 32, no. 4: 439-451.
———. 1983a. "A Comparison between Classical Chinese Thought and Thomistic Christian Thought." *Journal of the American Academy of Religion* 51, no. 3: 427-458.

————. 1983b. "The Perfected Person in the Radical Chuang-tzu." In V. Mair, ed., *Experimental Essays in Chuang-tzu*, pp. 125-149. Honolulu: University Press of Hawaii.

————. 1985a. "A Confucian Crisis: Mencius' Two Cosmogonies and Their Ethics." In R. Lovin and F. Reynolds, eds., *Cosmogony and Ethical Order: New Studies in Comparative Ethics*, pp. 310-327. Chicago: University of Chicago Press.

————. 1985b. "Freud as Creator and Critic of Cosmogonies and Their Ethics." In R. Lovin and F. Reynolds, eds., *Cosmogony and Ethical Order: New Studies in Comparative Ethics*, pp. 381-413. Chicago: University of Chicago Press.

————. 1985c. "Teachers and Saviors." *Journal of Religion* 65, no. 2: 225-243.

————. 1990a. "Bourgeois Relativism and the Comparative Study of the Self." In J. Carman, ed., *Thematic Comparison in the Teaching of Religion*. Mercer, Georgia: Scholar Press.

————. 1990b. "Education and the Intellectual Virtues." In S. Burkhalter and Ann F. Reynolds, eds., *Beyond the Classics? Essays on Religious Studies and Liberal Education*. Mercer, Georgia: Scholars Press.

————. 1990c. "Recent Work on Virtue." *Religious Studies Review* 16, no. 1: 1-9.

————. Forthcoming. "Chuang Tzu's Cosmic Identification." Wei-ming Tu, ed., *Taoist Spirituality*, vol. 10, *World Spirituality: An Encyclopedic History of the Religious Quest*. New York: The Crossroads Publishing Co.

————. Forthcoming. "Conflicts Among Ideals of Human Flourishing." G. Outka and J. Reeder, Jr. eds. *Prospects for a Common Morality*.

————. Forthcoming. "Hsün Tzu: Ritualization as Humanization." Wei-ming Tu., ed., *Confucian Spirituality*, vol. 11, *World Spirituality: An Encyclopedic History of the Religious Quest*. New York: The Crossroads Publishing Co.

Index of Names

267

Index of Subjects

Advantage, perceived. *See* Courage, semblances of; Motives, acquisitive and expressive
Analogical imagination. *See* Imagination: analogical
Analogy, 32, 40, 44, 57, 169, 181, 183, 185-203, 215n.5, 235n.17. *See also* "Similarities in differences and differences in similarities"; Imagination
Anger (*ira*), 19, 82, 87, 108, 120, 127, 140, 228n.16. *See also* Thumos
Apathy, spiritual (*acedia*), 87, 89, 91, 92, 137, 229n.30. *See also* Sorrow (*tristitia*)
Apprehension, real and notional, 66. *See also* Confrontations, real and notional
Aquinas: general comparisons with Mencius, 4-6, 27-28, 40-44, 48, 51, 56, 58-60, 158-59, 167-68, 170-82, 184-85, 189, 193-94; conscience in, 76-77, 219n.32; on courage, 118-43, 174, 193-94, 227nn.11, 12, 13, 228nn.16, 17, 18, 19, 23; developmental model in, 59, 78, 79, 95; on emotions, 79, 81-83, 96-106, 120, 186, 220n.41, 223n.62; understanding of ethos, 48-51, 76, 77; on expan-

sions of courage, 19, 33-35, 118, 121, 129-39, 141-43; and failures to be virtuous, 75, 84-95, 187; formation of emotions in, 82-83; emotions in courage, 119-23, 136-38; emotions in Gift of Courage, 141-43; and injunctions, 48-51, 75, 76, 77, 78, 171; interpretive difficulties, 27-28; list of virtues in, 29-36; method in, 32-35, 56-57, 159, 182-87, 199; and "open" religion and the relevant cosmology, 4, 42, 170; on parts of virtue, 29-30, 33-36, 181, 183-85; practical theory in, 43, 88, 93, 111, 147, 159, 167, 177-81; on reason's relationship to inclinations and emotions, 79-83; relationship of reason and nature in, 49, 57, 72, 75-78, 215n.6; on revelation, 78, 219n.34; secondary theory in, 88-90, 95, 103, 110-11, 147, 154-56, 158-59, 165, 167, 175-81, 189-90; on semblances of virtue, 17, 19, 33, 80-81, 83, 109-10; on sin, 86-95, 220nn.45, 46, 221n.47; Stoic reading of, 27, 75-77; structure of the self in, 72-75; concept of virtue in, 29-36, 56-57, 79-83, 89, 109-11, 172, 183-87

271